Military Conscription

Contributions to Economics

Christoph M. Schneider
Research and Development Management: From the Soviet Union to Russia
1994. ISBN 3-7908-0757-5

Bernhard Böhm/Lionello F. Punzo (Eds.)
Economic Performance
1994. ISBN 3-7908-0811-3

Lars Olof Persson/Ulf Wiberg
Microregional Fragmentation
1995. ISBN 3-7908-0855-5

Ernesto Felli/Furio C. Rosati/Giovanni Tria (Eds.)
The Service Sector: Productivity and Growth
1995. ISBN 3-7908-0875-X

Giuseppe Munda
Multicriteria Evaluation in Fuzzy Environment
1995. ISBN 3-7908-0892-X

Giovanni Galizzi/Luciano Venturini (Eds.)
Economics of Innovation: The Case of Food Industry
1996. ISBN 3-7908-0911-X

David T. Johnson
Poverty, Inequality and Social Welfare in Australia
1996. ISBN 3-7908-0942-X

Rongxing Guo
Border-Regional Economics
1996. ISBN 3-7908-0943-8

Oliver Fratzscher
The Political Economy of Trade Integration
1996. ISBN 3-7908-0945-4

Ulrich Landwehr
Industrial Mobility and Public Policy
1996. ISBN 3-7908-0949-7

Arnold Picot/Ekkehard Schlicht (Eds.)
Firms, Markets, and Contracts
1996. Corr. 2nd printing 1997.
ISBN 3-7908-0947-0

Thorsten Wichmann
Agricultural Technical Progress and the Development of a Dual Economy
1997. ISBN 3-7908-0960-8

Ulrich Woitek
Business Cycles
1997. ISBN 3-7908-0997-7

Michael Carlberg
International Economic Growth
1997. ISBN 3-7908-0995-0

Massimo Filippini
Elements of the Swiss Market for Electricity
1997. ISBN 3-7908-0996-9

Giuseppe Gaburro (Ed.)
Ethics and Economics
1997. ISBN 3-7908-0986-1

Frank Hoster/Heinz Welsch/Christoph Böhringer
CO_2 Abatement and Economic Structural Change in the European Internal Market
1997. ISBN 3-7908-1020-7

Christian M. Hafner
Nonlinear Time Series Analysis with Applications to Foreign Exchange Rate Volatility
1997. ISBN 3-7908-1041-X

Sardar M. N. Islam
Mathematical Economics of Multi-Level Optimisation
1998. ISBN 3-7908-1050-9

Sven-Morten Mentzel
Real Exchange Rate Movements
1998. ISBN 3-7908-1081-9

Lei Delsen/Eelke de Jong (Eds.)
The German and Dutch Economies
1998. ISBN 3-7908-1064-9

Mark Weder
Business Cycle Models with Indeterminacy
1998. ISBN 3-7908-1078-9

Tor Rødseth (Ed.)
Models for Multispecies Management
1998. ISBN 3-7908-1001-0

Michael Carlberg
Intertemporal Macroeconomics
1998. ISBN 3-7908-1096-7

Sabine Spangenberg
The Institutionalised Transformation of the East German Economy
1998. ISBN 3-7908-1103-3

continued on page 203

Simon Duindam

Military Conscription

An Economic Analysis of the Labour Component in the Armed Forces

With 21 Figures
and 5 Tables

Springer-Verlag Berlin Heidelberg GmbH

Series Editors
Werner A. Müller
Martina Bihn

Author
Dr. Simon Duindam
Open University of the Netherlands
Valkenburgerweg 177
NL-6419 AT Heerlen, The Netherlands

ISBN 978-3-7908-1203-9 ISBN 978-3-642-50005-3 (eBook)
DOI 10.1007/ 978-3-642-50005-3

Cataloging-in-Publication Data applied for
Die Deutsche Bibliothek – CIP-Einheitsaufnahme
Duindam, Simon: Military conscription: an economic analysis of the labour component in the armed forces; with 5 tables / Simon Duindam. – Heidelberg: Physica-Verl., 1999
(Contributions to economics)

Originally published by Physica-Verlag Heidelberg in 1999.

Softcover Design: Erich Kirchner, Heidelberg

SPIN 10720830 88/2202-5 4 3 2 1 0 – Printed on acid-free paper

Table of Contents

CHAPTER 1

Economics and Conscription

"Economics is the science which studies human behavior as a relationship between ends and scarce means which have alternative uses".
Lionel Robbins, An Essay on the Nature and Significance of Economic Science, London 1962, pp. 16.

Military conscription is a public phenomenon, which has been part of Dutch society since the Napoleonic age. Conscription is a complicated phenomenon. A number of committees studied the issue of conscription in the Netherlands, but could not come to the conclusion to abandon conscription. Contrary to many other social issues, conscription has not been at the centre of much attention. It was not until the last decades of this century that scientists showed interested in the economics of the conscripted soldier.

Practically none of the economists in the Netherlands involved themselves with conscription[1], although some of them referred to conscription as an example of a tax-in-kind, like Rudolf Goldscheid did in his "Staatssozialismus oder Staatskapitalismus"[2].

Nevertheless, military conscription is a very relevant economic subject, something Adam Smith already made clear in "The Wealth of Nations".[3] In this economic standard, Smith explains that the costs of warfare differ, depending on the society and the times. When societies consisted mainly of hunters, an army cost almost nothing, because the nature of the activities of the hunters did not change when they were going to war. This would also be true for a society of shepherds. If shepherds were going to war, the whole population accompanied them, and were not an extra burden for their leaders. After the shepherds, the

---

1 In the course of my literature research for this book I could only find 2 articles about conscription by Dutch authors: H. Volten, "Dienstplicht, legervorming en de Nederlandse economie, ESB, nr. 2577, 25-01-1967 en C.B.A. Spil, "Een economische verklaring van de dienstplicht", ESB, nr. 2553, 10-08-1966. Both articles are cited by P.G.A. van Bergeijk, Economie van de Oorlog, Rotterdam, 1986. An example of a reference to conscription as a tax-in-kind can be found in: L.G.M. Stevens, Elementair Belastingrecht, Deventer, 1989, pp.14.

2 R. Goldscheid, Staatssozialismus oder Staatskapitalismus: ein finanzsociologischer Beitrag zur Lösung des Staatsschulden-Problems, Wien, 1917, chapter 1.

3 Adam Smith, The Wealth of Nations, New York, 1937, Book V, chapter 1, pp. 653-669.

farmers appeared. Farmers with a little farm could easily be transformed into soldiers. Although a farmer had to be equipped with protection and armory, the costs for the farmers' community were not that high, if the war started after the sowing period and was ended before harvesting. Nature could do its work here, and the harvest could succeed without the help of the farmer, so that the farmer had his hands free to go to war. This is different for a craftsman, like a black smith or a carpenter. When they leave their work place, the source of income will dry up. Nature does not give them any slack. The craftsman has to do it all on his own.

Over the ages warfare has become much more complicated. In the beginning it was nothing more than a simple fight, in later times, a war existed of different campaigns, that lasted for almost the whole year. It therefore became necessary that the community should support the people who were fighting the wars for them, otherwise the loss of income would be to high for the soldiers.

The complexity of warfare has her origin in technological progress. Warfare is directed towards the production of combat power. Combat power is a combined result of both capital and labour, whereby the capital component both represents physical and human capital. If the technological process advances, different forms of effective combat power can be distinguished. But this is only possible if man becomes familiar with these complicated ways of combat power through education. The state of technology determines what kind of perfection is possible in a war. However, to achieve this kind of perfection it is necessary that warfare is the only and principal occupation of a specific group of the society, because here too the division of labour is the best method to improve the results.

With the progress of society, man has, in a way, turned his back to warfare. In such a society there are two methods to provide for the protection of the community, when this is necessary. In "The Wealth of Nations" these methods are described as follows:

"There are only two methods of providing for defence. It may either, first, by means of a very rigorous police, and in spite of the whole bent of the interest, genius and inclinations of the people, enforce the practice of military exercises, and oblige either all the citizens of the military age, or a certain number of them, to join in some measure the trade of a soldier to whatever other trade or profession they may happen to carry on.

Or secondly, by maintaining and employing a certain numbers of citizens in the constant practice of military exercises, it may render the trade of a soldier a particular trade, separate and distinct from all others.

If the state has recourse to the first of those two expedients, its military force is said to consist in a militia; if to the second, it is said to consist in a standing army. The practice of military exercises is the sole or principal occupation of the soldiers of a standing army, and the maintenance or pay which the state affords them is the principal and ordinary fund of their subsistence. The practice of military exercises is only the occasional occupation of the soldiers of a militia, and they derive the principal and ordinary fund of their subsistence from some other occupation. In a militia, the character of the labourer, artificer, or tradesman, predominates over that of the soldier: in a standing army, that of the soldier predominates over every other character; and in this distinction seems to consist the essential difference between those two different species of military force[4]."

In a standing or all-volunteer force a soldier is paid by the community and warfare is a professional occupation. The salaries of the soldiers are paid by the other members of society by monetary taxes.

In a militia, or conscription army, the occupation soldier does not exist in principle, but warfare is a temporary activity of people who actually have a different occupation. The community does not pay the conscripts a salary, so it does not have to raise taxes to pay for the salaries. The cost of warfare is borne by the conscripts, because during the war they are not able to acquire their normal income.

According to Adam Smith a conscription army is technically inferior to an all-volunteer force, because:

"The soldiers, who are exercised only once a week, or once a month, can never be so expert in the use of their arms, as those who are exercised every day, or every other day; and though this circumstance may not be of such consequence in modern, as it was in ancient times, yet the acknowledged superiority of the Prussian troops, owing, it is said, very much to their superior expertness in their exercise, may satisfy us that it is, even at this day, of very considerable consequence.

The soldiers, who are bound to obey their officer only once a week or once a month, and who are at all other times at liberty to manage their own affairs their own way, without being in any respect accountable to him, can never be under the same awe in his presence, can never have the same disposition to ready obedience, with those whose whole life and conduct are every day directed by him, and who every day even rise and go to bed, or at least retire to their quarters, according to their orders. In what is called discipline, or in the habit of ready obedience, a militia must always be still more inferior to a standing army, than it may sometimes be in what is called the manual exercise, or in the management and use of its arms. But in modern war the habit of ready and instant obedience is of much greater consequence than a considerable superiority in the management or arms[5]."

Smith adds to this statement that a conscription army that has taken part in a few campaigns can be regarded as an all-volunteer force.

§ 1.1. Conscription and taxation

From "The Wealth of Nations" we can learn that the costs of warfare depend on the alternative activities of those who have to fight the war. This is what

4 Smith, op cit., blz. 659.
5 Smith, op cit., blz. 661.

economic science calls "opportunity costs". The costs of warfare also rise, if the community develops itself. In addition, warfare becomes more complicated when a community develops itself. In earlier times hunters were going to war with shields, spears and hardly any technical training, in stark contrast to our technologically sophisticated times.

When preparing for war and executing the war, the size of combat power of the army is an important variable. Combat power is a combination of capital (spears, shields, education, ships, planes, etc.) and labour, whereby labour can be provided by volunteers or conscripts. The costs of labour in an all-volunteer force are borne by the whole community in the form of monetary taxes, in a militia, or conscription army, a tax-in-kind is paid by the size of the alternative earnings of the work that conscripts could have done if they would not have been in the army.

From an economic perspective military conscription is a tax-in-kind. Conscription is a compulsory contribution without receiving a reciprocal contribution from the receiver. From this definition a few questions can be derived: "What is the size of this tax-in-kind, is it possible that this tax can be avoided or evaded, and what is the total excess burden of this tax"?

Conscription is a tax on labour. A tax on specific goods means that the relative prices between the different goods change; the allocation in the armed forces is disturbed by conscription.

Military conscription causes a specific cost structure in the armed forces, because conscription can be considered as a subsidy on labour for the receiver of the subsidy, the armed forces. Every subsidy raises the amount used of the subsidized goods. In the armed forces these "goods" are the soldiers. Conscription stimulates the armed forces to engage cheap military, so that militia armed forces relatively have a lot of inexperienced and undereducated young soldiers.

Because of the changing relative prices by conscription an excess-burden appears: a loss of welfare in addition to the size of the tax-in-kind that conscription already involves.

§ 1.2. The vision on society

In economic science conscription can be regarded as a tax-in-kind, though this is not necessarily taken as a general point of view. It depends on the view one has on the relation between the individual and the community of which that individual is part of, and how the state should function in society.

Political scientists distinguish two major approaches in the relation between individuals and the state.[6] In the organic view on the state, the state is characterised as a natural organism. Every individual is part of this organism and

---

6 In this we follow the vision of Harvey S. Rosen in his book Public Finance, Homewood, 1988, pp. 4-8.

the government can be regarded as the heart of this organism. The individual only exists as a member of the state and the welfare of the individual is directly related to the welfare of the state. If the state is doing well, than the individual is doing well too. Thus, in the organic vision the individual is subordinated to the state. In Plato's republic an activity of an individual was only preferred, if this activity contributed to a 'fair' state.

When choosing between a conscription army and an all-volunteer force in a organic vision on the state, the interest of the state is of a higher concern. If the interest of the state is based on only financial parameters, than conscription is preferable to an all-volunteer force, because for the state a conscription army costs less than an all-volunteer force. If the state is doing well, than the conscript will be all-right too.

In opposition to the organic vision of the state is the mechanistic vision. In this vision the government is not the heart of society, but government is raised by all individuals in the society to care for the provision of all individual needs, that can not be provided by these individuals individually or in a small group. The individual in this vision is the central point of interest, rather than the government or social planner that takes care of the tasks of the government.

In this mechanistic vision conscription is a burden for society. This burden can not be found in the registers of the government, but is a burden for the community, because individuals will regard conscription as a burden. In the mechanistic vision the government exists for the well being of all the people. This is the vision adhered to by a lot of people in the Netherlands, and which will be used later in this study.[7]

If we accept that the government exists for the well being of the people, we still have the problem to show what welfare is, and how the government should promote it. In economics there is a subdiscipline, called welfare economics, that concerns itself with this problem. Welfare economics is an economic theory about the social desirability of alternative social situations.[8]

§ 1.3. Welfare economics and the welfare of conscripts

A welfare economics analysis,[9] which has a normative background, starts with a simple economy of two persons, who consume two goods with a given production of these two goods. The only economic problem here is the allocation of the two goods to the two people. As simple as this model is, the results of this

---

7 This does not mean that everybody has this view. The choice in this study is a normative one.

8 Rosen pp. 40.

9 This analysis is explained in Rosen, pp. 38 and further.

model can be used in a world with many people and goods.[10] The two-by-two model is chosen here because of its simplicity.

The two people are named here Hans and Leo, and the two goods, security and education. The allocation of the amount of security and education between Hans and Leo is shown in an Edgeworth Box.[11] In figure 1.1. the length of the Edgeworth Box, Os, shows the amount of security available in the economy, while the height, Or, shows the amount of education. The amount of goods consumed by Hans is measured by distance from point O; the amount of goods consumed by Leo is measured by the distance from point O'.

If we assume that both Hans and Leo possess conventional indifference curves, that reflect their preferences for security and education, we can use these curves in figure 1.1. Hans is 'happier' with indifference curve H3 than with H2 or H1 and Leo is 'happier' with indifference curve L3 than with L2 or L1.

The following assumption is that there exists an arbitrary allocation of security and education, such as - G - in figure 1.2., whereby Hans possesses Ox security and Ou education and Leo possesses O'y security and O'w education. Hereby HgHg represents Hans' indifference curve and LgLg represents Leo's. The question can be posited whether it is possible to reallocate the amount of security and education in such a way that Leo is better off without deteriorating Hans' position. If we take point - j -, we see that Leo is better off, because indifference curve LjLj represents a higher utility than utility curve LgLg, while Hans stays at his old indifference curve. The question is how far Leo's welfare can be increased, without deteriorating Hans' welfare?

In figure 1.2. we can see that this process can continue until point -k- is reached and Leo's indifference curve touches Hans' (HgHg). An allocation like in point -k- is called a Pareto-efficient point[12], because the welfare of Leo can only be improved by deteriorating Hans' position. Pareto-efficiency is used in economics as a standard to evaluate the desirability of an allocation of means. If an allocation is not Pareto-efficient, than in principle means are wasted, because it is possible to improve someone's welfare without deteriorating someone else's. A Pareto-improvement is nothing but a reallocation of goods, making at least someone better off without worsening somebody else' position .

Point -k- is not the only Pareto-efficient point, that could have been reached from point -g-. In figure 1.3. we see that k1 and k2 are also Pareto-efficient points and if we take a look at the whole Edgeworth-box, we can see a whole series of Pareto-efficient points. The locus of all Pareto-efficient points is called a contractcurve. The contractcurve is designed in such a way that at all points on the contractcurve the marginal rate of substitution of security for education of Hans and Leo are the same.

---

10 For a mathematical deduction of the general applicability of this model, see chapter 11 of Henderson and Quandt, Micro-economic Theory: a Mathematical Approach, New York, 1980.

11 Named after the great 19-century economist F.Y. Edgeworth

12 Named after Vilfredo Pareto.

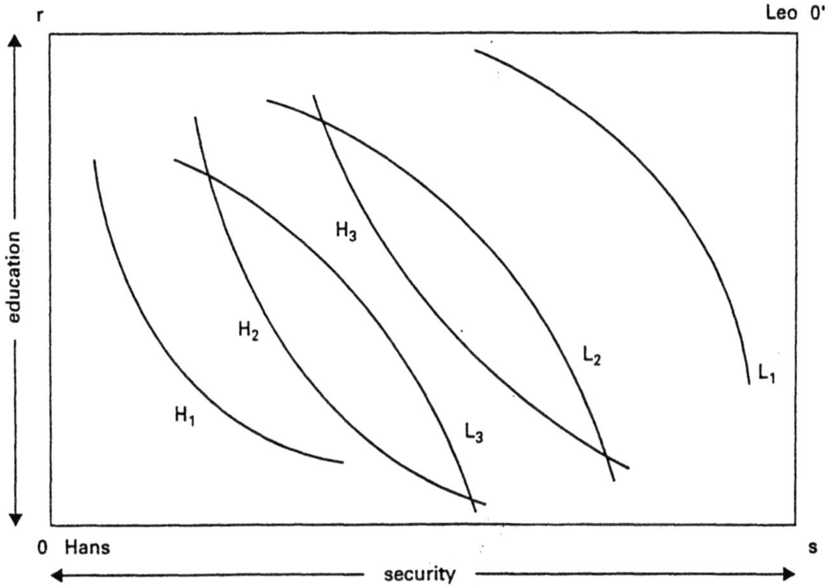

FIGURE 1.1 Indifference curves in an Edgeworth Box

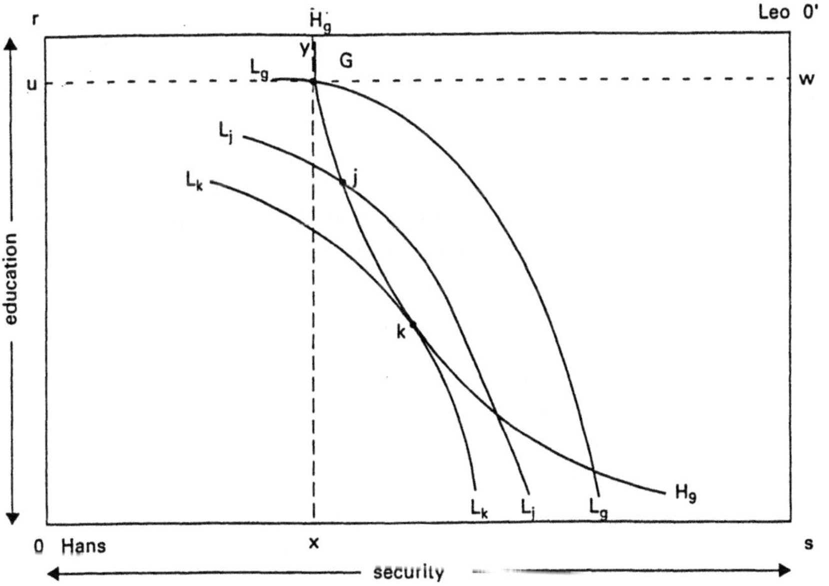

FIGURE 1.2 Pareto-efficiency

The analysis so far assumed that the production, and thus the supply of security and education, is constant. If production is made variable, the question arises of what happens with the conditions for a Pareto-efficient allocation. Pareto-efficiency is possible under variable production, but requires the condition to be extended. In addition to the equality in the marginal rate of substitution of security and education, Pareto-efficiency of equality of the marginal rates of substitution with the marginal rate of transformation of security and education is also necessary.

The marginal rate of transformation shows at what rate security can be transformed into education. If this marginal rate of transformation is expressed in terms of marginal costs, the incremental costs of one unit of security or education are known and the condition for Pareto-efficiency can then be interpreted in terms of marginal costs.

Pareto-efficiency now requires the rate of marginal costs between security and education to be equal to the marginal rate of substitution of security and education. When describing the necessary conditions for Pareto-efficiency, There is no indication whether in a real economy this ideal situation is actually reached. Will a market system reach the contractcurve in a natural way?

The First Fundamental Theorem of Welfare economics provides an answer. This theorem states that as long as producers and consumers act as pure competitors, take prices as given, under certain conditions a Pareto-efficient allocation will occur. These conditions are that the prices of goods should be equal to their marginal costs, where competition guarantees that this condition is satisfied. The marginal costs of goods are defined as the extra costs for society, the marginal social costs that should be made, when one additional unit of the same goods is provided. Thus, Pareto-efficiency demands that the marginal social costs of goods are reflected in its price. If there is a difference between the marginal social costs and the marginal physical costs or the price, this can mean that production is not socially efficient.

However, the criterion of Pareto-efficiency has its limitations too. This is because Pareto-efficiency does not provide sufficient grounds to declare whether a certain allocation of goods is really desired. This will need an explicit normative choice. Without these value judgments it can not be determined whether the original allocation is also fair.

Going back to the contractcurve of figure 1.3, we see that the contractcurve gives an implicit relation between the welfare of Leo and Hans. If the welfare of Leo is high, Hans his welfare is low, and vice versa. In figure 1.4. the utility of Leo is shown on the horizontal axis and Hans' utility on the vertical axis. The curve UU is the utility possibility curve and is derived from the contractcurve. The points k1 and k2 are equal to the points k1, k2 on the contractcurve in figure 1.3. All points on or below the utility possibility curve can be reached by Leo or Hans, or stated broadly the whole community, whereby all points on the UU-curve are Pareto-efficient points, but they represent differences in welfare. Which point would now be considered best?

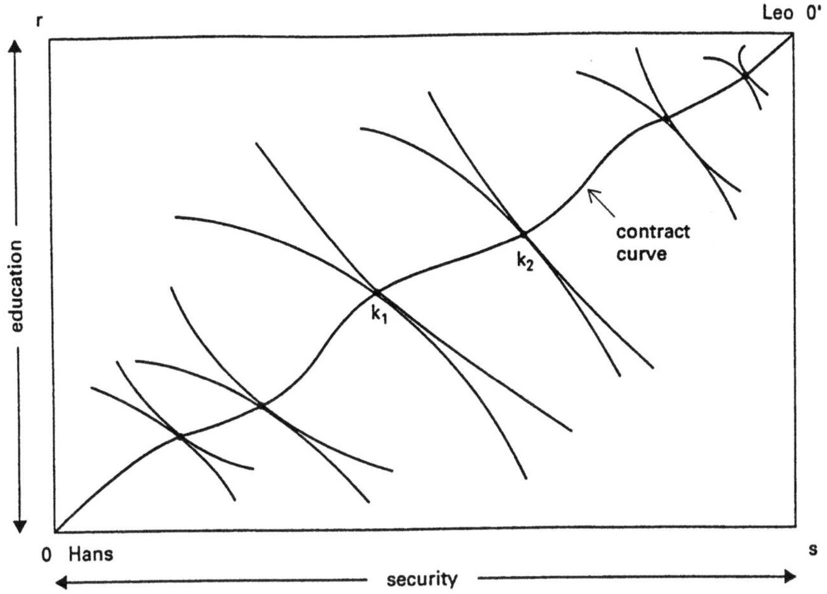

FIGURE 1.3 The contract-curve

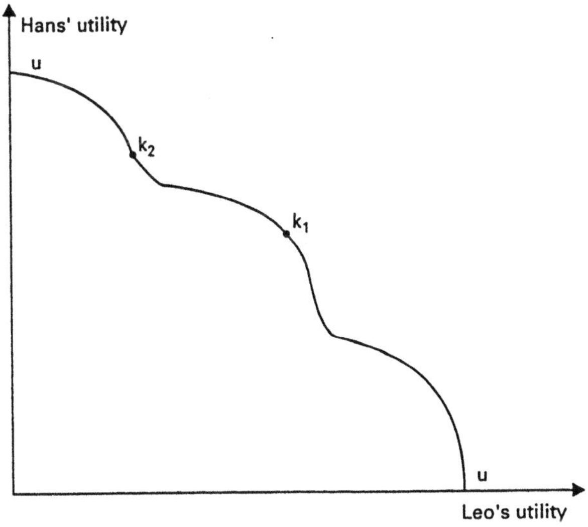

FIGURE 1.4 The utility-possibility-curve

The conventional way to answer this question, is to assume a social welfare function. This social welfare function (W) shows the maximum social welfare that can be attained and depends on all individual consuming and voting preferences (u).

(1.1.) W = F(uH, uL)

The consequence of this definition[13] is that in the social welfare function there is no place for elite preferences, paternalism, or a pursuit of power. The preferences of all individuals are in the foreground. When talking about individuals, it is not important that we talk about conscripts, general tax payers, civil servant, administrators etc. The community is better off if W increases, or in our limited case, Leo's welfare increases without making Hans worse off.[14] As an individual utility function for goods leads to a system of indifference curves, a social welfare function can lead to a system of social welfare functions, as shown in figure 1.5.[15]

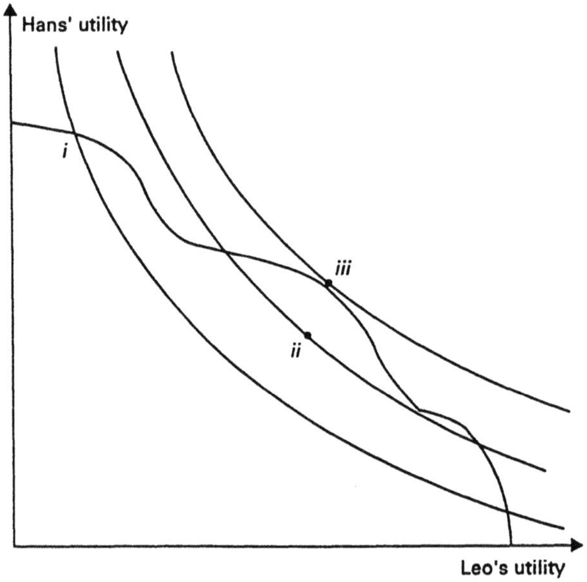

FIGURE 1.5 The maximalisation of social welfare

In figure 1.5. the utility possibility curve is added to the system of social indifference curves. From this figure we can derive that point -i- is not as favourable as point -ii-, while this last point is, opposite to point -i-, not Pareto-efficient. Point -ii- lies on a higher indifference curve and will be preferred to point -i-. It is not important that point -ii- is not Pareto-efficient. Point -iii- in

13 See D.J. Wolfson, Publieke sector en economische orde, Groningen 1988, pp. 33

14 We are not interested here in the fact how precisely the preferences of Hans and Leo originated.

15 Social welfare functions that only depend on the utilities of individuals are called "utilitarian" social welfare functions, from their association with the 19th century utilitarian philosophers.

figure 1.5. of course is most preferable. This point is both Pareto-efficient and most 'fair'.

The fundamental Theorem of Welfare Economics indicates that a system with full competition leads to an efficient allocation. However, there is no reason to believe that this will also lead to a situation where social welfare is at a maximum. Even if the economy provides an Pareto-efficient situation, government intervention can be necessary to achieve a 'fair' distribution of welfare in the community.

Let's return to military conscription. What is the relation between welfare economics and military conscription? It is important to state here that we live in a society, where the welfare of every separate individual is close to everybody's heart , which includes the welfare of the conscript. The welfare of conscripts is part of the total welfare of the community and thus plays an important part in the study of the economic aspects of military conscription. If we want to speak about a Pareto-efficient allocation, than we should include the social costs of conscription in our analysis. A Pareto-efficient allocation demands that the marginal social costs of conscription are visualized in the price of conscripts. If we do not take into account the welfare of conscripts, a difference is created between marginal social costs and marginal physical costs and social inefficiency is a result. Moreover, the individual approach in the analysis is very important, because by analyzing the opportunity costs of the individual conscript, not only the social costs of conscription can be discovered, but we can also see how the welfare positions of different groups in society are influenced by conscription.

On the basis of this individual approach we can get to a social cost-benefit analysis of the institutional design of the personnel part of the armed forces. Or in a more economic description we can say that the analysis has a micro-economic basis and uses micro-economic instruments, that ends in a macro-economic cost-benefit analysis.

§ 1.4. Conscription and scarcity

If we take a closer look at the definition of welfare, an other aspect of the economic dimension of military conscription becomes clear. "Welfare is the sum of individual utilities derived from handling with scarce alternative applicable means".[16] From this definition four elements come forward: (1) the subjective character of welfare as the sum of individual utilities; as Pigou, the founder of welfare economics, put it: "Welfare is in the mind".[17] In paragraph 1.3. we investigated extensively what this means; (2) the subjective utility aspect comes forward in the demand for alternative applicability. Utility is an external exchange rate and supposes that something can be used alternatively; (3) the

---

16 Wolfson, on cit, pp. 22 and further.

17 A.C. Pigou, The economics of welfare, London, 1962.

welfare concept has an open character. It contains every individual utility experience, even if it costs somebody's material gains. Finally (4) it is dealing with scarce resources, because without scarcity we do not have a choice problem, and can not speak about dealing with alternatives.

Scarcity collides with conscription, because conscription is not an issue of choice for the conscripts. Conscripts are obliged by law to fulfill their military service.

From this obligation it follows that the armed forces have a large amount of youngsters at their disposal. This supply of youngsters is so large that the armed forces have no incentive at all to see these people as scarce resources. So, a conscription army is a military that contains an infinite amount of conscripts, whereby the scarcity element of conscripts is very weak or non existing.[18]

On the face of it, economics should have some difficulty with conscription, because the central element, scarcity, is lacking. Lionel Robbins states:

"The economist studies the disposal of scarce means. He is interested in the way different degrees of scarcity of different goods give rise to different ratios of valuation between them, and he is interested in the way in which changes in ends or changes in means-from the demand side or the supply side-affect these ratios. Economics is the science which studies human behaviour as a relationship between ends and scarce means which have alternative uses[19]".

Considering that conscription eliminates the scarcity of labour in the armed forces, one can deduce that conscription is not of interest for an economist. But this would be completely missing the point. The obligation denies society the alternative use of certain means, but this does not mean that these means can be used alternatively. Conscription also has its social costs. Buchanan refers to Frank Knight about the principle of these costs:

"The opportunity cost notion is central. The cost of any alternative (simple or complex) chosen is the alternative that has to be given up; where there is no alternative to a given experience, no choice, there is no economic problem, and cost has no meaning. Economic cost, then, consists in the renunciation of some 'other' use of some resource or resource capacity in order to secure the benefit of the use to which it is actually devoted. The only

---

18 An all-volunteer force, or standing army is a force that has scarce resources, because the armed forces do not 'possess' a infinite large amount of conscripts. The scarcity element is very strong in an all-volunteer force. With the term conscription army we diverge from the normal term cadre-militia army, because the lack of scarcity of personnel had its influence on the whole organisation and not only on the conscription part of the armed forces. For the same reason a cadre-volunteer army is called an all-volunteer force.

19 Lionel Robbins, An essay on the nature and significance of economic science, London 1962, pp. 16.

general-cost theory which can be maintained will, after all, be that of alternative cost, ...,."[20]

Similarly, centralized economies, like the ones in Eastern Europe, before the end of the Cold War, are interesting for an economist, and because conscription introduces a centralized economy in the armed forces there is no reason to not treat the conscription issue from an economic perspective. Economics can show in this case how the situation could have been, if scarcity was really present in the armed forces. It can show the alternatives, and therefore the alternative costs. Thereby it does not only take a look at conscription as a production factor, but also at the alternative incentives that people in the armed forces receive as a consequence of the difference between the presence and absence of conscription. Scarcity introduces competition. This competition is necessary in order to really reach a Pareto-efficient situation. An armed forces without scarcity does not know the built-in incentives, that awakes the invisible hand of Adam Smith. Thus, conscription can only lead to a situation where Pareto-efficiency is almost unfeasible and can only be reached by chance.

In an investigation of conscription the search for the alternative situation leads the way. An investigation that starts with an analysis of the social costs of conscription to reveal the marginal social costs of conscripts. With these marginal social costs of conscription the all-volunteer force, the alternative situation, can be analyzed.

On the other side of the issue of the costs of conscription, there are the benefits of conscription. When discussing the benefits we are not only discussing the personal benefits of the conscripts, but also the benefits on a meso-economic and macro-economic level. Conscription brings many people into contact with different backgrounds, from different parts of the country, with different cultures and habits. Because of these contacts learning effects for the conscripts can occur, which are taken with them after the service has ended, to their own families and communities. Conscription brings integration into the community. This can most probably occur in a country that does not have many alternative communication means. Conscription brings interaction between different parts of the community, both for certain groups in society and for certain parts of the country.

Conscription also brings interaction between society and the armed forces. When analyzing conscription it has to be clear what the alternative implications for this point are in a situation where conscription no longer exists. Adam Smith says the following about the interaction between society and the armed forces in "The Wealth of Nations":

"Men of republican principles have been jealous of a standing army as dangereous to liberty. It certainly is so, wherever the interest of the general and that of the principal

---

20 J. M. Buchanan, Cost and choice, Chicago, 1969, pp. 15.

officers are not necessarily connected with the support of the constitution of the state. The standing army of Ceasar destroyed the Roman republic. The standing army of Cromwell turned the long parliament out of doors. But where the sovereign is himself the general, and the principal nobility and gentry of the country the chief officers of the army; where the military is placed under the command of those who have the greatest interest in the support of the civil authority, because they have themselves the greatest share of that authority, a standing army can never be dangereous to liberty. The security which it gives to the sovereign renders unnecessary that troublesome jealousy, which, in some modern republics, seems to watch over the minutest actions, and to be at all times ready to disturb the peace of every citizen. Where the security of the magistrate, though supported by the principal people of the country, is endangered by every popular discontent; where a small tumult is capable of bringing about in a few hours a great revolution, the whole authority of government must be employed to suppress and punish every murmur and complaint against it. To a sovereign, on the contrary, who feels himself supported, not only by the natural aristocracy of the country, but by a well regulated standing army, the rudest, the most groundless, and the most licentious remonstrances can give little disturbance. He can safely pardon or neglect them, and his consciousness of his own superiority naturally disposes him to do so. That degree of liberty which approaches to licentiousness can be tolerated only in countries where the sovereign is secured by a well-regulated standing army. It is in such countries only, that the public safety does not require, that the sovereign should be trusted with any discretionary power, for suppressing even the impertinent wantonness of this licentious liberty[21]"

With this opinion Smith is diametrically opposed to the opinions of Machiavelli, who stated more or less the opposite in his "Dell'arte della guerra"[22]. Machiavelli regarded an all-volunteer as a great danger for society. The interaction between society and the armed forces and the problems that are attached to alternative forms of the armed forces, can not be overlooked in an analysis of military conscription, just like the "sister" of military conscription, social service, and their "cousin" compulsory education.

§ 1.5. The structure of this book and the research questions

Conscription poses a lot of questions, which are elaborated and explained in this paragraph. In the next chapters, we will try to answer these questions extensively. When answering the questions a certain structure will be followed. This structure follows from chapter 1 and can be separated into two outlines. The first outline follows conscription as a tax-in-kind, while the second outline concerns conscription in a public-choice environment. The former concerns questions like the development of conscription as a tax-in-kind, the size of the

---

21 Smith, on cit., pp. 667.

22 See e.q. M.L. Tiesinga, Dienstplicht van militaire, naar sociale?, Armex defense magazine, 1992.

conscription tax, the excess burden of the conscription tax, and the effects of scarcity questions connected to conscription. With the answers to these question we like to show the social costs of conscription. In this outline a micro-economic analysis is central, both in the separate chapters as in the whole book.

With the help of the alternative costs we can take a different look at the public choice process concerning conscription. Main question is how the welfare positions of different groups, like conscripts, general tax payers, people who are concerned about the interaction between society and the armed forces, and the individuals who stress the technological and quality aspects of the armed forces, are influenced by the establishment of an all-volunteer force. The results of both outlines will then be used to make a macro-economic cost-benefit analysis of the possibility of changing a conscription army into an all-volunteer force.

Because military conscription originally concerns a set of public rules, that can be found in the constitution of the Netherlands, the analysis in this book can be situated in the field of "Law and Economics". From this description it can be derived that the analysis primarily concerns a juridical question, that is analyzed with economic methods and techniques.

Because of the special characteristics of conscription, both the Law and Economic approach, as well as New Institutional Economics are used in this book. These special characteristics primarily concern the lack of 'real' scarcity in the armed forces. The New Institutional Economics concentrates on economic theory and the improvement of this theory, by pointing to until recently neglected subjects in economics, such as the design and choice of certain institutions.

If we translate the structure of this book to specific questions, we get the following research questions:

- (1) Military conscription is a means to supply labour to the armed forces. Armed forces that primarily have the task to produce combat power, so the needs for the defense of the common good can be fulfilled. What economic aspects are attached to the defense of the common good and which actors play a role in the production process, taken into account that the defense of the common good is brought about with the help of the budget mechanism and the public choice process.
- (2) Military conscription is a phenomenon that did not appear overnight. What is the origin of conscription in the Netherlands, are economic explanations for conscription available? Moreover, we can ask ourselves, why has conscription been the norm for such a long time?
- (3) Conscription is a tax-in-kind. What is the size of this tax, what is the distribution of the tax, and what other direct costs are connected to this tax-in-kind?
- (4) Conscription disturbs the allocation in the armed forces. This disturbance causes a relative change of prices and an excess-burden. What is the size of this excess-burden, and what effect has conscription on the use of production factors in the armed forces?

- (5) The alternative for a conscription army is an all-volunteer force. Which economic aspects play a role in the composition of an all-volunteer force? Which tasks does an all-volunteer force have, and can the market mechanism fill the needs of production factors in an all-volunteer force against social costs that are acceptable, or are certain rules really necessary to get effective and efficient armed forces.
- (6) Which alternatives can replace or even improve conscription as a means of interaction between society and the armed forces? What is the role for economics in this process?
- (7) When a conscription army is transformed into an all-volunteer force a reorganisation of the armed forces is necessary. Is this transformation preferable? If the transformation of a conscription army into an all-volunteer force is possible, how should we organize this transformation process and which instruments are necessary.
- (8) In constrast to military conscription the Netherlands does not have social conscription/service. Can we compare military conscription with social service and can we learn from military conscription when we discuss the possibilities of social service? What are the benefits of military conscription and is social conscription really an alternative, if we concern the benefits of military conscription.

CHAPTER 2

The public good "Defense"

"Strategy and costs are as interdependent as the front and rear sights of a rifle".
Charles J. Hitch and Ronald N. McKean, The economics of Defense in the Nuclear Age, Cambridge, 1960, p.3.

§ 2.1. Defense and economic theory

Military conscription is part of the manner in which members of a society want to protect themselves against attacks from outside their society. In other words, military conscription is part of the public good defense.

Defense is a public good, because it is impossible to exclude those who don't want to pay, and because the demand of one person for the good does not diminish the possibilities to consume for another person (non-rivalry). Exclusion and rivalry are the central ideas in the theory of public goods. This theory states on the basis of characteristics of goods, why markets can fail as an information-, finance- or sanction mechanism, and why it can be preferable to finance some goods collectively. When using the theory of public goods, including defense, three elements are central[1]:

1) To see which characteristics of goods and efficiency motives are responsible for deciding to finance public provisions collectively
2) Efficiency is not the only motive for government intervention. Government intervention can also be motivated by external effects, monopolies, cost considerations, cultural and public opinions, and the total deficiency of markets.
3) If the government is paying for the collective good, it doesn't mean that the production of the collective good should also be done by the government.

The reasons why defense is paid by public funds has to do with the characteristics of the public good defense. An individual cannot reject defense, if he or she doesn't want it, but an individual cannot be excluded from the good either. Defense is non-excludable, because the delivery of the public good defense cannot be restricted to those people who are ready to pay the existing market price. Moreover, the consumption of the collective good defense does not restrict the consumption possibilities of another person for the same collective good. There is no rivalry in this case, but joint-consumption. In other words, the

---

1 D.J. Wolfson, Publieke sector en economische orde, Groningen, 1988, p. 46.

marginal costs of an additional unit consumption of defense is zero. It would follow that the price should be zero, and as a consequence the public good defense should be provided without charges. In the case of defense it should be added that the actual demand for defense is based on the international security situation and not on the individual demands of one person or a group of persons. The theoretical vertical aggregation of demand curves for collective goods, as done by Samuelson[2], is not suitable in the case of defense.

This means that the finance of defense becomes rather complicated, because it is not possible to prevent free-rider behaviour. The real preferences for defense are no longer clear, and as a result the provision of the public good defense fails. That is why the government finances the public good defense.

The government also provides the production of the public good defense. This does not have an economic reason, but rather a legal justification. This legal reason shall be explained in § 2.2. If the government provides the production of the collective good, it does not mean that the economic laws concerning producing the good efficiently, can not be accounted for in the defense sector.[3]

Using production means in the defense sector means that means are redeemed from the civil sector, where these means are relatively scarce with regard to the appearing needs. So, it can be said that means in the defense sector are scarce. From a military point of view, it is sometimes said, that the use of economic criteria in the armed forces is limited, because of the specific character of the armed forces. Some even go further by stating that the necessity of economic conduct in the armed forces can be called into question. However, Hitch and McKean say:

"The problem of security might in theory be regarded as one big economic problem. The nation has certain resources - now and prospectivily in the future- which are conventionally classified by economists as various sorts of land, labor, and capital. These subjects can be used to satisfy many objectives of the nation and its individual citizens - national security, a high standard of living, social security, and a rapid rate of economic growth, and so on. These are, of course, competing objectives. In general the more resources the nation devotes to national security, the less it will have for social security and vice versa".[4]

Every organization tries to make a product with the efficient use of its available capital and labour. In the armed forces this production is called combat power. In practice the term combat power is not very often used. Usually, the product of the armed forces is described in terms of inputs, like the amount of soldiers,

---

2 Paul. A. Samuelson, The Pure Theory of Public Expenditure, Review of Economics and Statistics 36, 1954, pp. 387-389.

3 See for example: K.A.M. Bogaert, Aspecten van het economisch handelen in de militaire organisatie, Maandschrift economie, 1965, pp. 378-381.

4 Charles J. Hitch en Roland N. McKean, The Economics of Defense in the Nuclear Age. Cambridge ,1960, p 3.

tanks, or planes. However, it is more correct to describe the product of the armed forces in terms like: "the defense of the Northern-German plains during a period of 100 days" or "the ability to fight two wars in two separate parts of the world, plus the possibility to fulfill the wishes of the UN to take part in 3 UN-missions". This 'abstract'-output is decided by the international security situation and the public choice mechanism and not by the armed forces themselves. The armed forces are asked to produce the public good 'defense'. The 'output' of the armed forces may be decided outside of economic markets, but in regards to the input factors there is no reason to exclude the armed forces from economic market conditions.

This distinction is very important, and is stressed by Wolfson in his third point considering the theory of collective goods. The presence of a pure collective good, like defense, means that the government takes care of the finance of that good. Who produces the collective good is an entirely different question. This theory includes pure collective goods too. For example, dikes for protection against the sea are financed collectively, but are built by private constructing companies.

In a situation where the output of the armed forces is decided by the international security situation and the public choice mechanisms, an efficiently operating armed forces is based on the minimization of its inputs, capital and labour. In the armed forces efficiency should be prominent too. There may be a public conflict about the question how much money to spend on several public provisions, but once it is decided how much money is to be spent on defense, it is its task to provide this collective good against minimal costs. There is not a single conflict between military strategy, technology to provide combat power, and the efficient use of means in the armed forces. Hitch and McKean say:

"There is a conflict between defense and other goods in deciding on the size of the military budget. Economizing involves deciding how much of other things to sacrifice in the interest of military strength. But in decisions on how to spend the military budget - on what kinds of equipment and forces to implement what kind of strategy - there is no such conflict. Strategy, technology, and economy are not three independent "considerations" to be assigned appropriate weights, but interdependent elements of the same problem. Strategies are ways of using budgets or resources to achieve military objectives. Technology defines the possible strategies. The economic problem is to choose that strategy, including equipment and everything else necessary to implement it, which is most efficient (maximizes the attainment of the objective with the given resources) or economical (minimizes the cost of achieving the given objective) - the strategy which is most efficient also being the most economical".[5]

In conclusion we can say that economic theory can be used to analyze the armed forces without restriction, and that these armed forces should conform to

---

5 Idem, blz. 3.

economic laws. If they do not , an inefficient production will follow, which does not only have severe consequences for the armed forces itself, but for society as a whole.

§ 2.2. The monopoly of violence of the government

Other than the financing of the public good defense, the government also takes care of the production of the same good. The public good defense is produced by the armed forces, consisting of the Royal Army, Royal Navy, Royal Air Force and Royal Military Police. As mentioned before, this has a legal cause. Only the government is allowed to use violence. It alone possesses the monopoly of violence.

The armed forces employs both military personnel and civilians . In addition, within the armed forces a distinction can be made between combat groups and non-combat groups. This distinction is called the "teeth-to-tail-ratio". The teeth of the armed forces are those sections considered violent (combat groups) and the tail of the armed forces consists of the parts supporting the task in the production process of the defense (non-combat groups). The involvement of the government is necessary for the combat groups, because these parts of the armed forces use violence. The other supporting parts can be done by civilians or private initiatives, because these tasks do not have an element of violence.[6]
The distinction made between combat positions for soldiers and non-combat positions for civilians differ from the "Regeling inzake het aanmerken van functies als organieke militaire- of burgerfuncties". According to article 2 of this regulation:

"Organic military positions are described as:
a. positions that have as their main or secondary task the use of a weaponry or a weapon system, as well a positions that have a direct relation to these positions.
b. positions that need military expertise.
c. positions which in exceptional circumstances need military authority or where military authority can be delegated to, or positions which demand military hierarchy in war times."[7]

Positions mentioned under a. are clearly combat positions. The question is why positions mentioned under b. and c. can not be fulfilled by civilians. From the explanation to article 2 it becomes clear that positions under b. are:

---

6 It says "can be done", because it is not a natural thing to do. The supporting parts of the armed forces can be supplied by civilians of private initiative, if they are cheaper than the military. Otherwise these tasks could also have been provided by the military. In chapter 5 this will be investigated thoroughly.

7 Regeling inzake het aanmerken van functies als organieke militaire- of burgerfuncties, in: Maatschappelijke Raad voor de Krijgsmacht, advice nr. 16, Verhouding burger- en militair personeel, The Hague, august 1989, pp. 36.

"With military expertise - which can only be acquired by having a military career - a more than average knowledge of personnel and material means is meant, as well as the experience and abilities needed to use these means effectively."[8]

Military expertise is an objective phenomenon, which can be acquired by knowledge of the organization and the means in the organization. It becomes clear from the explanation that this knowledge can only be acquired by having a military career. But we can find a lot of people in the world who have an excellent knowledge of the armed forces, without having such a career. Within the armed forces too, there are a lot of people who have military expertise without the military career. Military expertise is mostly obtained, by acquiring knowledge about the armed forces. A military career is not strictly necessary for this. So, there is no reason to deny the positions under b. to be fulfilled by civilians.

The positions under c. can also be filled by civilians, if we keep in mind that in situations described under c. formal responsibilities of civilians get a military character. In other words, for these positions it is not necessary to have a military career, but it is sufficient that civilians can handle military hierarchical relationships in extreme circumstances. The task of the civilian does not change. The legal relationships do change.

The difference between positions with a combat character and those with a non -combat character is not only found in the armed forces. In research in the efficiency and effectiveness of the police, in most cases a difference is made between 'real' police work and positions that only need 'restricted' tracing authority or no authority at all. Boorsma and Bokkes state in their research of the economic benefits of deputies:

"The fact that,...., in different amounts partly authorized or non-authorized personnel is used and one sees possibilities to allocate work to non-authorized personnel points out to the fact that the possibilities are underestimated on this issue.[9]"

The difference between combat positions and non-combat positions are also found in the peace-operations of the United Nations. With peace-keeping it is tried to keep the disputing parties apart, without using violence. The UN-weapons are only serving as a means of self-defence. So, a position in a peace-keeping unit is in principle a non-combat position. If violence is used, this is for self-defense. In practice we see that next to troops also civilians are used to perform UN-peace-keeping duties. Strictly speaking, military personnel is not necessary in an UN-peace-keeping operation. That military personnel is used is because no alternatives are available. Only the Swedes got a specific UN-

8 Ibid, pp.39.

9 P.B. Boorsma and W.T.M. Bokkes, De economische baten van hulpagenten, in: Openbare uitgaven 23, nr.5, september 1991.

department. This department is a independent part of the Department of Defence. People who are sent abroad for peace-keeping operations are selected from a labour pool and get a civilian contract.[10] Only when an UN-task changes from "peace-keeping" into "peace-enforcing", military participation is necessary, because the use of violence is an explicit part of the assignment now.[11]

§ 2.3. The organization of the armed forces in the Netherlands

In paragraph 1 of this chapter we have seen that the armed forces are an organisation of capital and labour, which produces combat power. With this combat power they try to keep the enemy out, both on land, at sea and in the air.

For this task an efficient organization is necessary. In this paragraph an overview will be given of the organizational structure of the armed forces. This overview serves as a reference structure for the rest of this book, where we speak about the organization of the armed forces or about parts of the armed forces.

The organization schedules are based upon the 'Defensienota 1991'. The structure of the 'Defensienota 1991' also served as a starting point for the analysis in this book. After the 'Defensienota 1991' the 'Prioriteitennota 1993' appeared. Because the 'Prioriteitennota 1993' has the same structure as the 'Defensienota 1991' the analysis is not changed for the 'Prioriteitennota 1993'. The taxonomy is the same, only the extent of the changes is a little bigger in the 'Prioriteitennota 1993'.

The top of the military organization in the Netherlands is called the "Centrale Organisatie". Main task of this central organization is to steer all the parts of the armed forces, Royal Navy, Royal Air Force, Royal Army and the Royal Military Police, in terms of putting at disposal the necessary means for production. The structure of the central organization is given in schedule 2.1.
The secretary-general is the most important civil servant at the Ministry of Defense. He is among other things responsible for the information streams to the ministers and the integration and coordination of the general policies of the armed forces. The Chief of the General Staff is the highest advisor on operational policies. He has an important role in steering the parts of the armed forces. Each of the directors-general are charged with the development and advice about headlines of these policies. Each director-general has a specific task in this field. This task is coupled to the instruments, which are used by the central-organization to steer the separate parts of the armed forces. Beside this the central organization has a few supporting groups, like the unit Housing, Works and Grounds, the unit Computerization, the unit Telecommunication and the unit Scientific Research.

---

10 Information received through interviews with Swedish civil servants, Mr Kirsten Lindholm, head of the education section, UN-department, Stockholm, august 19, 1991.

11 In chapter 6 the UN-operations and its implications are elaborated.

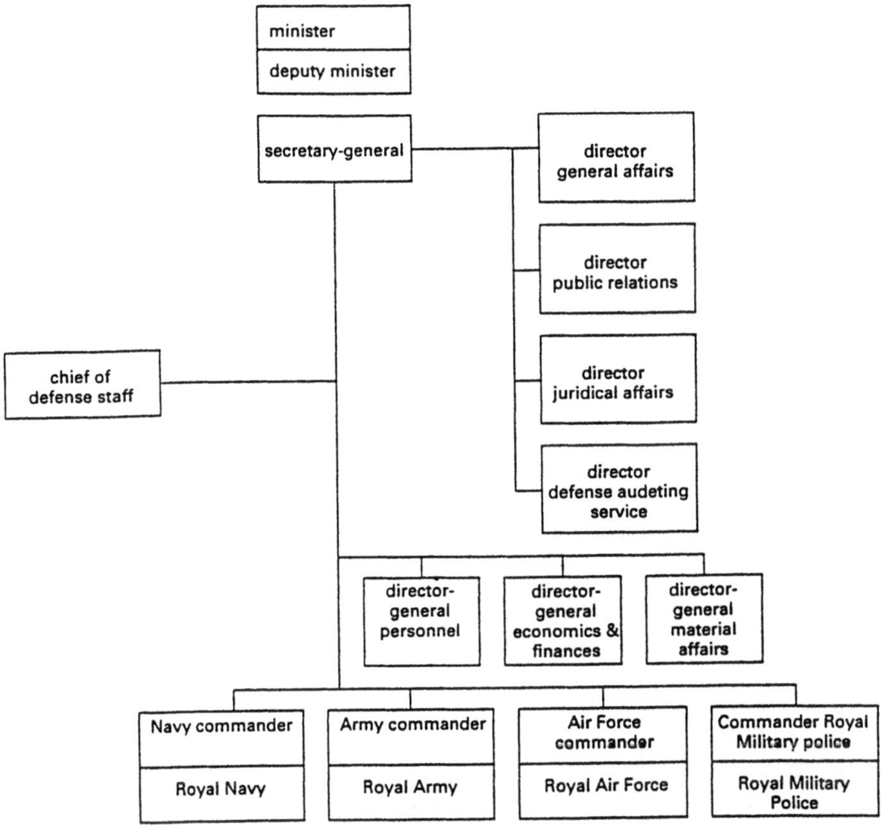

SCHEDULE 2.1 The central organisation

At the top of each of the parts of the armed forces, there is a commander. The commander is responsible for the policies and the execution of these policies in his part of the armed forces. For reasons of clarity only the organisational structure of the Royal Army will be elaborated upon. The organisation of the other parts of the armed forces, have more or less the same structure, only the names of the operational parts are different[12].

12 These organization schemes can be found in the Defensienota 1991, pp. 217-230 and pp. 241-247.

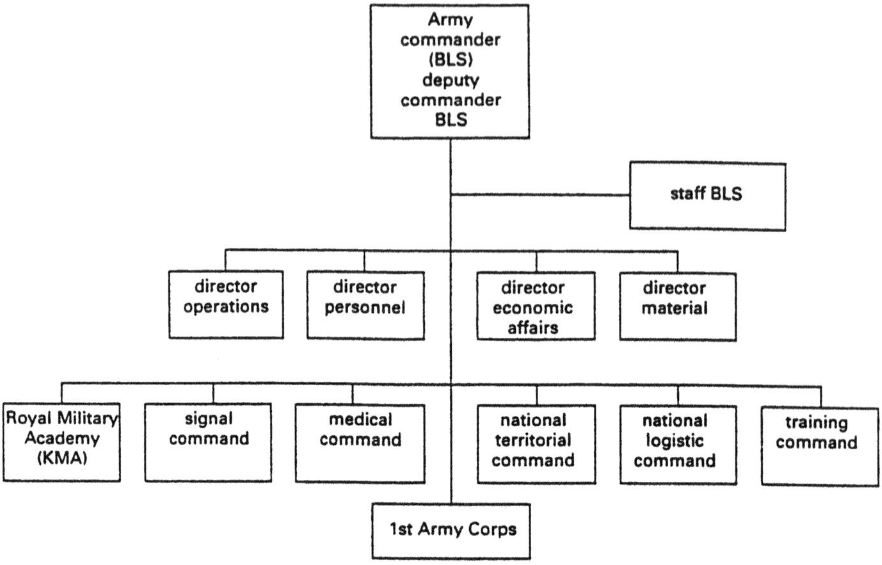

SCHEDULE 2.2 The Royal Army

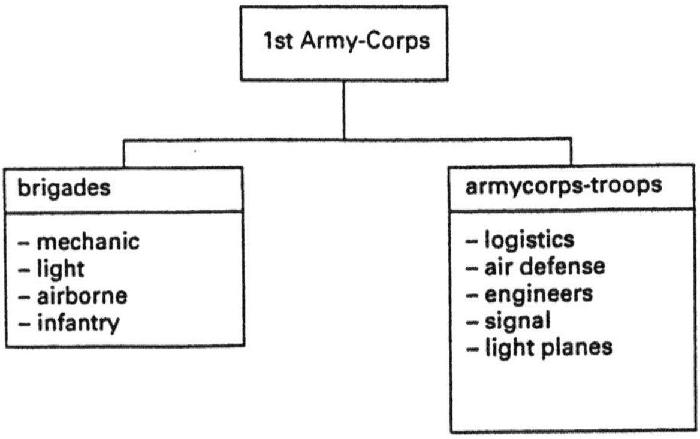

SCHEDULE 2.3 The 1st-Army-Corps

Directly under the Army commander are the Army Staffs. These are summarized in schedule 2.2.. Of all the parts in the Royal Army, the First Army is meant to keep the enemy out of the country. In order to get a better view on the organization of this First Army, the First Army is divided into brigades and army troops in schedule 2.3. The brigades deliver the real combat power, but for a decent execution of their task they depend directly on the army troops.

In this book the First Army can be seen as the combat troops. All other units are non-combat troops, because on the one side these units deliver no direct combat power, and on the other side because some of these units are not meant for external purposes, but have a domestic character.

The armed forces are an organization of capital and labour. Just because of this labour component the armed forces are a dynamic organization, that is a child of her employees. Employees, or in these case bureaucrats, have specific tasks in the armed forces. Next to this task, bureaucrats also have personal interests. The next paragraph elaborates upon the role of human beings in the armed forces, especially the bureaucrats and the civil servant in temporarily service, the conscript.

§ 2.4. Defense, conscription and the role of bureaucrats

As we have seen earlier, defense is a public good. This means that the process of pay, say and benefit about one good can not be united in one person. Demand and supply are not united by the market, but by public choice. The budget mechanism tries to take over the price mechanism in order to produce public goods. The budget mechanism can only be efficient if a lot of people cooperate, but every human being has their own peculiarities. In the public sector, and also in the armed forces, the behaviour of the producers of the public good, the bureaucrats, also play an important role[13].

In early literature the behaviour of civil servants played an subordinate role. Partly this has to do with the organic thoughts about the state. In a state where the organic view prevails, individuals are subordinate to the goals of the state and the personal goals of civil servants are not regarded as relevant. Every organization, private or public, is seen as an indivisible organic entity, from which the acts of his servants do not differ a lot from the behaviour of the organization as a whole. This opinion, also called the holistic organization opinion, can not be used properly to analyse the behaviour of very big bureaucratic organizations, like the armed forces.

Here, the mechanistic vision of the state is central. In this vision the role of the state is subordinate to the one of the individual. This will say, various individuals have founded a government, in order to get a better provision of their needs. In this mechanistic vision, there is also space for research about the internal and external behavior of government bureaucracies, like Downs and Niskanen have done.[14]

From these investigations it becomes clear that the behaviour of civil servants can have an important effect on the existence of military conscription. The departing point in these investigations is that the civil servant is no longer an 'impartial' part of the organization, subordinate to the goals of the political

---

13 For the next part of this paragraph, the following books has been used: J.G.A. van Mierlo, Ambtelijk gedrag in bureaucratische organisaties, in: A.F.A. Korsten and Th.A.J. Toonen, Bestuurskunde, Leiden, 1988 and N.A.A. Baakman (ed), Overheid en onderneming, een inleiding, Open Universiteit, Heerlen, 1991.

14 Downs, A., Inside Bureaucracy, Boston, 1967 and W. Niskanen, Bureaucracy and Representative Government, Chicago, 1971.

leadership, but an individual who strives for the maximization of his own goals within the institutional context he or she works in.

Downs analyses the internal behaviour of members of bureaucratic organizations, both in the private as in the public sector. Bureaucratic organizations, or in short bureaus, are organizations who specialize in the supply of those provisions, of which some public organization wishes that the amount of this provision exceeds above the amount that is produced by the market and whereby that organization is not prepared to contract with a profit-seeking organization.

According to Downs, bureaus have the following characteristics:[15]

1. They are big.
2. Most employees work full-time, almost their whole life for bureaus and get most of their income from these bureaus.
3. Employees are engaged, stay and are promoted on the basis of an expected role within the bureau.
4. Most of the production of the bureau is not evaluated directly or indirectly in external markets, on the basis of quid pro quo transactions.

According to Downs, the members of the bureau, in our case the civil servants of the Ministry of Defense, are driven by motives of their own interests attached to the benefits that belong to their positions.

Niskanen has analysed the external relation between politicians and civil servants with the help of a mathematical-economical model, in which politicians demand public goods and services and give civil servants production orders in exchange for public funds. This model is an example of a principal-agent model.

It is assumed that the principal, in our case the parliament, has less information about the production process than the agents. Because of this situation of asymmetric information, it is difficult for the principal to check if the work is done according to its will. As long as the results are not too far off from the expected results, the agent can handle the situation as he or she wants. They get the liberty to strive for their own goals, within certain boundaries.

Under the variables that influence the goals of a civil servant are the next: salary, status, power, the size of the bureau, the comfort with which the civil servants achieves changes and the comfort with which he or she manages a bureau. All these variables, except the last two, are a monotonous climbing function of the total budget of the bureau.

Niskanen concludes that civil servants strive for budget maximization and without exception. Even civil servants with a preference for low wages and a relative huge motivation to change things for the benefit of the people, will strive for the maximization of their budgets.[16]

Budget maximization is a necessary, but not sufficient condition in the theory of Niskanen. Bureaus and civil servants are restricted in their urge to expand by

---

15 Downs, pp. 24-31.

16 Niskanen, pp.38.

the expected output from the principal, who gives him his money. Niskanen summarizes both conditions, as follows:

"Bureaucrats maximize the total budget of their bureau during their tenure, subject to the constraint that the budget must be equal to or greater than the minimum total cost of supplying the output expected by the bureau's sponsor."[17]

This implies that civil servants have an incentive to change the perceptions of the sponsor with the help of promotional activities, analogous to promotional activities in the market sector. Civil servants of the Ministry of Defense can do this for example by stressing the international security risks in the world.[18]

Conscription appears, where the bureau reaches the boundaries of his budget. This is because a bureau is not only dealing with a principal, but with three kinds of groups: 1) the public organization who provides the bureau of money (the principal), 2) the suppliers of production factors and 3) in some cases consumers who pay for certain services a price-per-unit. For the armed forces this means that parliament is the sponsor and with the suppliers of production factors, the producers of army equipment and the suppliers of labour, like conscripts, are meant.

The relation between the civil servants of the Ministry of Defense and their principal is already explained. Parliament votes every year about the defense budget and after approval of the budget the armed forces have the means to produce their product. In this paragraph it will be assumed that parliament has a passive role. It knows the amount of money it is willing to spend for the production of a certain amount of combat power, but does not have the means or possibilities to acquire the information what is minimally necessary to generate this amount of combat power.

The second relation, the one between the armed forces and the suppliers of production factors, is in this study of military conscription of eminent importance. Most bureaus attract their labour and capital on competing markets. They pay the same price for equal sorts of production factors. Under these conditions there will not be much difference between bureaus and profit-seeking enterprises concerning attracting capital and labour.

The first base for wage- and factor price discrimination, of which conscription is one form, is that bureaus are the only provider of some services. These bureaus have a monopoly as a demander of labour skills and capital, that are necessary for the production of these services. A second base for wage- and factor price discrimination is that such bureaus often want to make a first claim

---

17 Ibid.

18 After the release of the Meijer-report a fierce discussion appeared in the media about the international security analysis in the report. Supporters of the draft drew attention to the chaotic character of the international security situation and the threat that could follow from that situation. The supporters of this vision could mainly be found under those defense employees who were responsible for the operational tasks.

on sources, which seem to be of public ownership, like air, nuclear material, ground, but also young, healthy and intelligent people.

The possibilities of monopsonistic competition will be used by bureaus, because it enlarges both its budget and its output. The execution of wage- and factor price discrimination is mainly limited to national bureaus, like the armed forces, police, health care, elderly care etc., because these bureaus have a bigger monopoly power, use complicated materials and possess common resources. However, this must not be seen as a general characteristic of bureaus.

Wage- and factor price discrimination is a risky business if the interests of the people, who supply labour and capital, are represented in parliament. In such a case a bureau will not use its possibilities, because it is running the risk of loosing the support of the sponsor. But if the owners of capital and labour are not represented strongly in the sponsor organisation, as is the case for draft suitable youngsters, bureaus will continuously try to use its possibilities for wage- and factor price discrimination. Often this appeal is justified by stressing the rights of the state and the civil duty.

The analysis of bureaus, that use wage- and factor price discrimination, leads to the following hypothesis given by Niskanen:

"Some bureaus, specifically those that operate in the budget-contrained region[19] and face increasing prices for specific factors, may exercise factor price discrimination. They have a larger budget and output of services (and a lower average budget per unit of output) than other bureaus with similar demand and cost conditions that pay competitive prices. Such factor price discrimination is most likely to be used on those specific factors which are weakly represented by the officers of the sponsor organization"[20].

In his theory, Niskanen makes a distinction between a bureau that operates in a "budget-contrained-region" and a bureau that operates in a "demand-contrained-region". Considering the consequences for conscription, it is good to think about this distinction.

In the first case we are dealing with an ordinary principal-agent relation, whereby the budget of the bureau has been tied up by the principal. If the principal has complete information about the bureau, budget maximization is fully consistent with cost minimization at the equilibrium level of production. In such a case wage- and factor price discrimination, or in our case conscription, is almost impossible to realize. This is because the sponsor will account for the costs of conscription in his political choice. This doesn't mean that conscription is impossible, but not very likely to appear.

In the case that a bureau is working in a "demand-contrained-region", external affairs play an important role by declaring the budget. The bureau escapes from the strict supervision of the principal, because the bureau has to

19 The explanation of this concept is given in the next part of this paragraph
20 Niskanen, pp. 50.

take care of the provision in all circumstances. For the armed forces this means that they have to resist the enemy with all available means.

This point also makes clear why in the armed forces, there is the idea that economic behavior is not really necessary, because the armed forces have a special task. If a bureau is situated in a "demand-contrained-region", the bureau will not be very interested to acquire costs savings and will be insensible for rising costs that lower the output of the bureau too, without leaving the "demand-contrained-region". If the principal asks for budget savings, a bureau that deals with several services, will try to lower the costs on his "budget-contrained-services, while the costs of the "demand-contrained-services will be raised as high as possible, so that the budget will run out and costs savings seem to be impossible.

In the Cold War it could be stated that the armed forces were situated in the "demand-contrained-region". A situation that did not need a costs savings mind. With the end of this war, the armed forces are under the threat of falling back completely to the "budget-contrained-region" with all possible consequences.

The costs of the armed forces will play an important role and parliament will play her old role as a principle again, by clearly stating the output of the armed forces. The civil servant within the armed forces will be hampered in his pursuit for power and status and will possible be forced to slow down.

In the following chapters the aspects of bureaucracy considering conscription and the armed forces will play an important role. In chapter 4 and 5 the cost aspects of the armed forces are narrowly analysed, and chapter 8 takes a look at the conflicts and problems that appear when the transformation of a conscription army in an all-volunteer force is taken into account.

In summary, we can say that the principal-agent theory and the connecting behaviour of civil servants can be linked to the institution military conscription. A connection that becomes very clear when the armed forces are asked to get smaller, because in such a situation the budget of the armed forces is not based on the ideas about the enemy, but based on public choice. A cost minimizing armed forces will collide with the budget maximizing civil servants in the same armed forces. However it is not correct, that conscription only results from the behavior of civil servants, the public choice process also has her effect on the public good defense and conscription.

§ 2.5. Conscription, voluntary service and the role of public choice about the size of the public good defense

In the last paragraph we have seen that conscription is not a self-evident feature. Bureaus try to use wage- and factor price discrimination in their pursuit for budget maximization. Conscription is one example. As we have seen in chapter one, conscription can be regarded as a tax-in-kind. If we think about the fact that fiscal choice is not a given fact, but the consequence of a public choice process, we can also analyse the choice for conscription with our economic tools.

This paragraph tries to analyse conscription from an alternative perspective.[21] The standard analysis uses a personal market orientated choice; the size and composition of the budget for the public good defense are taken as assumed and then the effects of alternatives in fiscal choice (conscription or all-volunteers) on the allocation of production factors and distribution of income are taken into account.[22]

§ 2.5.1. The model

We assume that we live in a "two-good-world" with "butter" and "canons", whereby butter is a substitute for all civil, non-military services and canons a substitute for all the military services. In this two-good-world n-individuals are present, who vote by majority about how much butter and how many canons will be supplied.[23]

We start with the description of the budgetary balance, that results if the input factors capital and labour are provided voluntarily in the production process of the canons. In § 2.5.2. conscription will be introduced and the results of this introduction in terms of budget allocated to canons is investigated.

Every individual (i) has a utility function $Ui = Fi\ (B,K)$, whereby B represents the amount of butter that is available for every individual and K is the amount of canons that is available for the whole community, of which individual (i) is taking part. Every individual (i) maximizes its utility under the budget restriction $PbB+PkK=Ii$, whereby Ii is the income of individual (i) and Pb and Pk are the prices of butter and canons.

For every individual (i) applies that $Ti = Ti(K)$ represents the amount of taxation that has to be paid for the amount of canons supplied. This amount of taxation also represents the amount of butter that the indiviual (i) is willing to give up for the canons.

21 This analysis is based on: Richard E. Wagner, Conscription, Voluntary Service, and Democratic Fiscal Choice, in: Buchanan and Tollison, Theory of Public Choice, 1972, pp. 136-152.

22 The original choice between conscription or no conscription and the existence of conscription is analysed in chapter 3, paragraph 5. In this paragraph attention is paid to the size of the public good defense, as a result from the decision for or against conscription.

23 The model used looks like the Samuelson model, considering the choice about the size of public goods, but is not the same. In this thesis and in this paragraph the size of the public good is mainly based on the international security situation and only secondly by the public choice proces, and the latter only as a consequence from the choice between fiscal alternatives.

Vi = Vi(K) represents the value of the amount of canons supplied to the individual (i). As long as Vi'(K) > Ti'(K) the individual (i) has a preference for an expansion of the amount of canons, because his marginal utility for canons exceeds the marginal utility of butter he has to give up.

The optimal amount of canons, the budget for military services for individual (i), is that amount for which Vi'(K) = Ti'(K) applies.[24] If we translate the preferences of one individual in the community to the whole community we get the following vectors:
T = (T1'(K), T2'(K),.........,Tn(K)) is a vector of marginal taxprices, whereby T>0 and V = (V1'(K), V2'(K),........,Vn(K) is a vector that represents the value of marginal expenses to canons, whereby V>0. From these vectors a third vector can be derived for the net marginal preference P, so that P = -T + V. When choosing for a marginal expansion of the amount of canons, an individual will agree as long as Pi>0. A common decision to expand the amount of canons will be reality as long as Pi>0 for m>(n+1)/2 individuals, whereby n is an odd number.

An equilibrium in the common supply of canons will appear if:

- Pi>0 for (n-1)/2 individuals i=1,2,.......,j-1;
- Pi=0 for 1 individual i=j; and
- Pi<0 for (n-1)/2 individuals i=j+1, j+2,.......,n.

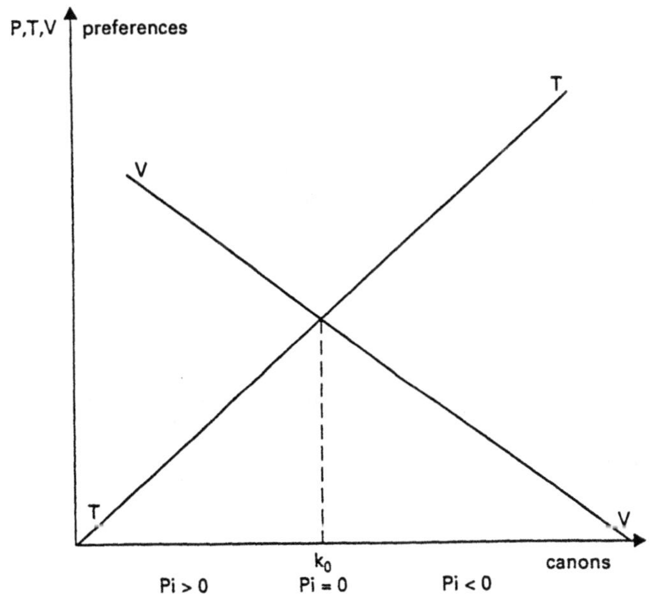

FIGURE 2.1 The median-votermodel and the preferences for butter and canons

---

24 It is assumed here that the second-order conditions Vi''(K)<0 and Ti''(K)>0 apply.

The first group has above median preferences, the last group has preferences below the level of the medium voter and individual (j) is the median voter. In this median voter model K0 canons will be chosen. Individual taxation will be equal to t=K0Ti'(K) and total tax receipts (R) will be R = K0Tμ.[25] Graphically this choice process is presented in figure 2.1.

§ 2.5.2. The introduction of conscription

Conscription is a tax-in-kind. If we add conscription to the existing monetary taxes, we find that conscripts pay a higher price for canons than non-conscripts with an equal income. The imposition of conscription can also be seen as an income transfer from conscripts to non-conscripts. λ = (λ1,λ2,.....,λn) is a vector of multiplicators, that make K0Tμ = K0Tλ.[26] Conscription changes the structure of taxation in such a way that λ1>1 for conscripts and 0<λ1<1 for non-conscripts. The per unit tax price gets Ti'(K)λi, and individual taxation gets K0Ti'(K)λi. This change in tax structure will also have its effect on the public choice process, and as a result of that on the amount of canons that will be chosen by the community.
We will investigate how a change in the tax system will have its effect on budgetary policy, both in the case that conscripts are excluded from voting, as in the case they are allowed to vote as a member of the community.

If conscripts are excluded from voting, their preferences will not influence the public choice, except in the case that there are people in the rest of the voting community who are more interested in the interests of specific conscripts than in their own interests. Because Ti'(K)λi<Ti'(K) for non-conscripts, individuals who had already a Pi>0 under a voluntary service will have it now too.

For the median voter Pi>0 in the case of conscription. And of the (n-1)/2 individuals who had Pi<0 under conscription, some will have a Pi>0 now.[27] Expansion of the amount of canons is the result, because Pi>0 for m>(n+1)/2 individuals in the voting population. This expansion will continue until a new equilibrium K1 is reached. This new equilibrium satisfies the conditions for an equilibrium under majority voting, which we have seen before.

If conscripts have voting rights, the analyses will change and hereby we assume two extreme cases. In the first case we assume that all conscripts belong to the group for which Pi<0 applies under a voluntary service. Even if this group consists completely from conscripts (i.e. (n-1)/2 part of the community is a conscript) the above described written analysis holds without exception, whereby Pj = 0. If there are less than (n-1)/2 conscripts, some individuals who

25 μ is a vector, that is necessary to express R into one number.

26 μ is a monetary tax, while λ is a tax-in-kind with the same value as μ

27 For analytical purposes it is assumed here that the population of the community has a normal continual distribution regarding their preferences for butter and canons.

experienced $P_i<0$ first, will have a $P_i>0$ now because of the change in the tax structure and an expansion of canons is the result.

The possession of voting power of conscripts can only influence the outcome of the public choice process in the second case, whereby some conscripts belong to the group for which under voluntary service $P_i>0$. Conscription means that for some conscripts $P_i<0$ and the question appears where the new equilibrium K1 will arise. This new equilibrium will depend on the restructuring of preferences of both conscripts and non-conscripts.

If the amount of canons raises to K1, the budget for canons will raise with (K1-K0)Tl, expressed in terms of sacrificed butter. For the minority, the conscripts, applies that $K1Ti'(K)\lambda i>K0Ti'(K)$ because $K1>K0$ and $\lambda 1>1$. However, for the majority in the community, the non-conscripts, $K1Ti'(K)\lambda i>=<K0Ti'(K)$ applies, because $K1>K0$ is opposite to $\lambda 1<1$. When any inelasticity in the demand for canons exists, total payments by non-conscripts will be lowered, though with less than the rise in burden for the conscripts. In a situation of conscription the marginal costs for the majority of the voters, which are per head:

$$\left(\sum_{i=1}^{j} T'i(K)\lambda\, i\right)/j \quad ,$$

are less than the costs for the whole community, which are per head:

$$\left(\sum_{i=1}^{j} T'i(K)\lambda\, i\right)/n + \left(\sum_{i=j+1}^{n} T'i(K)\lambda\, i\right)/n$$

Because the choice of a community is based on the marginal costs of the majority, that are less than the marginal social costs of the whole community, tax discrimination leads to the Pigou-critique about the difference between marginal private costs and marginal social costs and a larger amount of canons.

In this paragraph we have seen that it is probable that a conscription army produces a larger amount of output (canons) than an all-volunteer force. The expansion of the amount of canons is not the result of the behaviour of budget maximizing bureaucrats, but the result of a democratic decision process, whereby a majority imposes the burden of defending the community to a minority.

§ 2.6. Summary

This chapter has shown a variety of analyses, which can all be used to investigate the specific aspects of the public good defense and the producer of the good: the armed forces. As a conclusion we can say that economic theories do not lose their values within the armed forces, but can even bring forward very interesting features. This chapter has also shown us several economic tools. Other than the tools of general economics and public choice, the literature study will also be used. The combination of neo-classical economics and public choice is important, because with these instruments the analysis of military conscription can be given a different face. In an investigation after the personnel component in the armed forces not only the describing or fundamental analysis of the factor labour is important, even more interesting is the behaviour of people in the armed forces, because of conscription. Both the behaviour of individuals, and groups of individuals like departments or even the whole armed forces are central in this analysis. An application of the theories will be shown in the following chapters. In these chapters we will use the methods and instruments described here.

CHAPTER 3

The history and existence of conscription in the Netherlands

For many ages now, mankind has been busy with the protection of its possessions. Sometimes the enemy is water and dikes and mounds are erected. Other times human beings rise up in arms and require them to defend themselves man against man. In the thousand-year period that proceeded the introduction of the general and personal conscription system in the Netherlands, military service has been a class privilege up until the beginning of the middle ages, becoming a profession until the downfall of the Republic, and after which it became an obligation, which was assigned to one class, especially to the poorer classes in society. In contradiction to earlier times it became a privilege to be exempted from military service.[1]

In this chapter the origin and the existence of conscription will be studied. In the first part of this chapter the historical development of conscription is central. In this part a special place is assigned to the case of replacement. In the second part of the chapter the emphasis is on the theoretical aspects of the existence of conscription in a democratic environment.

§ 3.1. The origin of military conscription in the Netherlands

In the course of the ages military conscription has known times of prosperity and times of decline. In the middle ages military conscription was almost unknown, but the issue of conscription as it appeared during the Roman empire returned in the period of the Renaissance. However, the primitive structure of the state in the sixteenth century did not allow it to become practice, as was intended in article 7 of the Union of Utrecht (1579). Despite some formal attempts, the deficiency of a powerful organizing body and the absence of a feeling of unity made all regulations dealing with military conscription a dead issue.

The idea of military conscription returns at the end of the eighteenth century with the French Revolution. The "levée en masse", which placed all men between 18 and 40 at disposal of Paris, provided France an army of 650.000 men

---

1 See e.g. F.C. Spits, Klassedienstplicht in de negentiende eeuw, plaatsvervanging en afkoop, in: Driekwart eeuw historisch leven in Den Haag, 1975, p. 201.

in 1793. As a consequence of the actions in France, the Netherlands formally re-introduced military conscription in 1798.

The execution of conscription did not take place until 1810, and becomes a fact of daily life after the annexation of the Netherlands by France. Each year some part of the Dutch youth is added to the armies of the French emperor by a lottery-system.

After the collapse of the Napoleonic Empire in 1813, the Netherlands come under the influence of sovereign of the Netherlands, king Willem I. One of his tasks was to organize new armed forces. At first he tried to get volunteers, but this being insufficient, he later starts a "last-reserves" and a militia. The militia would be formed of people between 17 and 46 years old. A lottery would decide, which persons had to serve, whereby it was permitted to replace some one else. With these two systems a conscription-force developed slowly next to an all-volunteer force, based on the same military conscription principle that was so much detested under Napoleonic rule.

In 1814 a general, personal conscription system is introduced in the constitution and as a consequence in 1815 the first militia law is brought about. Practical facts teach us that the recruiting of the stand-by force was not very successful, because those who wanted to be a volunteer could do this more profitably by serving as a substitute. By Royal Decree it was then decided to merge the national militia with the volunteers. This announced the beginning of the abolishment of the standing army , and the armed forces were developing themselves into a conscription army. "Bij gebrek aan vrijwilligers had het Napoleontische conscriptiestelsel gezegevierd"[2], Campagne stated.

§ 3.2. Replacement

One of the main causes for the failure of a standing army can be found in the replacement system within the conscription-system of the nineteenth century. During these times the conscription system was more or less accepted. Everybody was obliged to fulfill his duty in the defense of the country. However, in reality this obligation was limited. For an amount that depended on supply and demand, a rich man could be replaced by someone else.

In principle, replacement was hardly discussed. Replacement was a system that was existing practice and accepted throughout Europe in those days. Replacement was morally accepted too, because it was felt that if war was really eminent, the inequality between the rich and the poor would disappear, because the rich would also volunteer to defend national territory. In the nineteenth century the time between mobilisation and concentration of troops would take months before a war would follow. In a slowly starting war there would be

2 "Because of a lack of volunteers the Napoleonic conscription system triumphed". in C.T. Campagne, Over het ontstaan en de ontwikkeling van het instituut van de militaire dienstplicht, in: Kernvraag 4, pp. 5-24, 1968.

plenty of time for the rich to prepare for the dealing with arms. According to a lot of writers during that time the rich would take part in the defense of the country voluntarily if the need was really there.[3]

However, in time of peace it had to be possible to have oneself replaced. Personal conscription during peace time would create inequality, because someone who was going to be replaced was predestined for "liberal" professions, that needed a lengthy and expensive education. It would not have been in the interest of the citizen and least of all for the state to disturb such an education. The time of the citizen was expensive. It was felt that a few months of his life could not be compared with the equal amount of time for a common man, who would be clothed, fed and sheltered even better than he normally would be used to. From this social and economic justification the opportunity cost principle of conscription becomes clear. This idea is elaborated in chapter 4 and applied to our age.

The replacement system was also politically useful according to many people, because it gave the common people a place to work, where almost everybody was able to work. Moreover, the replacement system diminished the possible danger from having too many idle hands, for the state. And the substitute had a higher moral, because he was serving voluntarily. The replacement system was legally untouchable too, because the system was driven by voluntary consent.

However, the execution of the replacement system gave rise to a lot of complaints. The compliance costs were very high. In articles these complaints, all the inconveniences and the problems for the ones who were replacing themselves were described in all depths. Spits[4] gives an example of these inconveniences below. This example not only exposes the problems of the system, it shows why it was so difficult to fill the whole army with volunteers.

"The amount of problems this system created! One could buy a substitute at a 'soul-merchant'; it was also possible to find a substitute yourself. When one did have a substitute, the real trouble began: the delivery to the state. This was a task that should be done personally. One was asked to go to the militia council with the substitute to test him. After this meeting, one should keep him in personal custody for 14 days. When one was lucky, one could find the substitute back, because it often happened that at the day of delivery one could look everywhere for the substitute. Kruseman, writer of a pamphlet published in 1853[5], draws us the next example, which will be presented here in a short version, wherein the problems for a respectable father who wants his son to be replaced are exposed.

---

3 See e.g.: Handelingen van de Tweede Kamer der Staten Generaal, 1847-1848, p. 808; I.M. Engelberts, Moet de plaatsvervanging bij de militie worden afgeschaft, Nijmegen, 1848, p. 22, en A. Kruseman, Over de nationale militie en remplacement, Amsterdam, 1853, p. 43.

4 Spits, pp. 193-195

5 See footnote 3

On an evening in autumn An entire family is gathered enjoying each others company. It is cold outside, and everyone is happy to sit inside together..
They speak about the events of the day, about the future of the eldest son, who was lucky to find a substitute, about the money the substitute costs and about the inconveniences one meets when one wants to free himself from military service. Almost the whole evening is gone and it is rather late, when the door bell rings.
Who could be there? A servant brings the unpleasant message, that the substitute of the master is there.
Shortly after the announcement a man with a uncomfortable step, whose dirtiness is visible in his face, enters the living room, a human being who is utterly bad inside, but externally fit to fulfill the duty of soldier. It seems that he is looking for some fun and wants to play 'a game of cards' with the father of the house and his son. Reluctantly, the request is granted. After playing for huge amounts of money, the man lights up a pipe to avoid falling asleep, starts to smoke and fills the lovely room with a terrible smoke like a stinking Aeolus.
After smoking silently during the play, he seemed to have an awful taste in his mouth. He asked: "hey, do you still have that very tasteful brandy, like you had last time?
"No, man", was the most modest answer, "it is gone, and you had your part of it". The substitute insists to be served something else. "Your punch will be okay too, won't it? I have to drink, for heavens sake! Because my throat is extremely dry."
The Family is so good to serve the drinks late in the evening. To be short, after playing on for a few more hours with drinking en toasting with the guest, hearing his awful and mean language, the substitute gets sleepy and goes home with a lot of guilders in his pocket, and an old sweater and hat, that he needed, "not to keep" , as he said, but only "on loan"
This is not the end of it. The heavily tried father can expect other difficulties. He has to bother himself with the payment to the closest receiver and subject the minutes of the contract with the substitute to the judgment of the militia council. After that he can move up to the real contract. Moreover, during eighteen months he depends on the good faith, or simply the bon vouloir of the substitute, before the case is finished and he can sit back easily. He is still responsible for the man and must offer an other substitute etc., if the substitute deserts. Such an offer can also be demanded if the substitute has some disabilities, with the exception that a distinction is made between injuries that are the consequence of serving in the armed forces or not.[6]

From the perspective of the substitute, following the opportunity costs principle, it is easy to explain the behaviour of the substitute. For him it would not be advantageous to join the armed forces immediately as a volunteer, because the replacement system offers a much higher expected income. A substitute weighs the costs and benefits of joining the armed forces under both systems. The chance that someone was elected to join the armed forces as a conscript was not big, the salaries in the armed forces were relatively low, so the choice between a reward according to his own low opportunity costs and the opportunity costs of a rich man, who is looking for a substitute, turns out to be negative for immediate volunteership. The replacement system provides a much bigger reward. Or in

6 See footnote 4

economic terms: the expected value of joining voluntarily is lower than the expected value of conscription.

The statement of Campagne in last paragraph, that because of a lack of volunteers the Napoleonic conscription system triumphed is not stated by the facts. The lack of "real" volunteers was caused by the replacement system, not by conscription. Substitutes enough, as long as the armed forces paid enough. Moreover, the lack of volunteers was even more harrowing, because the conditions for joining the armed forces voluntarily were absolutely minimal. No attention was paid to provide reasonable care and housing, the premiums for volunteers were low and his prospects for the future were miserable. In the nineteenth century the armed forces were not able to compete on the labour market with civil society. The armed forces were lacking the incentives to do so, because the provision of labour power was arranged legally. This is a situation that existed until the abolishment of conscription in 1996, although since 1993 the situation was improving.[7]

In the 1861 militia law many regulations in the replacement system were softened. For a few members of parliament this was still not enough. They were looking to other countries, where replacement could be bought off. According to them this was the only way to replace the disadvantages of the replacement system completely. The supporters of the ransom could be found in a reactionary-conservative party in parliament. They strove for the recovery of the old system, in regards to the organization of the armed forces, an army with volunteers. They rejected conscription. According to them it could be possible to ask the civilians to defend themselves in the case of an invasion, but for all the other services the armed forces should be filled with volunteers.

According to member of parliament Van Goltstein compulsory service did not bring anything than misery

"The conscripts were extracted from their families, halted in their general development, and disturbed in learning a profession. When they return from the armed forces, they have lost the desire for working and are unsuitable for domestic purposes".[8]

In addition, the quality of the armed forces was critical. This had to do with the large amounts of substitutes. Van Goltstein also saw them as the cause of a lot of drinking problems in the armed forces.

"The replacement of the replacement system by a ransom could turn all that evil. The government should deliver the substitutes herself and should form a fund from all the ransom money, to cover the costs of better premiums, wages and pensions in a standing army. This would be beneficial for all parties. The stand-by troops of the armed forces would gain strength, and would improve in quality too, because of increased demands for joining the army. The burden for the civilian would be lowered; for every extra volunteer

---

7 This is investigated in chapter 6 and 7.

8 See Spits, pp. 196-197.

a conscript could stay at home. For the soldier, things would get better too; the threatening prospects of poverty and needs would not enhance him any longer. All this could be achieved, because the state could compete in this system with the private companies in getting substitutes.[9] She did not need the profits and could give much better guarantees".[10]

According to the reactionary-conservatives in Parliament, ransom was preferable. However, the arguments put forward were not convincing enough for the liberals. They talked about the traditional Dutch aversion to a professional army, that could increase from the ransom system. Every year fewer conscripts would be taken into the armed forces and fewer trained men would be given back to society. They argued that the civilian spirit would no longer be present in the armed forces, and the military spirit in society would be weakened. The gap between civil- and military society would get bigger and bigger.

With these arguments the liberals referred to the fundamentals for conscription, as put down by Machiavelli (1469-1527) in his "Dell'arte delle guerra". Machiavelli distinguishes three reasons to prefer conscription to a voluntary army. A conscription army would be cheaper, conscription would raise civilian spirits and conscription would prevent the possibility that someone would acquire the means to take over power against the will of the people.

The discussion between the liberals and the reactionary-conservatives was won by the opponents of buying off conscription, with the argument that buying off conscription would take away the security of filling the vacant positions in the armed forces every year.

"If what they feared was true, that the main cause of not joining the army, did not come from a low premium or low wages, but from the traditional aversion of the military profession, with the possibility to earn their income somewhere else, it would follow that the optimistic predictions of the supporters of the ransom, that enough volunteers would always be available, could not be true.[11] Besides, how should the price for the ransom be determined? If the price was too high, than the system was a privilege for very wealthy people. If the price was put too low, than many people would use the system and large shortages would remain in the armed forces. It could be possible to fill up these shortages with extra people, but then the least wealthy in society would suffer again".[12]

---

9 The practises of the private companies, institutions who concerned themselves with intermediate trade and delivery of substitutes, were notorious. They collected a large sum of the money that was asked for substitution. Most of the time the substitute only received half of all the money involved.

10 Handelingen van de Tweede Kamer der Staten Generaal, zitting 1860-1861, pp. 759, in: Spits, pp. 197. If we change the word ransom in the quotation by personal income tax, the discussion of 1861 can be replaced to our times, because in 1992, the discussion also concerned the substitution of a tax-in-kind by a tax in money.

11 See chapter 6 for a detailed report about the labour conditions and -circumstances and the attractiveness of the military profession.

12 Handelingen van de Tweede Kamer der Staten Generaal, zitting 1860-1861, pp. 910, in: Spits, pp. 199.

The government was supported by experiences abroad. The ransom system did not function quite well over there. So, Parliament was not convinced to follow the conservatives and the replacement system survived. If we look back on the discussion regarding conscription in 1861, we can say that the arguments for and against conscription did not change a lot since then. Both in the discussion of 1976, and 1992, the arguments used in 1861 appeared again.

§ 3.3. The period after 1870

The war between France and Germany (1870-1871) brought a mobilization of the armed forces in the Netherlands. This mobilization showed a lot of abuses in the armed forces. The mobilization report of September 20th recognized three big mistakes[13]: a too weak cadre, underdevelopment of the conscripts (20% of the men were substitutes) and unsuitableness of the marksmen. The leaders of the armed forces and the government concluded immediately that there was a need for personal conscription without the replacement system.

The man who introduced the real personal conscription, was Minister of War K. Eland. The law of July 2nd 1898 made personal conscription reality. From that moment, the Dutch armed forces developed itself into an almost pure conscription army with only a few professionals.

Also after the Second World War conscription survived. Conscription time varied between 18 and 24 months between 1945 and 1966. Conscription was often adapted to external circumstances caused by the Cold War. Civil labour conditions also played an important role in shortening or extending the length of conscription.

After 1960 conscription appeared again on the political agenda. In the hundred years after the discussion between the liberals and the reactionary-conservatives there had not been a lot for changes for the conscripts. The income of the conscripts was nothing more than an token allowance, the labour conditions were extremely poor, conscripts were transported in second-hand trains and were treated by professional soldiers like second-hand civilians. The changes in the armed forces and politics after 1960 fit in the general circumstances of these times, but have a specific cause in the armed forces too. At the beginning of the sixties the registration system of conscripts was computerized. By computer selection the highly educated people were allocated to low functions, where they never had appeared when the allocation of conscripts had been done by hand. The new allocation method caused a difference between skills and functions, and caused a lot of turmoil among the conscripts. In this atmosphere the Vereniging Van Dienstplichtige Militairen (VVDM) [Union of Conscripts] arose on august 4, 1966.

---

13 See Campagne, pp. 8-9.

The soldiers union VVDM took on the arguments as laid down by Van Goltstein in 1861. Originally as an interest group, but later on as a real union of conscripts the VVDM pleaded for the improvement of labour conditions and labour circumstances of conscripts. Successes were easily obtained in both material and immaterial aspects. According to the VVDM the civilian standards and values should be mirrored in the armed forces. Although it could expect severe resistance from the professional branch of the military, because it decreased the power of these professionals, the VVDM found its place at the negotiation table by influencing politicians and by joining the general labour union FNV. That resistance from professional soldiers was to be expected has already been described by the Niskanen model in chapter 2.

The VVDM had been a supporter of conscription for years: conscription was the ideal way to integrate the armed forces with civil society. On the other hand the VVDM provided the groundwork for an armed forces with only volunteers, by trying to change all labour conditions of conscripts in such a way that they would equal the labour conditions in civil society.

In 1992 the VVDM departed from its old vision on conscription, and from then on she put all its efforts into achieving the needs that should be necessary to transform the conscription force into an all-volunteer force.

Since 1960 the discussion about conscription in the Netherlands continued. In 1976 the Mommersteeg-committee investigated conscription and concluded that conscription could not be abolished on a short term notice. After the end of the Cold War in 1989 the Meijer-committee started to investigate the matter again in 1991. After a one-year study the committee concluded that conscription could not be abolished either. The committee had four reasons why the armed forces should not be transformed into an all-volunteer force. (1) The international security situation does not allow for an all-volunteer force, (2) there is not enough supply of professional soldiers on the labour market, without which the all-volunteer force can not be filled, (3) an all-volunteer force is too expensive and (4) the constitution needed to be changed if conscription were to be abolished.

Nevertheless, the Dutch parliament was of the opinion that conscription had to be abolished. The government followed this opinion and stated that conscription should be ended at December 31, 1997. This date was later changed to august 31, 1996.

§ 3.4. The existence of conscription in a democratic environment[14]

In chapter 2 we have seen that conscription is not just a fact of life, but the result of a democratic decision. The existence of conscription is also influenced by

14 This paragraph is based on Robert D. Tollison, The Political Economy of the Military Draft, in: Buchanan and Tollison, Theory of Public Choice, Ann Arbor, 1972, pp. 302-314.

public choice considerations. This paragraph shows a simple model, that describes the political origin and existence of conscription. The model is closely related to the model used in paragraph 5 of chapter 2. With the use of this model it is evident why conscription had prevailed for 180 years and why the arguments of the discussion in 1861 and those of 1992 are essentially the same.

§ 3.4.1. The model

The model tries to give an explanation for the fact why conscription exists and can survive in a democratic environment. The model corresponds with the model of chapter 2, paragraph 5, and possesses explanatory power. The model presents an individualistic choice model of conscription in a referendum-type democracy. In paragraph 3.4.2. the assumptions of the model are relaxed to show how the introduction of more realistic collective condition tends to reinforce the choice process depicted in the model. Sincere attention is given to the fact, that the model still has explanatory power. Individuals in the model base their voting behaviour on how they expect the conscription issue to affect their present wealth positions. They are perfectly able to discount the present wealth impact of the draft issue. This discounting condition applies to the tax-in-kind associated with being drafted and to the potential subsidy generated by lower budgetary plans for manpower under a draft system.

In the model it is assumed that the voting population is rectangular distributed by age. Every age group has the same amount of people and all the conscripts have voting rights, the choice for or against conscription is the only issue on the political agenda and all costs of collective decision-making on this issue are negligible. This assumption rules out complications of logrolling and political decision-making costs at this point.

The last assumption is that every approved conscript joins the armed forces and that this group is sufficient to fulfill the needs of the armed forces. For the initial choice for conscription the same assumption applies, as we have seen in chapter 2, paragraph 5. For voters older than 18-20 years, the conscription age, conscription brings tax savings. This group will support conscription under the terms of the model.

Draft-age individuals must calculate the net present-wealth impact of conscription. This would be the balance of the relinquished income while being a conscript and the subsidy received in future budget periods as a veteran. Let it be assumed that this balance is negative. The draft-age group in the model would thus vote against the issue. Depending on the sizes of the groups for and against conscription, conscription will be executed.[15] Once the conscription issue is passed and put into operation, the effect of the ongoing conscription system on the individual voter's present wealth can be used to show how the draft would

15 See chapter 2, § 4.1.

tend to remain in operation over a conceivably long sequence of future generations. Let it be assumed at first that the voting rule and voter-age distribution which prevailed when the issue passed in the initial period continues to prevail in all subsequent voting periods. Also, it is assumed that the draft has to be re-legislated every two years. In this setting the viability of the draft depends on how the present draft-age group will choose on the issue once they have served their two years and become beneficiaries (veterans) in the collective process. The voting behaviour of veterans is critical since the requirement that all must serve means that at some future point the entire non-draft-age segment of the voting population will be veterans.

The veteran in the model faces a distinctly different choice situation than he faced in the initial voting period. The opportunity cost imposed on the veteran by conscription is a sunk cost which was subjectively capitalized in the initial period. In subsequent periods this cost is conceptually irrelevant to the veteran's voting decision on the conscription issue. Although the future veteran capitalizes the expected subsidy in the initial period, the continued receipt of the subsidy over time depends on the choice behavior of the individual in all future referenda on conscription. In terms of the voting decision the veteran faces a positive return on voting for the conscription issue in all post-conscription voting periods and will rationally choose for the process to be continued regardless of how he chose on the issue at the conscription-age.

Conscription creates its own continued existence in the model by channeling each generation of 18- to 20-years olds into their post-draft existence with a vested interest in seeing that the process goes on. This existence is confirmed in practise, when we analyse the discussion about conscription in the Netherlands in 1861 and 1992.

§ 3.4.2. Variations on the model

The model in paragraph 3.4.1 has a few assumptions, that will be changed in this paragraph to more realistic assumptions. First, the assumption of perfect discounting of the tax-in-kind and subsidy is central to the choice problem posed by the model. Without this condition the wealth effects of the conscription issue can be distorted by imperfect, illusory, or uncertain perceptions on the part of individual voters. The choice problem would become more unpredictable under these circumstances. The most probable case is the one in which the tax-in-kind is accurately and confidently capitalized and the subsidy is not. The tax is a specific burden which the individual would bring little difficulty in perceiving and capitalizing. The subsidy consists of a reduction in the general budget, that is generally dispersed over the collectivity. It is quite possible under these conditions that individuals perceive imperfectly their share of this reduction. If this condition is held in extreme form, in which the subsidy created no impact on the present wealth positions of non-draft-voters, the initial legislation of the conscription issue would not be possible. Only in the case in which the subsidy has no value at all for the non-conscripts, conscripts can abolish conscription. As long as the non-draft-group in the model perceives the existence of the subsidy to any extent, the choice process described in the model will be operable. It does not seem unrealistic adhere to this view. In times of discussion about conscription, like in the case of the recent Meijer-committee, people become aware of the real value of the conscription subsidy.

Secondly, once other issues and political agreement costs are introduced to the model, the complexity of the choice problem facing the individual voter is increased. In such a case coalitions and logrolling will play an important role, through which it can be decided to abolish conscription. To the extent that the conscription issue represents an intense minority facing a non-intense majority, the probability of political trades to abolish conscription would be increased. On the other hand, it is also possible that coalitions and logrolling will occur that prevent the abolishment of conscription. These new coalitions can appear, because the discussion about conscription brings new issues connected to conscription into focus, issues which were not present prior to the discussion. The political practise in the Netherlands is that the conscription issue is treated quite independently from any other issue, and that the possibility of logrolling or coalitions is rather low.

Thirdly, the model was built on the assumption that everyone qualified will indeed serve in the armed forces. If the assumption is relaxed by not drafting every qualified man, like in practise, the group non-conscripts will be even bigger as assumed in the initial group and abolishment of conscription can not be expected quickly. But, if the assumed age group of 18- to 20- years old is not enough and conscription is extended to 21- years old, then the chance becomes greater that conscription is going to be abolished. In practise this will not happen quickly, because a small change of the age is already sufficient to fill the vacant functions in the armed forces, and the threshold to change to decisions on conscription requires larger changes most of the time.

At last, we have the assumption that all conscripts have a negative perception about conscription in the initial period. However, realistic features like patriotism can create divergent attitudes towards conscription and would probably lead to a existence of conscription.

The introduction of more realistic conditions to the analysis does not significantly influence the conceptual validity of the choice process of the model. Indeed, in many cases the realistic conditions tend to reinforce the inference that something like this choice process explains the existence and stability of real world draft systems.

The lesson from studying the process in this paragraph is that conscription maintains a political issue and this paragraph showed that conscription can be initialized and exists in a democratic environment. This paragraph also showed that the historic development of conscription as described earlier in this paragraph, is not just an event. The model also helps explaining, why the discussions about conscription in 1861 and 1992 are more or less similar.

§ 3.5. Summary

In this chapter the origin and existence of conscription is investigated. Conscription is imported from France, but became reality through the joining of conscription with the replacement system. Attempts to abolish conscription failed because of a lack of incentives by politicians and armed forces. After 1861 conscription existed without discussion until the 1960s. From this moment a process of change started, partly because conscripts themselves took action. This change also influenced the political debate, as the different committees investigating conscription since 1966 showed. But it remains a question whether conscription is going to be abolished, because of this change of process. Groups in society that benefit from conscription are much bigger than the group that bears the burden of conscription. Moreover, conscripts are young and do not have much influence in the political debate themselves. This is even strengthened by the fact, that the costs of conscription are sunk costs after the moment conscription is finished for the conscript. Veterans will plea for the existence of conscription, because they benefit from this existence. Not only in money, but also in power and status. The existence of conscription takes care of the fact that veterans are not a dying group, and the veterans can hold their position of power.[16] Although the Meijer-committee concluded in its 1992 report that conscription could not be abolished. Yet parliament and the Lubbers-3 government decided to transform the conscription force into an all-volunteer force.

16 An example in the Netherlands are the KNIL-soldiers from the former Netherlands-Indies, who are still a very powerful group and the many letters send to newspapers form former soldiers against the possible abolishment of conscription. Within the Departement of Defense there is also a lot of attention for veterans, as is showed by the special taskforce "Post-actives", which have their own consultation discussions within the department.

CHAPTER 4

The conscription tax

Conscription provides the possibility to keep the budgetary costs of military labour low and can be seen as an instrument of economic policy. Because conscription lowers the tax that has to be gathered by society, conscription can be seen as a tax. It can be defined as a compulsory contribution without a reciprocal contribution by the party who receives the contribution. Conscription also provides the possibility to bypass the market in the process of filling the open positions in the armed forces, at which point it also raises a few economic questions. This does not infer that the choice for or against conscription can be made on the basis of economic arguments alone, but it does indicate that the use of conscription has economic consequences for the armed forces in particular and for society in general.

One of the characteristics of taxes is that they cause inefficiencies, no matter how important these taxes are. In chapter 1 we have seen what kind of inefficiencies conscription brings. In this chapter we will take a look at a couple of these inefficiencies. Next to the size of the conscription-tax, we will also take into account the division of the conscription-tax and the costs associated with the collecting of the tax, as well as the detection and deterring of evasion en avoidance of the tax.

§ 4.1 The size of the conscription tax

In the production process of the collective good defense, the costs of the armed forces naturally play an important role. There are different ways to look at the costs of the armed forces, from which two are of specific interest[1]. The first

---

1 These different ways are based on: S.H. Altman en A.E. Fechter, "The supply of military personnel in the absence of the draft", American Economic review, mei 1967; A.C. Fisher, "The cost of the draft and the cost of ending the draft", American Economic Review, juni 1969; W.L. Hansen en B.A. Weisbrod, "Economics of the military draft", The Quarterly Journal of Economics, vol 81, 1967; C. Lingle, "On the real costs of military conscription", South African Journal of Economics, vol. 57, 1989; W. Oi, "The economic cost of the draft", American Economic Review, mei 1967; A. Roux, "The economics of alternative

standard is the budgetary burden of the military labour forces, which has to be paid by the general tax-payer. The second standard - which is less visible, but is very important from a social viewpoint, concerns the economic costs of the military. The economic costs of the military are defined as the value of labour that is used in the armed forces. The difference between economic and budgetary costs is especially important in times of conscription, because, as we have seen earlier, conscription provides the armed forces the opportunity to pay less than the market wage for military personnel. In competing or free markets, economic and budgetary costs in general will be equal to each other, but if the government intervenes, it can happen that both standards will differ, in some cases even considerably so.

Since we have defined the economic costs of a military man as the opportunity costs of someone who works in the armed forces, we have to see how big the costs are for a conscript. For that we can take (1) the opportunity costs for society in terms of lost production, or the opportunity costs for the individual conscript.

The reason for the first definition is that by joining the armed forces, society will lose production, otherwise provided by the conscript. Traditionally and empirically this first or narrow definition is measured by the civil income of the conscript, under the assumption that this income reflects the value of his labour in society.

The reason for the second definition is that by serving in the armed forces, the conscript not only misses his civil income, but also the positive or negative non-pecuniary benefits of his civil job. An example of the negative is that conscription is not employment by choice, and because the conscript is forced to join the armed forces, most of the time he is far away from home and the conscript is treated totally different than he was used to in civil society.[2] But in the armed forces he can also learn things that he is not familiar with in civil society. When missing the positive benefits from civil society the conscript says he is "sick-to-death". For that reason the positive or negative non-pecuniary benefits will in short be called "sick-to-death"-premium. The recognition of this "sick-to-death"-premium is essential for the analysis, because resulting from this recognition is the fact that for the accounting of the costs of conscription the costs for the conscript are the central point in the analysis. As a result the costs of the whole institution conscription will follow from this analysis.

The second or broad definition is measured by the reservation wage of a conscript: the wage at which he will join the armed forces on a voluntary basis. This reservation wage or supply price of every individual conscript is simply the

---

national service", South African Journal of Economics, vol. 59, 1991; R.V.L. Cooper, Military manpower and the all-volunteer force, Rand Corporation, Santa Monica, 1977.

2 In chapter 6 all elements of the military profession are investigated in detail. The positive and negative non-pecunairy benefits will be treated extensively. In the text only an indication is mentioned.

sum of his alternative civil wage and his sick-to-death premium. In the rest of this chapter the broad definition will be followed.

At the beginning of this chapter we could see that a tax is a compulsory contribution, without a reciprocal contribution by the party who receives this contribution. This description of a tax is a small revision of the definition Cort van der Linden of "tax" in 1887: "Belasting is iedere bijdrage aan de algemene middelen verschuldigd, onafhankelijk van enigen bijzonderen dienst der overheid".[3]

From annotations to this and other definitions of the term "taxation" it becomes clear that military conscription is also a tax[4]. The conscript is forced to join the armed forces and for that he receives a salary. As a result, the burden of military conscription or the conscription-tax is characterized by the difference between this salary and the opportunity costs of a conscript. If we want to visualize this conscription-tax, than we have to know the size of the civilian wage, the sick-to-death-premium and the salary of every conscript.

Table 4.1. shows the net civilian wage of a conscript[5]. It also shows the percentage of youngsters per year-wage-class, the cumulative amount of boys in the Netherlands with the same age and the absolute amount of conscripts per year-wage-class.[6] This last column is calculated by multiplying the total amount of conscripts in 1988, 44,671, with the percentage youngsters in the same year-wage-class. This is possible, because there is a general draft system in the Netherlands, without many exemptions. The chance to join the armed forces is almost equal for every Dutchman, so that every section of the Dutch community will be represented[7].

In 1988 the average net salary for a conscript was 12,000 guilders per year. The size of the sick-to-death premium is a more difficult to estimate. Cooper states that as the demand for military people rises, all things being equal, the armed forces should offer a higher premium to get these people within the armed forces on a voluntary basis.[8] With that he assumes a positive relation between the

---

3 "Taxation is every contribution owed to the general means, independent from any special service of the government", Cort van der Linden (1887) in L.G.M. Stevens, Elementair belastingrecht, Deventer 1985, pp.272. In Stevens we can find another 20 definition of taxation. All have more or less the same meaning.

4 See for example, L.G.M. Stevens, Elementair belastingrecht, Deventer 1989, pp.14.

5 Statistics A and B: Statistisch zakboek 1991, Centraal Bureau voor de Statistiek, pp. 99. Statistics C en D: Jaaroverzicht dienstplichtgegevens 1988, Ministery of Defense. All presented statistics are concerned with the year 1988.

6 The cumulative amount of boys with the same age is based on the test results of 1988. In 1988 118,566 boys were tested. Because of rounding-up differences the total of column C is different from the actual figure. To make column D with the help of column B it is assumed that every year-class contains the same amount of boys (app. 118,000) and that the average wage of a conscript is 20 years. This last figure is in correspondence with reality.

7 In paragraph 3 of this chapter this assumption will be elaborated.

8 Richard V.L. Cooper, Military Manpower and the All-Volunteer-Force, Santa Monica 1977, p.70.

sick-to-death premium, the amount of conscripts and the alternative civilian wage. Cooper's study shows that the sick-to-death premium can be estimated at about 20% of the difference between the civilian wage and the salary in the armed forces[9]. Because it is technically impossible to calculate the exact size of the sick-to-death premium, the estimated figures that pertained to the United States are also applied to the Netherlands.[10]

Table 4.1. Civilian wage of a conscript.

	Year-wage-class 16-24 olds (gld)	Amount of young-sters in %	Boys cumulative	Conscripts (absolute)in year-wage-class
	A	B	C	D
1	< 10.000	5.6	6,640	2,507
2	10,000-12,000	6.4	14,228	2,865
3	12,000-12,500	1.6	16,125	716
4	12,500-15,000	9.6	27,507	4,297
5	15,000-17,500	13.9	43,888	6,222
6	17,500-20,000	22.9	71,140	10,253
7	20,000-22,500	21.9	97,106	9,803
8	22,500-25,000	11.0	110,148	4,924
9	25,000-27,500	4.1	115,009	1,835
10	27,500-30,000	1.7	117,024	716
11	30,000-32,500	0.6	117,736	269
12	32,500-35,000	0.3	118,091	314
13	35,000-37,500	0.1	118,210	45
total				44,671

The line SS' in figure 4.1. represents the civilian wage of the conscripts, as the sick-to-death premium is represented by the difference between the lines BB' and SS'. W_1 is the salary of the conscript. The distance Ob represents the demand for military personnel in the armed forces.

9 Ibid, pp. 70-74.

10 Interviews with members of the Dutch soldier unions and own field research when visiting army barracks show that the 20% sick-to-death premium is a reasonable measure.

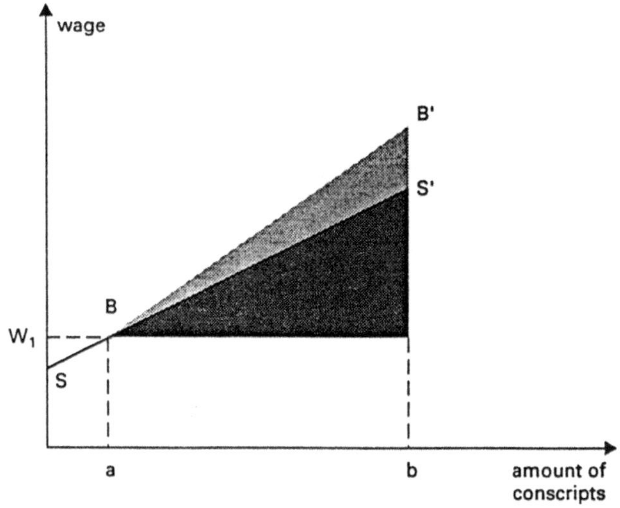

FIGURE 4.1 The conscription tax

If the demand for conscripts in the Netherlands would be filled according to the "Lowest-supply-price-drafted-first" criterion, then the shaded area under the SS'-line would represent the conscription-tax. Under normal circumstances (being without the force of conscription law,) people with the lowest opportunity-costs would have joined the armed forces already at the salary SS' on a voluntary basis. For them there is no sick-to-death premium. However, the Netherlands selects on the basis of a lottery system, which means that conscription concerns everybody, and not just the people with the lowest opportunity costs. In this system the sick-to-death premium plays an important role. The conscription-tax therefore consists of the shaded area under the line BB'. The total size of the conscription-tax in the Netherlands can be calculated by adding the conscription-taxes of every individual conscript. For example, every person in group 5 in table 4.1. has an average after-tax salary of 16,250 guilders, while a conscript from this group only receives 12,000 guilders. So, the conscription-tax for this conscript will be (16,250-12,000) x (1+20%[11]) = 5,100 guilders. If this calculation is made for every conscript, It comes to a total amount of 360 million guilders conscription-tax in the Netherlands.

---

11 The 20% is the size of the sick-to-death premium.

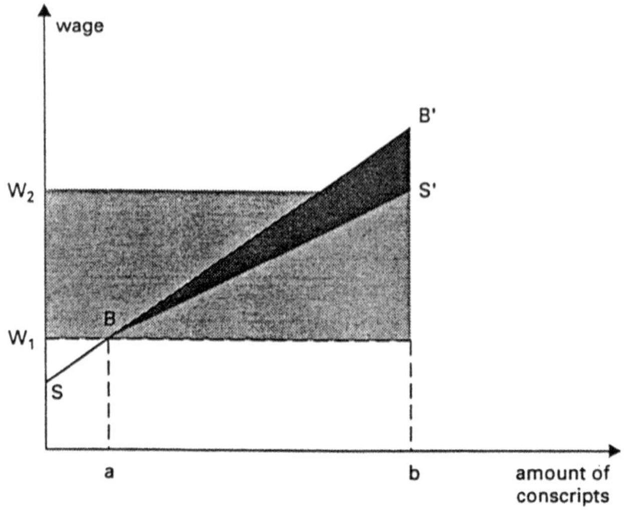

FIGURE 4.2 The "broad" conscription tax

However, this interpretation of the conscription-tax has one problem. It uses the implicit, but crucial, assumption that confiscation of 'economic rent' by the government is no taxation. In normal circumstances the government doesn't force people to fill its vacancies, and gives the surplus that is generated with consumption or production to the people who deserve it. However, by forcing people into conscription, the government does owe these rents. Figure 4.2. shows that the armed forces have to offer a competing salary, W2, in order to obtain enough volunteers to fill the demand Ob. The result is that volunteers receive a surplus equal to the difference between the competing salary W2 and their own supply price. The surplus is equal to the 'economic rents' that the government receives through conscription.

Considering this, Sjaastad and Hansen state:[12]

"...[the] narrow definition of the conscription tax reflects an implicit assumption that the confiscation of economic rent does not constitute taxation. Conscription can be viewed as a means of coercion whereby the government reduces the budgetary cost of military manpower procurement, and only part of that reduction takes the [narrow] form of tax defined above, the remainder being rents foregone. A persuasive argument can be made however, that the tax should also include forgone rents. In procurement of manpower for civilian functions (i.e., the Post Office) or procurement of materials, the government abides by the ethical norm of our society that surpluses, be they generated in production or consumption, are properly the property of the person to whom they actually accrue. While it is true that these rents are not necessary to attract individuals to military service, it is

12 Larry A. Sjaastad and Ronald N. Hansen, "The conscription tax: An empirical analysis", on cit. pp. IV-1-2, in Cooper, 1977, pp. 81-82.

also true that similar rents are in fact collected by the sellers of goods and services to the government in virtually all other cases. It is only in the case of certain military manpower procurement that coercion is systematically employed to reduce rents".

If we take into account the broad definition of the conscription-tax, the tax can be measured by the greater of 1) the difference between the market wage (W_2) and the military salary (W_1) or 2) the difference between the supply-price and the military salary. The amount of W2 is 19,095,- guilders, the salary that should be offered to get 44,761 boys into the armed forces on a voluntary basis[13]. In figure 4.2 this is the whole shaded area. The importance of the difference between the two measures of the conscription tax is not the size of the conscription tax, but the effect on the distribution of income by conscription. The narrow definition of the conscription tax doesn't recognize that individuals on the lower side of the supply curve are taxed too by conscription, because they earn the same as in civil society. However, they miss the economic rent. Moreover, the narrow definition of the conscription tax conceals unwanted social and public effects of conscription in general. Expressed in monetary terms, these extra social costs total 90 million guilders. This brings the total amount of the conscription tax to 450 million guilders[14]; 10,000 guilders per conscript.

§ 4.2. The interrupted career

In paragraph 4.1. the central issue was the real price of labour in the armed forces. We've seen that the social cost of labour in the armed forces is much higher than the actual cost, because of the conscription tax. The consequences for the allocation of production factors in the armed forces and the supply of volunteers for the armed forces will be discussed in chapter 5 and 6. In this paragraph another aspect of conscription will be discussed that can be associated with the conscription tax. Until now we've only discussed the conscription tax, while being in the armed forces. Conscription also has a delayed aspect, which will be called the effect of the interrupted career. Conscripts will be able to supply themselves on the labour market a year later than other people in the same age group, who won't have to join the armed forces. On the other side, conscription can also have a learning effect, which can be rewarded by employers, resulting in a better position for ex-conscripts in civilian live than that of those who didn't have to join the armed forces.

---

13 For 44.761 approved boys, 61,000 non-tested boys are needed, because the test percentage is about 73%. The minimum wage that should be offered to get 61,000 boys into the armed forces on a voluntary basis can be read in table 4.1., column A and C, and is on a yearly basis 19,095 guilders.

14 The size of the conscription tax consists of: narrow definition conscription tax: 300 million, sick-to-death premium: 60 million and 'economic rents': 90 million.

Research for the civilian effect of conscription has mainly been done in the United States of America. Rosen and Taubman[15], Swartz[16] and Crane and Wise[17] showed that Vietnam-veterans earned less than non-veterans, while DeTray[18], and Berger and Hirsch[19] on the other side showed positive effects between Vietnam-veterans and non-veterans with different age and education groups. Researchers from the Veterans Administration[20] found a generally positive effect for veterans in comparison to non-veterans. The war in Vietnam played a significant role in understanding the income differences and it was not possible to isolate the consequences of conscription as an independent phenomenon. However, recent research by Joshua D. Angrist[21] shows that the difference in income is caused by conscription and by the Vietnam war. Angrist shows that Vietnam veterans earn on average 15% less than the comparable non-veteran group. A loss of income that is caused by the loss of 2 years of experience in civilian life, because of conscription[22]. Should Angrist his results be compatible with the Dutch situation, than the length of conscription of 1 year in the Netherlands would have resulted in an income difference of 7,5% between veterans and non-veterans.

Expressed in guilders this means an extra income loss or conscription tax for all former conscripts of 927 million a year.[23] The problem with this result is that it is based on research from the United States. This does not naturally translate to the situation in the Netherlands. In appendix 4.1. of the chapter an attempt is

15 S.Rosen and P. Taubman, "Changes in Lifecycle earnings: What do Socialsecurity Data show?", Journal of Human Sciences, summer 1982.

16 S. Schwartz, "The relative Earnings experience of Vietnam and Korean era Veterans", Industrial and Labor Relations Review, july 1986.

17 J.R.Crane and D.A. Wise, "Military Service and the Civilian Earnings of Youth, in D.A. Wise (ed), Public Sector Payrolls, Chicago, 1987.

18 D.N. DeTray, "Veteran Status as a Screening Device", American Economic Review, march 1982.

19 M.C. Berger and T.Hirsch, "The civilian Earnings Experience of Vietnam Era Veterans", Journal of Human Resources, Fall 1983.

20 Veterans Administration Reports and Statistic Service, Research monograph 15: Education and Income Characteristics of Veterans, March 1979, Washington,1981.

21 Joshua D. Angrist, "Lifetime Earnings and the Vietnam Era Draft Lottery, Evidence form Social Administrative records, American Economic Review, Vol.80, June 1990.

22 For this research Angrist uses a new lottery system that was used in the USA during the last years of the Vietnam war. The big difference with other lottery systems in the USA was, that only a few exemptions were left. For that reason the conscription system is comparable with the Dutch system.

23 Assumed is a set back in income of conscripts of 7,5% ten years after they finished their duty, where the age of conscription is assumed to be 20. The average wage of a 30 year old is fl 26,800.-. Thus the average wage of a veteran is fl 25,537.- (M). The average wage of a non-veteran is fl 27,608.-. Burden interrupted career: (M-N)x44.761 = fl 92.7 million per year per year class. For the total burden it is assumed that there are ten yearclasses, who all bear the burden of 7.5% now (10 x 92.7 million = 927 million guilders). Statistics: Statistisch Jaarboek 1991, CBS pp. 99.

made to analyse the Dutch situation. Results on a short term won't be expected, because of technical problems.

The Dutch Central Bureau of Statistics started in 1984 with a Social Economic Panel research. On the basis of this research project the CBS expects to obtain some results in the year 2010[24]. Currently, the Social Economic Panel research describes the situation of about 5,000 households, with about 40 former conscripts, concerning many aspects of the economic situation of a household, such as income, social benefits, the purchase of durable goods etc. This interview is done twice every year, attempting to get as complete a profile of the same households as possible. On a long term basis the CBS gets a life time profile. But for our purposes, the amount of conscripts is too small now to make significant remarks about this group.

§ 4.3. The distribution of the conscription tax

In 1988 39% of the Dutch boys joined the armed forces. Figure 4.3. shows us that this is not an extraordinary figure in the twentieth century. The percentage has been quite stable around 35%, except for the years 1952-1960, when the percentage rose to 55%.

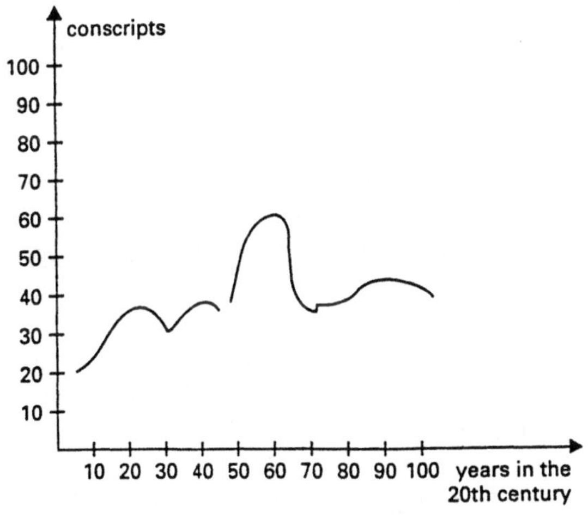

FIGURE 4.3 The distribution of the conscription-tax

If we compare the distribution of the conscription tax between generations, we can say that this distribution did not become more unfair. Within one generation however, the situation is completely different. 39% of all boys in the Netherlands or about 20% of all youths pays on average a tax of 10,000 guilders, while the

24 Based on interviews with employees of the CBS, October 7, 1992.

other 80% escapes from paying the tax. In this paragraph we will see if conscription as a tax-in-kind is fair or not according to the distribution principles of De Langen.

On the basis of empirical research De Langen has made six main principles, which form the basis of all tax laws in the Netherlands[25]. Three of these principles are principles of justice or principles of distribution, which will be discussed hereafter. The other three principles of efficiency, the welfare principle, the principle of the least pain and the principle of the maximum benefit, won't be discussed in this paragraph.

The first principle is the means principle. This principle states that tax can be levied according to the means of the tax payer. Means can be based on various grounds, such as income, consumption or wealth. The basis of the means principle is the principle of equality between every person. This means that people with the same income, should pay the same taxes. If they have an unequal income, their means are not equal and the tax to be paid should be different too. When deciding about the measure of inequality the theory of proportionate utility sacrifice plays an important role. According to this theory the tax tariff should be implemented in such a way that everybody sacrifices a proportionate utility of his income. If we want to achieve the situation in which everybody sacrifices the same percentage of pleasure, it means that someone with a high income should relatively pay more taxes, because the pleasure of one guilder diminishes, when income rises. This will result in a progressive tax structure.

The conscription system does not know any horizontal equity. People with the same background (young men) are not taxed equally, because in reality only 39% has to fulfill their military service and pay the conscription tax. Conscription also violates the concept of vertical equity. According to the theory of proportionate utility sacrifice people with a higher income pay more taxes than people with a low income, while in the case of conscription the situation is completely opposite. People with a low income (youth) pay a high tax, while people with a higher income don't have to pay the taxes. From this section, the conclusion follows that according to the means principle conscription is not a fair tax.

The second distribution principle is the benefit principle. Application of the benefit principle implies that taxation is based on the benefit that people get from public provision. The benefit can be a rise in wealth or a saving in costs. Therefore the benefit principle is sometimes called the compensation principle. According to the benefit principle, people will be taxed when they benefit from public provisions paid with public money. According to the compensation principle those people who damage society and force the government to spend extra money, are taxed. But a conscript doesn't damage society or the government, government causes damage to the conscript, without compensating the damage. The benefit that conscription brings for a conscript can be neglected, as we have seen in last subparagraph. Moreover, research from the Royal

25 See, L.G.M. Stevens, Elementair Belastingrecht, Deventer, 1985, pp. 3-5.

Military Academy[26] shows that a veteran does not benefit from conscription in finding a job, compared with non-veterans. From this section we can conclude that according to the benefit principle conscription is not fair.

The last distribution principle is the principle of privileged acquirement. Taxation according to this principle implies that a special tax can be levied if the person who obtains the benefit is in privileged situation when acquiring this benefit. There must be a situation of a stroke. But when analyzing conscription nowadays, we can not speak about a stroke. Therefore it is better to speak about the principle of difficult acquirement. According to this principle tax deductions are permitted to those people, who have to bring extra efforts to obtain there income. In Dutch tax laws this principle doesn't play a big role, but could bring a solution to solve the question of fairness of the interrupted career by conscription. During some time after serving in the armed forces conscripts get an extra deduction on their tax bill. For this section we can also conclude that conscription is unfair.

So far one element of the distribution of the conscription tax has not been investigated. This is the question whether every group in Dutch society really has the same chance to join the armed forces on an involuntary basis. Siccama[27] poses the question, "who does really serve?". Therefore, he suggests four hypothesis:

1. The chance not to be forced to join the armed forces will increase if the education records (and therefore the income record) of the father and the boy are higher.
2. The chance not to serve increases, if one has a political opinion that is more to the left side of the political spectrum.
3. The probability of joining the armed forces increases, if one visits the church more often than others.
4. The chance to serve is smaller, if one lives in a city, such as the "Randstad", than if one lives in rural areas.

These four hypothesis combines Siccama to the statement that it is much more probable that the son of a Zeeland peasant will join the armed forces, than the son of a socialist professor from Amsterdam. This statement is investigated by the Meijer-committee in its mission to investigate the complete conscription issue. It comes to the conclusion that the Siccama-hypothesis is not supported in practice.[28]

---

26 E. Smidt (et al): Een verloren jaar; de relevantie van militaire dienstplicht voor de arbeidsmarkt, in: Maatschappij en Krijgsmacht - Den Haag, august 1992, nr. 14, pp. 1-15.
27 J.G. Siccama: Militaire dienstplicht, ondoelmatig en onrechtvaardig, in Dienstplicht: afschaffen of uitbreiden?, C. Homan en J.G. Siccama (red), Clingendael, 1990.
28 Appendix report to official report "Naar dienstplicht nieuwe stijl", conscription-committee Subpart "dienstplichtigen over dienstplicht", by Dr R.M.W. van Gelooven, appendix 3, pp. 36.

But even if the statement is true, it is not true that a large amount of men is avoiding conscription in the Netherlands, as was the situation in the United States. Table 4.2. also shows that the distribution between groups in society is reasonably fair. This table is based on a comparison between education of conscripts and the education of people who just finished their last school career and are trying to find a job on the labour market. Some differences are visible, but it can not be concluded that large groups don't have to join the armed forces and personal conscription is avoided on a large scale.

Table 4.2: conscripts and recent graduates[29]

School type	Conscript in %	Graduates in %
Lower vocational (LBO)	12.25	22.33
Middle general (MAVO)	6.76	8.40
Middle vocational (MBO)	46.76	41.33
Higher general (HAVO/VWO)	10.84	10.07
Higher vocational (HBO)	16.90	9.46
Scientific (WO)	6.33	8.16

§ 4.4. The perception costs of the conscription tax

Every tax has to be collected, if the government wants to use the taxes in a productive way. For the collecting of taxes the government uses a big administration: the tax agency. Conscription is a tax and as a natural consequence the collection of the conscription tax includes a lot of costs too. Costs that have to do with the testing, training, housing and clothing of a conscript, but also with avoidance and evasion of the conscription tax.

If conscripts want to function in the armed forces, they need a training. In the Netherlands conscripts get a training programme of about 2.5 months on average. In 1992, after this program they were stationed at the stand-by troops for about 9.5 months. In order to get an army with 36,000 stand-by troops, 45,500 are necessary, because 9,500 men are in training. If the conscription period would have lasted for 19 months and 2.5 month training, than only 4,750 were in training. Thus, the length of the conscription period is inversely proportional to the amount of men in training and the costs of training. If we shorten the time of conscription and if we keep the amount of stand-by troops constant, the proportion productive/non-productive time will decrease, and more trainers will be put out of productive functions into supporting functions, and probably the

29 Statistics: SMK-VVDM report september 1991, and Statistical Yearbook 1991, CBS, pp. 413. In the calculation the percentage of drop-outs per schooltype is classed under the second-highest group.

production of the stand-by troops will decline. In 1991, the training of conscripts cost 500 million guilders a year.[30]

The costs of clothing and housing of conscripts were 265 million guilders and the costs of testing 22 million[31]. After the expense of these costs the conscripts are finally productive. The costs of training, clothing, etc. are still visible, but how about the costs made for avoidance or evasion of the conscription tax? In the last years the use of the Law for Conscientious Objectors has grown dramatically. Legal advisors earn a lot of money by advising so called "Objector yuppies" who are using this law to stay out of the armed forces for ever. Rough estimates are pointing in the direction of about 2.5 million guilders a year[32].

The costs involved with the execution of the Law for Conscience Objectors are also costs following from conscription. Without conscription, the law would not have existed. Each year about 25 million guilders is related to this law. The last way to avoid conscription is deferment of study. Such deferment will involve costs too if this deferment will get a definite character, when students will stay in school or university for ever, to avoid conscription.

In paragraph 4.1. we've seen that the benefits for the government of the conscription tax are about 450 million guilders. If we contrast this amount of money with the collecting costs of the tax, it becomes clear that conscription is an extremely inefficient way to tax people. For every tax guilder there is more than one guilder of collecting costs. Other taxes have much lower collecting costs[33], even if we add the extra burden of the conscripts.

§ 4.5. Final remarks

The social consequences of conscription are enormous. For the younger people conscription means a large loss of income. This tax doesn't stop after the service is over, but lingers because of the loss of civil experience during their military service. Conscription is a tax, but can not be found in our national ledgers. The collective tax burden is an important economic and political indicator in the Netherlands. It is defined as the sum of the burden of all taxes, social premiums and non-tax income of the state. When measuring the tax burden all direct and indirect taxes that are levied by the State or lower public administrations are relevant. However, conscription is not a part of this, because the conscription tax doesn't involve a cashflow. But this is not in correspondence with the idea behind the collective tax burden. This indicator should show the burden for the whole

---

30 Answer from the Ministery of Defense to questions in parliament by Mevr. van Heemskerk (VVD), Tweede Kamer 1990-1991, 21.800X, nr.39.

31 Ibid

32 Estimates based on interviews with these legal advisors.

33 See for example: M.A. Allers, Kosten van overdrachten voor particulieren en huishoudens, Onderzoeksmemorandum, nr.483, Instituut voor economisch onderzoek, Faculty of Economics, Rijksuniversiteit Groningen, Groningen, 1992.

society to finance our collective goods. The national accounts show us that consumers and companies are also part of our nation, and not just the government. Conscription is a burden for society and should be calculated into the figures for the collective tax burden.

Moreover, conscription is an unfair tax, because no principle of distribution is in agreement with the distribution of the conscription tax. It is true, that the conscription tax is distributed over all classes in society, but as individual burden only tangible with 20% of the youngsters, while 80% escapes from the tax.

Appendix 4.1.

A research description to find differences in income between veterans and non-veterans.

The aim of this project is to find differences in income between veterans and non-veterans on a long run basis. In order to execute this programme a large amount of data is needed:

1. A file with about 3,000 men from one birth year.
2. From all these men it is necessary to know whether they joined the armed services and when.
3. Over a period of ten year we need to know the income of these 3,000 men.
4. The last education records of these 3000 have to be known. This is necessary to exclude differences of income by education.
5. These data are asked for by the CBS in their Social Economic Panel research, which started in 1984 on a very minimal level

Working method

A) Each person gets a number. Attached to this number are the month of military service, education and income during the years 1980-1990. The combining of the figure is done with the help of a notary public, in order to respect privacy.

B) Statistical methods are used in order to prepare results.

C) This analysis can be put into practise when enough figures are available. As mentioned in paragraph 4.2. the CBS can hopefully do this in the year 2010. At this moment it is technically not possible to execute the research programme.

CHAPTER 5

Conscription and the allocation of production factors

"The larger point is that force structure itself should be a function of the costs of the specific inputs."
Richard V.L. Cooper in: Military manpower and the All-Volunteer-Force, Santa Monica 1977, pp. 275.

§ 5.1 Theory

As demonstrated in chapter 2, the use of production means in the armed forces, implies a withdrawal from such means from civil society. In civil society these means are relatively scarce with regard to occurring needs. Therefore, it can be said that means of production in the armed forces are also scarce. The output of the armed forces may be provided outside a market regime, however in regards to their inputs they are actually taking part in a civilian exchange process. Both on the labour market and on the capital market the armed forces have to satisfy the market demands.

When defense output is based on the international security situation, efficient armed forces imply the minimization of input costs, labour and capital. In this chapter the international security situation, as written in the "Defensienota 1991", is taken as a point of departure. In the armed forces the following means of production can be considered as specific inputs: capital and labour, whereby the production factor labour can be divided into conscripts, professional military personnel and civilians.

Micro-economic analysis teaches us that if the cost of specific production factors rise relative to the costs of alternative factors, production factors will be redistributed by replacing expensive inputs, with less expensive inputs. This principle also holds for the armed forces and this means that force structure itself should be a function of the costs of the specific inputs, given the amount of combat power needed as follows from the Defensienota 1991.

Conscription disturbs allocation in the armed forces. There are two reasons for this phenomenon. The first reason is that conscripts earn about 58% of the salary of a professional troops with the same rank. This means, there is "cheap" labour available in the armed forces. The second reason is that mandatory service by conscripts results in labour not being scarce anymore in the armed forces. Therefore military labour has a "free" character.

The armed forces are losing information about the real costs of their means of production, because these costs are not based on market prices, but legal rules. This is not an absolute loss, if the armed forces keep in mind the real civil costs of the conscripts and not just the budgetary cost, when making decisions. Efficiency losses by conscription will be kept at a minimum, when the salary of the conscripts doesn't differ from the salary they would have earned elsewhere in society, combined with the idea that the conscript is not a free lunch.

In practise everything is different. Conscripts get a salary that is far below the market standard and the armed forces show a huge need for conscripts.[1] The consequences for the division between labour and capital in the armed forces are that in the armed forces much more labour is used relative to capital, when we compare this with capital-labour relations in civil society. In peace time this expresses itself in boredom. Conscription implies that the armed forces have a lot of people, a lot of military and a lot of inexperienced people. This would change if military labour would become expensive and scarce.

In a model this will result in the following.[2]
The technological relation between inputs (capital, labour, professional military, conscripts and civilians) and output (combat power) is based on the production function:

1) $Q = f\,(X_1, X_2)$

Q is equal to the combat power needed.
X1 is equal to the first input.
X2 is equal to the second input.

The costs of these inputs are based on a costs function. In our case this is:

2) $C = p_1X_1 + p_2X_2$

C is equal to the total costs of the inputs.
The different p's give the price of each specific input.

An optimal allocation of inputs can be achieved by maximizing equation 1 under the budget restriction of equation 2, or minimizing equation 2 under the restriction of the necessary combat power from equation 1. A necessary

---

[1] In other words, because of the conscription tax the social cost of conscripts is far above the real cost.
[2] For a general theoretical background see: A. Koutsoyiannis, Modern Microeconomics, London 1975.

restriction for an optimum is that the relation marginal product/price is equal for every input:

3) $Mx1/p1 = Mx2/p2$

$Mx1$ is equal to the marginal product of input 1, etc

If we take for input 1, Labour (L) and for input 2, Capital (K), then equation 3 says that the ratio between the marginal product of labour and the marginal product of capital (the technical rate of substitution) is equal to the ratio between the price of labour and the price of capital.

4) $MxL/MxK = w/r$

MxL is the marginal product of labour
MxK is the marginal product of capital
w is the wage or the price of labour
r is interest or the price of capital.

The marginal products of labour and capital are positive, but decreasing functions of the amount of labour and capital. Equation 4 implies also that if the ratio w/r changes, the ratio K/L should also change. If wages rise relative to the costs of capital, the amount of capital (K) will rise in relation to the amount of labour (L).

This model provides the basis for research after the allocation of different input factors in the armed forces. The model shows us that:

a) Combat power is directly related to the used inputs, so that an efficient management will be reached by combining the right choices of these inputs.

b) The classification of inputs in broad categories, such as capital, labour, conscripted military, professional military, and civilians, is a useful method to investigate alternatives concerning personnel and the cost of personnel.

c) The optimal allocation of military resources is a function of the relative cost of the inputs.

Using this method, the following issues will be studied in the remainder of this chapter: boredom, the ratio capital vs. labour in the armed forces, the ratio civilian vs. military in the armed forces and the ratio of inexperienced vs. experienced employees in the armed forces.

§ 5.2. Boredom

Boredom is a structural experience in the armed forces. Boredom is caused by conscription and involves being idle during labour time. Conscription causes mandatory participation in the labour process in the armed forces, whereby it is impossible for conscripts to quit the job voluntarily. Because the provision of labour is dealt with legally, there are no incentives for the employer to meet the wishes of the employees. Troublesome people can be removed and replaced without any difficulties.

Boredom results from the mandatory character of the duty and can only disappear, if the mandatory character of the job is abolished or when there is a possibility for the conscripts to quit voluntarily. Even if conscripts would receive a professional wage, boredom will survive.

The amount of boredom depends on labour costs. One can expect that the amount of boredom will be lower with a professional wage, than with a salary of 58% of this wage, as is the case for conscripts. This follows from the fact that the demand for labour will be lower, when the price of labour is higher, and less people are bored.

There are two principle reasons to assume why, on a long term basis, the demand for military labour will be a decreasing function of the labour costs. The first is the substitution effect, because labour will be exchanged for capital if labour becomes more expensive. The second is the income effect, because a rise in the budgetary burden of labour costs for defense will on a long term basis be accompanied by a lower demand for defense and military as a consequence, although this effect is not so strong, due to reasons of international security.
The amount of boredom thus results from the fact that the armed forces have too much or too few people in relation to a social optimum, as is described in figure 5.1. by the intersection of the demand and supply curve in point a.

If conscripts would have been expensive and scarce, than on the basis of the substitution effect it can be expected that these conscripts would have been substituted for capital. Not by regular tanks, but by better exercise (human capital), advanced tanks and other weapon systems, catering services and a better basic training. There will also be substitution of conscripts for civilians. Under a market regime the waste of labour is expensive and should be prevented. Besides, we haven't even mentioned the fact that the armed forces are under the ongoing threat of losing their personnel, when the consequences of boredom have their effects on the job satisfaction of their personnel.[3]

In the Dutch armed forces, 75% of the conscripts say that they are bored more than two hours a day during labour time[4]. On average this means that boredom is about 25% of the labour time. If we take this 25% of labour time as a proxy for the inefficiency in the armed forces, an efficient army would not need 44,761 soldiers (OB, figure 5.1.), but only 33.570 (OA). This should be accompanied by a market wage of 17.864 guilders (W_2) in stead of the 12,000

---

[3] See chapter 6, paragraph 1.

[4] Research by AVNM: Verveling in dienst, Utrecht 1989

guilders after tax that a conscript gets (W1).[5] The amount of boredom is equal to the dashed square in figure 5.1. and would have been 40.5 million guilders if the conscripts were selected with the LSPDF-principle.[6] In the Netherlands we have personal conscription. This causes an even higher amount of boredom. An estimate shows the amount of 188 million guilders. This estimate can be made by subtracting the area of the pentagon OSaD'B from the area under the line SS'.

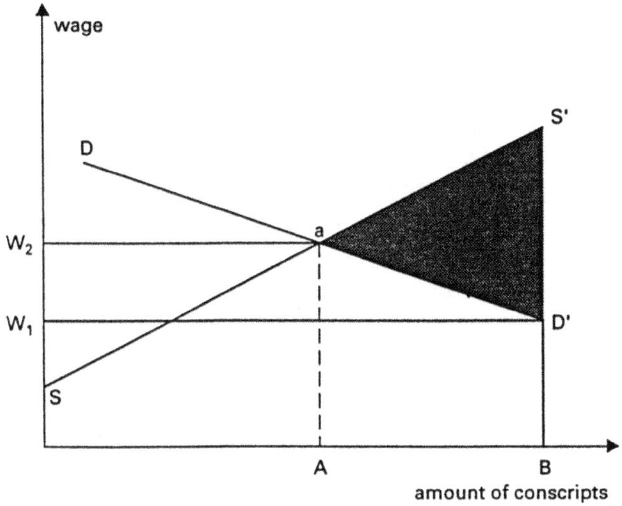

FIGURE 5.1 Boredom

§ 5.3. Capital-labour substitution

In last paragraph we've seen that the demand for capital will rise, if conscription were to be abolished and military personnel becomes expensive and scarce. Conscription creates a situation in the armed forces, in which the capital/labour ratio is lower than were to be expected, if the market could have done its job. Substitution between labour and capital seems to be mainly possible in these parts of the armed forces that have a great similarity with sectors in civil society.

The comparison with the civil sector can probably provide a reasonable insight in the opportunities for substitution. This is surely the case if we keep in mind that 75% of the armed forces work in a function that is more or less comparable to a position in civil society. This 75% follows from the "teeth-to-tail"-ratio in the armed forces of about 68% tail(civilian)positions and the fact that within the combat forces a lot of logistic positions can be discovered which are comparable to positions in civil society.

---

5 For 33.570 approved boys, you need 45.987 tested boys, because only 73% gets through. The wage that is needed to get the last well-tested boy in to the armed forces is *f* 17.684 net a year. For calculations see appendix 5.1.

6 See for calculation: Appendix 5.1.

In a discussion about substitution possibilities it is important to make this comparison on the basis of existing technology. Capital-labour substitution is surely possible within the combat forces, but in order to achieve such a substitution new advanced technology is often necessary. New technology that is less needed in supporting parts, because most of the time this new technology is already available in civil society.

An example is the guarding of military complexes in the Netherlands. Guarding activities are one of the main activities for the armed forces. To accomplish this job, the armed forces trust heavily on human activities by soldiers. This soldier is supported by a walkie-talkie, his personal weapon and the fence around the barracks. That guarding is mainly done by soldiers has to do with the financial aspects of guarding. Most of the job is done by conscripts, who are very cheap, because the guarding activities are only partly compensated in time. Added to this is the fact that this time is also very cheap, because conscripts just get a salary that is far below a normal wage for guarding. The possibility for consuming this compensation time is also limited, and will only be given when there is totally nothing to do and conscripts end up very bored.

If labour would have been more expensive, a professional wage for conscripts or a civilian guarding team, then the expensive labour force would have been substituted for capital. One can think about an alarm system or video guarding. How far this substitution process will go on depends on the marginal costs of labour and capital.

The examples of boredom and guarding can be seen easily in practise, but are not enough to pose the general statement that the capital labour ratio in the armed forces is lower than this ratio in civil society. Confirmation of this statement would require more empirical research.

Research from the United States shows there is a clear difference between both capital labour ratios.[7] In the twenty years after the second world war each 1% change in the labour-capital costs ratio in civil society seemed to be followed by a 1.4% change in the capital-labour ratio, despite the fact that society was getting more and more services orientated. In the mean time in the armed forces a rise of 40% in the ratio labour-capital costs seemed to be accompanied by a rise of 1% in the ratio capital-labour. Each percent rise in the labour-capital costs ratio thus results in a 0.025% change in the ratio capital-labour.

An analysis for the Netherlands can not support the research for the United States. This is mainly caused by a lack of good data. In the period 1972-1990 it appears that the armed forces are more capital intensive, but a division between investments and use of capital between combat forces and supporting parts of the armed forces is very difficult to make. Up until now the conclusions about capital-labour substitution are based on global observation. Empirical studies will still need to be elaborated for the Netherlands.

---

[7] Richard V.L. Cooper, Military Manpower and the All-Volunteer Force, Santa Monica, 1977, pp. 286.

As a preliminary conclusion we can say that when activities in the armed forces are comparable activities in civil society substitution of labour for capital seems to be possible. Theory and American empirical results show that is possible to gain from this substitution.

Although it may be possible to substitute labour for capital in daily life, some political obstacles should not be overlooked. This is because the parts where most gains can be expected in terms of capital-labour substitution, are not the parts that always attract the attention of the general staff or parliament. They focus mainly on big expenses in the combat divisions, while most gains can be collected in the supporting parts. Moreover it is important to show that capital expenses are profitable on a long term basis, because generals and politicians often focus on the short term without considering the long term profitability.

The analysis in this paragraph has shown that by substituting capital for labour in the long run budget savings can be achieved. Or in other words, long term savings can be achieved by re-allocating means, rather than cutting in combat power; a re-allocation that is necessary if conscription is going to be abolished. However, it should be stressed that these re-allocation processes will in the short run lead to extra expenses.

§ 5.4. Military personnel and civilians[8]

Within the armed forces there are many positions filled by non-military personnel, i.e. civilians. Civilians are used in the armed forces to fill positions that don't provide a direct contribution to combat power, but certainly do in an indirect way. Military personnel should fill the combat positions, because these positions involve the element of violence.

Table 5.1. gives us a survey about the amount of combat positions, that result from the Defense report 1991. The combat positions in the army concern "The first Army", in the Air Force, "The pilots of the F-16, transport planes and helicopters, and the positions for air defense", and in the Navy "the marines and the personnel for the ships". The positions that are necessary to organize and to command the mobilization parts in the army and for the relief of personnel in the Navy are taken into account in table 5.1.[9]

---

8 This paragraph is based on: M. Binkin, The Military Pay Muddle, The Brookings Institution, Washington DC, 1975; M. Binkin, H. Kanter and R.H. Clark, Shaping the defense civilian work force, The Brookings Institution, Washington DC, 1978, and Stichting Maatschappij and Krijgsmacht, The price of defense, The Hague, 1983.

9 See parliamentary question nr 207 and 211, Tweede Kamer, Vergaderjaar 1990-1991,21991X, nr. 8. The amount of combat positions for the Navy and the Air Force are estimated on the basis of the Defensienota 1991. The amount of marines is put at 3.000 and for the personnel on the ships (including relief) a ship-shore ratio of 3:7 counts. This ratio is well known in the United States. All other figures are based on the Defensienota 1991. The background of the number in training of 1.500 is given in paragraph 5.6.

Table 5.1. Amount of combat positions

Unit	Combat positions
Army	26,500
Navy	6,500
Air Force	2,000
Military Police	3,000
In training	1,500

Total	39,500

In 1992 the Dutch armed forces enlisted about 90,000 military. Although the reduction of the armed forces will also diminish the amount of military personnel, the question why are there so many troops relative to the amount of combat positions remains.[10]

An answer to this question can probably be found in the costs of military and civilian labour. If a soldier is cheaper than a civilian to fill a certain position than it is profitable to employ a military person in that position. If we want to analyse the military-civilian problem we have to look at the cost ratio of these sorts of labour.

A surplus of military can be explained if the average costs of military are lower than the average costs of a civilian. The big problem when comparing the costs of civilians and military is the presence of enormous amounts of non-pecuniary payments to the military, like training, clothing, and the costs of (early) retirement . In order to get the average costs of every group, the budgetary costs of every group should be divided by the amount of people that is present in every group. This method gives us a reasonable insight of all the costs, but is not perfect because the enormous cost of training of military and civilians is not incorporated perfectly.

Table 5.2. shows the average costs of different groups of employees in the armed forces, using the figures of the budget of the defense department 1992, nr. 01, 02, and 03 for every chapter. In this table five different groups are distinguished: civilians, conscripts, professional soldiers, military (conscripts + professionals) and military (+). This last group shows us the cost of military personnel, if the social costs of conscription are discounted in the price of soldiers. The costs in-kind concern facts like travel expenses, costs of clothing etc. Facts that have no rewarding character.

10 The amount of military should be diminished to 86.696 in 1995 on a total of 107.573. Source Defensienota 1991. Because of the Prioriteitennota 1993 these figures are out of date now, but this is not relevant for a analysis of conscription.

Table 5.2.: Average costs employees armed forces in guilders

Average costs	amount	wage cost	pension	in kind	total
Civilians	23,177	58,700	1,872	5,276	65,848
Conscripts	37,965	19,177	5,789	6,613	31,579
Professionals	51,651	59,949	25,126	10,512	95,587
Military	89,616	42,930	16,934	8,866	68,730
Military (+)	89,616	48,997	16,934	8,866	74,797

From the table, it can be concluded that the difference in costs between civilians and military is small (about 3,000 guilders). The present allocation of personnel within the armed forces can without a doubt be confirmed on the basis of present cost relations.

The cause of the present allocation can also be found in table 5.2.: conscription. Because of conscription the average costs of military labour are lower than they would have been in the case of an all-volunteer force. Conscription conceals the costs of the military. If conscripts would have been paid a professional salary, than military would have been substituted by civilians on positions where this is possible.

This problem becomes even more evident when we recognize that the costs of military training are much higher than that of civilian training. Military people are trained inside the armed forces, whereas most of civilians get their training in civil society.

It is also important to recognize, that by using the substitution possibilities, cost reductions are possible without losing combat power. Substitution of military by civilians can produce a lot of money, but we have to keep in mind that the pecuniary aspect is secondary to the fact if it is possible to substitute a soldier for a civilian.

The primary question concerns the combat character of a position. Military personnel should occupy the combat positions and civilians the supporting positions, if civilians are cheaper than military personnel. In table 5.2. we have seen that civilians are cheaper and that the substitution of military by civilians on supporting positions should take place, if we want to get an efficient organisation.

In we want to make a distinction between civilians and military the combat- and costs characteristics are the only valuable criteria. These criteria are objective and give only little discussion. This in contradiction to criteria as tradition or bureaucratic rule[11], which have a subjective reason and are therefore not suitable for a comparison between positions for civilians and positions for military personnel.

---

11 See chapter 2, paragraph 2.

In the case of analysing conscription, the possibility of substitution of military for civilian personnel is of eminent importance. Because of conscription, the demand for military personnel should in principle be very large. This also explains why there are so many military in the armed forces. Abolishing conscription makes military personnel scarce and also expensive, as shown in this paragraph. The strict distinction between combat positions and supporting positions is very important, because this distinction reveals the real demand for military personnel. That civilian personnel is also cheaper is then of secondary importance in a discussion about conscription. In a social efficient armed forces the substitution of military for civilian personnel should always have taken place. Moreover, a larger amount of civilians supports the socialization of the armed forces.[12]

In real life the military-civilian substitution does present a few problems. Experiences from the United Stated show us that the military-civilian-substitution receives a lot of public support, but moves to the background if the armed forces are capable of easily being filled with volunteers, without bringing the amount of troops needed to a minimum. In such a situation the conscription problem is solved, but does not necessarily result in an efficient armed forces. Charles Moskos states that an all-volunteer-force is certainly not cheaper than an conscript-force[13]. He reaches this conclusion after analyzing the costs of the United Stated armed forces, where an explosion in the costs of retirement and early retirement are visible. What Moskos doesn't mention is the fact that the increase in costs is not the result of introducing an all-volunteer force, but of insufficient substitution of military personnel by civilians. The American people were liberated from conscription and this was enough to continue the traditions from the past. The social costs of an all-volunteer force were of secondary importance and simply forgotten.

For the conscription discussion in the Netherlands this is also an important aspect. If the military-civilian-substitution is moved to the background, then considerable cost increases concerning retirement can be expected. From table 5.2. it can be deduced that the costs of professional troops are so high, because of high retirement costs. Navy personnel retires at only 50-years, other branches do so at 55.

Another problem concerning the substitution of military personnel for civilians is the fact that these substitutions can only be executed in supporting-positions. However, the combat positions receive almost exclusive attention from the politicians and the general staff, whereby the other part of the armed forces, with most of the personnel, are virtually ignored. This example expresses again that the solution to the conscription puzzle must be found in the non-combat positions and not in the amount of tanks, ships or planes.

---

12 See for extension of this problem: chapter 7.

13 Charles Moskos, L'armee de métier Americaine (1973-1990): Constat de carence; Fondation pour les études de défense nationale, Paris, February 1991.

Contrary to the problems with the substitutions of capital and labour, the military-civilian substitution has the advantage that cost reductions are immediately visible for politicians. Moreover, the socialization of the armed forces is also an important political point.

A big practical problem of military-civilian substitution in the armed forces is military tradition. A military tradition, that is put under pressure when the loss of uniform, rank, power and status is considered. If the substitution of troops for civilians will really be a success, than these points of consideration should be taken into account. In chapter 8, paragraph 5 we will analyze this problem and we will also suggest some possible answers.

§ 5.5. The substitution between inexperienced and experienced personnel

The military personnel system is a closed-shop system. For most of the military positions, people are selected from their own ranks. In order to keep sufficient experienced personnel in a closed shop system like the armed forces, it is necessary to get enough new young people. There is a dynamic balance between the amount of experienced and inexperienced personnel, because on the one hand a huge amount of youngsters can mean that there is not enough space to flow trough the organisation, but on the other hand too few youngsters can mean that there are less possibilities to select the right people for the right place.

The mix between experienced and inexperienced personnel plays an important role in the armed forces. From an allocation perspective it is therefore important to make a distinction between these two groups and to see these two groups as specific production factors.

Economic theory teaches us that when inexperienced and experienced personnel can be substituted for each other, a rise in the wage for inexperienced personnel will lead to a re-allocation of resources, whereby inexperienced personnel will be replaced by more experienced personnel. In reality we see that the armed forces rely heavily on conscription and thus on inexperienced personnel. A rise in military pay for conscripts to the professional pay level will thus lead to a change in the mix for inexperienced/experienced personnel in such a way that more experienced personnel will be employed. The question attached to this change is: how big will this change be? An answer can be given by looking at the productivity of both groups.

If inexperienced soldiers are doing work that can better be done by experienced personnel, it results in a loss of productivity. In other words, inexperienced soldiers can be substituted by experienced personnel on lower than one to one basis without the loss of combat power. Research from the United States shows us that 100 people with 4 years of experience can replace 180 inexperienced people without any loss of combat power.[14] The substitution of inexperienced conscripts by experienced personnel can thus result in important productivity gains of cost reductions.

Regarding the importance of the mix between inexperienced and experienced personnel, it is important that we look at possible issues facing this possibility of substitution. The first is that due to a lack of scarcity, the mix of inexperienced and experienced under conscription has always been seen as a question of organization, not as a question of required personnel. In the case of an all-volunteer force it would be necessarily to regard the latter question. The second issue is that the armed forces have valued their seniors mainly as supervisors, in stead of as executing personnel. Currently professional military are ordinarily found behind a desk and not in the field. A last issue is that the mix between inexperienced and experienced personnel is not a problem of too many people in the higher ranks, but is a problem a too many people in non-productive positions. A general as a infantry-soldier can be more productive than a general behind a desk.

§ 5.6. The need for personnel in an all-volunteer force

This chapter has as a motto a quotation from Cooper:

"The force structure itself should be a function of the costs of the specific inputs".

This quotation is of eminent importance, if we want to get sufficient insight in the possibilities to substitute a conscription-force for an all-volunteer force. Because of the "free" character of conscripts the need for inexperienced troops is "infinitely" large. In an all-volunteer force this "free" character disappears, and a search for alternatives for inexperienced personnel is needed.

In this chapter we have seen that alternative production factors are available and should be found in using capital, civilians and experienced military. Strictly speaking contracting out should be added too, but will be seen so far as a combination of capital- en civilian substitution. In chapter 7 we will analyze contracting out as a special case of the interaction between the armed forces and civil society. In this chapter we restrict ourselves to the alternatives that are possible within the armed forces.

In 1976 conscription and the transition to an all-volunteer force is investigated by the Mommersteeg-committee.[15] This committee concluded that it was favorable to abolish conscription, but it was practically impossible to make

14 Gay, Robert M., Estimating the cost of on-the-job training in military occupation: A methodology and pilot study, The Rand Corporation, Santa Monica 1974.

15 Committee Mommersteeg, Verplicht of vrijwillig dienen, Den Haag 1976.

this transition. The same conclusion was stated by the Meijer-committee in her "Naar dienstplicht nieuwe stijl" in 1992.

The possibility to transform a conscription-force into an all-volunteer force depends on both the supply and the demand of volunteers. In chapter 6 we will analyze the supply side thoroughly. In this paragraph we will quantify the real need for personnel in the armed forces using the methods shown in this chapter. In chapter 6 this will also be analyzed, but with other methods. Both methods are complementary, but are treated separately to keep an overview on the subject. In this paragraph the restriction of personnel due to allocation processes will be central. In chapter 6 specific labour market instruments will be analyzed to look at possible restrictions in the amount of military needed.

With the analysis in this paragraph we can see whether the Mommersteeg and Meijer-committee were correct in stating that the transition to an all-volunteer force was not possible. The Meijer-committee used the Defensienota 1991 and the Defense budget 1992 as a starting point for its analysis. In this paragraph we will do the same, as we already did in the whole chapter.

Table 5.1. teaches us that there are 39,500 combat positions. By capital-labour-substitution it must be possible to reduce the Army positions by 5%. Special emphasis in this substitution process should be placed on the positions in the Army-supporting combat troops within the First Army.

The savings on military expenses by the substitution of inexperienced conscripts by experienced personnel is estimated moderately on 10% of the Army positions. Gay's study[16] shows that even savings up to 45% are possible, but in this paragraph some caution with this figure is taken into account. A 10 % savings seems to be more reasonable. However, the armed forces should be working on this figure by stimulating long-term contracts and re-entering of veterans.

After the execution of these substitutions 35,000 military positions remain. This number of 35,000 is less than the amount of professional troops that is present in the armed forces in 1992.[17] The amount of civilians in an all-volunteer force rises considerably. According to the Defensienota 1991 the amount of civilians declines to 17,000. By substituting troops for civilians, extra civilians are needed for maintenance, guarding, management and training positions. The maintenance positions are mostly positions within the Navy and the Air Force and are estimated for the whole armed forces at 10,000. The amount of guarding positions are estimated on 2,000 and when we consider management positions, we generally mean positions on a barracks level like that of general management, warehouses, and human services. The amount of positions involved is estimated at 6,500.

The training positions are derived from the amount of troops in training. With 35,000 combat positions it is estimated that each year 3,000 positions will

16 Zie footnote 14.

17 See table 5.2. In 1992 the Netherlands had 51,.651 professionals

become available.[18] With an average basic training of 6 months, 1,500 troops would have to be trained as is expressed in table 5.1. A rule of experience from the United States teaches us that for every person in training one trainer is needed. Nowadays this ratio is 14:8, but because of expected intensified training of professional military personnel in different skills, it is possible that this ratio will become 1:1. As a consequence 1,500 civilians are needed to train these troops. Some of these civilians will need a military background in order to provide the proper training.

Finally the substitution processes will result in an additional 20,000 civilians, which brings the total amount of civilians to 37,000. The Meijer Committee did not investigate the possibility of attracting this amount of civilians to the armed forces, so it cannot immediately be assumed that this will be the case.

After all the substitutions the armed forces still have 72,000 positions. Compared to the starting figure of 112,000 this means that 40,000 positions will disappear. These 40,000 positions include savings due to a cut in combat power resulting from the Defensienota 1991, a gain in productivity by substituting labour by capital, inexperienced personnel by experienced personnel and a reduction in bureaucrats that follows from the transition to a more society orientated armed forces.

However, these reductions pale in comparison with the savings in personnel employed in training positions. In 1992 22,000 people were permanent busy in the Army alone with receiving training or giving training. This amount is reduced to 3,000 for the whole armed forces in the case of an all-volunteer force.

The Meijer-committee arrived at very different results. The demand for personnel was estimated much higher, because it used the principle that one conscript should be replaced by one professional.

The Mommersteeg-committee investigated the conscription-force in 1976. If we want to make a closer investigation of the report of this committee, we have to go back to the international security situation described in the Defensienota 1974. According to this white paper the armed forces had a demand for 99,000 troops and 25,800 civilians. In the case of scarcity, when abolishing conscription, this will result in a demand of troops for about 45,000. An estimation of the amount of civilians needed, according to the method described above an amount of 48,000 result.

On the basis of these figures we cannot conclude differently. Saying that an all-volunteer force would have been possible during the period of the Mommersteeg-committee, because the figures only differ slightly from the figures for the Meijer-committee.

However, there is one big obstacle. The research shows that it is possible to transform a conscription-force into an all-volunteer force, if we compare the

---

18 In 1992 the armed forces needed 4,550 professional military each year to fill their positions on 51,.000 positions totally. This means that in an armed forces with 35.,00 professional military positions, about 3.000 positions have to filled each year.

organisation of the armed forces under both institutions in peace time. However, the armed forces have to prepare for a war and in a war mobilizing forces also play a role. Only if there is also an alternative to fill the reserves, we can be sure about the fact that the results from both the Meijer-committee and the Mommersteeg-committee were wrong. The reserves are discussed in chapter 8, because the alternatives for the mobilizing troops become really clear after treating the supply of volunteers in chapter 6 and the interaction between society and armed forces in chapter 7. Although this question about reserves is important it remains obvious that both in 1992 and in 1976 an all-volunteer force is possible

§ 5.7. The budgetary consequences of the transition of a conscription-force to an all-volunteer force and the "excess burden" of a conscription force

Now that we have specified the demand for military and civilians, we can combine the costs of the production factors to get the budgetary consequences of a transition from a conscription force to an all-volunteer force.

When combining the costs figures of 1992 (table 5.2) with the personnel figures of paragraph 5.6 the total personnel costs will be 6.4 billion guilders: civilians 2,436 million guilders, military 2,466 million guilders and pension costs 1,517 million guilders.[19] In the long run personnel costs can decline to 5.1 billion[20] guilders, because of the decline in pension costs and a relative younger professional force. In 1992 the total personnel costs were 7,7 billion guilders a year. The abolition of conscription in combination with reductions in the combat power according to the Defensienota 1991 will lead to a savings of 2,6 billion guilders a year with regard to the 1992 budget, whereby most of the money comes from savings in training costs and a decline in pension costs.

In the short run this sum will probably be lower, because restructuring a big organisation like the armed forces always costs a lot of money and because of the labour savings investment that take a lot of money too. However, in the long run the transitions costs will disappear and the abolishing of conscription will save a lot of money. An all-volunteer force is not expensive like the Meijer-committee stated in her report.

The cost savings that could have been accomplished, if the Mommersteeg-committee had given the green light to an all-volunteer force, are in so far interesting, because these costs savings can shed a light on the excess-burden of conscription.

---

19 Civilians 37,000 x 65,848 = 2,436 million guilders, military: 35,000 x 70,461 = 2,466 million guilders.

20 Civilians: 37,000 x 65,848 = 2,436 million guilders, military: 35,000 x 74,797 = 2,617 million guilders.

Contrary to the Meijer-committee the Mommersteeg-committee had to express an opinion about conscription during times when there was no discussion about reducing combat power caused by changing international circumstances. The aforementioned amount of 2.6 billion guilders as cost savings has the disadvantage, that this sum is partly caused by the reduction in combat power and partly by the abolishing of conscription. Because of this combination the excess burden of the conscription tax can not be measured. An investigation of the Mommersteeg report can give us the "burden of conscription added on to the conscription tax", because in 1976 no combination was present.

In 1976 we had 99,000 troops and 25,800 civilians. In 1992 guilders this would have resulted in 8,502 million guilders personnel costs.[21] In an all-volunteer force we have 45,000 troops and 48,000 civilians. This brings us 6,527 million guilders personnel costs.[22] Next to these costs we have training, clothing and housing costs. In chapter 4 we've seen that the training of conscripts cost 500 million guilders a year. Most of these training costs are discounted in the costs of personnel and thus won't be added in calculating the excess burden to avoid double counting. The costs of clothing and housing (265 million guilders) will also exist partly in an all-volunteer force. In an all-volunteer force the amount of troops will decline by about 55%.[23] If we assume a proportionate decline in the cost of housing and clothing 120 million guilders still remain, so the excess burden will be 145 million.

The cost of testing conscripts also includes an excess burden (22 million), as is the cost that are made for avoiding conscription (2,5 million) and the cost for conscience objectors (25 million). In total this results in a 2,170 million guilders burden for society above the conscription tax each year, on the basis of the size of the armed forces in 1976 and the cost of production in 1992 guilders.

Conscription disturbs the allocation process. By changing the relative prices of production factors a considerable excess burden occurs of about 2 billion guilders a year.

§ 5.8. Conclusion

The central problem in investigating the feasibility of an all-volunteer force is the problem of scarcity. The possibility of an all-volunteer force depends heavily on the sensitivity of the armed forces for changes in the cost of production, which follow from abolishing conscription. Conscription gives the armed forces an artificial cost structure, which results in an inefficient organization with too many

---

21 Military: 99,000 x 68,730 = 6,804 million guilders + civilians 25,800 x 65,848 = 1,698 million guilders.

22 Military: 45,00 x 74,797 = 3,336 million guilders + civilians 48,000 x 65,848 = 3,161 million guilders.

23 (99,000 - 45,000)/99,000 = 0.55

people; too many troops; and too many inexperienced personnel. In the armed forces Leibenstein X-inefficiency is clearly visible.

The need for production factors changes in an all-volunteer force from inexperienced conscripts, to capital, civilians and experienced troops. Scarcity makes looking for alternatives attractive. This implies both the organization of the armed forces in peace time, as we have seen in this chapter as the occupation of the reserves as we shall see in chapter 8. An investigation for the feasibility of an all-volunteer force should be aware of the fact that an all-volunteer force implies a totally new concept of analysis.

Both the Meijer-committee as the Mommersteeg-committee are not aware of this new concept and are not solving the puzzle.

In this chapter we have also seen that the methods used are not just important for judging conscription. They also give us the possibility to realise cost reduction in the armed forces without decreasing the combat power of the armed forces. The armed forces can be much more efficient which will be advantageous to everybody in Dutch society.

Appendix 5.1.

	Wage class 16-24year old (guilders)	amount of youth in %	Boys cum.	Conscripts absolute
	A	B	C	D
1	< 10,000	5.6	6,640	2,507
2	10,000-12,000	6.4	14,228	2,865
3	12,000-12,500	1.6	16,125	716
4	12,500-15,000	9.6	27,507	4,297
5	15,000-17,500	13.9	43,988	6,222
6	17,500-17,684(L)	1.7	45,987	761
7	17,684-17,913	2.1	48,493	939
8	17,913-19,095(J)	10.8	61,316	4,838
9	19,095-20,000	8.3	71,140	3,715
10	20,000-22,500	21.9	97,106	9,803
11	22,500-25,000	11.0	110,148	4,924
12	25,000-27,500	4.1	115,009	1,835
13	27,500-30,000	1.7	117,024	716
14	30,000-32,500	0.6	117,736	269
15	32,500-35,000	0.3	118,,091	134
16	35,000-37,500	0.1	118,210	45
				_44,761(G)

This table has been used earlier in chapter 4 (table 4.1). For an explanation of all statistics, see the contents of chapter 4.

Test percentage (E) = 73,0% approved.
Conscripts salary (F) =fl 12,000,-.

1. Narrow definition conscription tax (H) = $1{,}2 \times \sum_{i=3}^{16}((Ai - F) \times Di)$ = 360 million guilders.

2. For 44.761 conscripts G/E = 61,316(8C) boys are needed. Wage(J) = fl 19,095.-(8A).

3. Broad definition conscription tax = $(J - F) \times G + \sum_{i=8}^{16}((1{,}2Ai - J) \times Di) =$ 450 million.

4. 33.570 = K. K/E = 45,987(6C). Wage (L) = 17,684(6A).

5. Boredom LSPDF = $\sum_{i=3}^{8}((Ai - F) \times Di) - (G - (D1 + D2)) \times (L - F) \times 0{,}5$ = 40.5 million.

- Boredom lottery system = $1/1{,}2 \times H - (G - (D1 + D2)) \times (L - F) \times 0{,}5$ = 188 million

Statistics A en B: Statistisch jaarboek 1991, CBS blz. 99.
Statistics C, D, E en G: Jaaroverzicht dienstplichtgegevens 1988, Min. van Defensie.
Statistics: Archive VVDM (Dutch soldiers union).

CHAPTER 6

The demand for and the supply of volunteers

"Enlargement of the interested supply and a better way of reaching the supply can mean that the need for volunteers can be narrowly accomplished, but for the conversion of a conscription army into an all-volunteer force it is necessary that the armed forces shed a light on its needs and procedures.

Research voor Beleid in "Naar dienstplicht nieuwe stijl"-rapport Commissie Meijer, Den Haag 1992.

In chapter four and five we used the "opportunity cost" instrument to investigate military conscription. With the opportunity cost instrument we analysed the social costs of conscription in terms of the conscription tax and we used these social costs for the social cost price of conscripts to analyse the allocation questions in the armed forces.

Thus, in researching the conscription issue, the search for the alternative scarce situation is central. This alternative situation is the all-volunteer force. If we want to analyse the social costs of conscription completely, we also have to investigate all the ramifications of an all-volunteer force with the same opportunity cost instrument.

In this chapter this investigation method appears around three central subjects. The first subject concerns the supply of volunteers for the armed forces. Before volunteers put themselves at the disposal of the armed forces for a combat position , they will make some kind of decision. Weighing their options the potential volunteers put the salary and the intrinsic value of the position in the armed forces, such as the molding of human capital and the element of adventure, against the alternative possibilities in civil society. As such becomes clear what the alternative costs are in this process.

The search for the opportunity costs of a potential volunteer will be analyzed in paragraph 6.1. This will be done in general terms, because for a concrete evaluation the tasks of the armed forces should also be clear. In paragraph 6.2. these tasks are also made part of the decision making process after which it will be investigated how the possibilities and the desires in terms of salary and other forms of rewards of the potential volunteers can be matched with the tasks of the armed forces. In these two paragraphs attention is also paid to the manner in which the armed forces should respond to wishes of potential volunteers, in order to give potential volunteers the chance to use special skills that can be used both in the armed forces and in civil society.

The second central subject of this chapter corresponds with the latter idea. In paragraph 6.3., specifically, we will look at the selection process in the armed forces. The armed forces make pick from the supply of volunteers by selection. This choice bears a certain amount of costs. These costs are not only in terms of losses of opportunities for a volunteer on the micro-economic level , but also can be spoken about 'opportunity costs' in macro-social terms. Specifically in the selection process the comparison between a conscription army and an all-volunteer force in terms of 'opportunity costs' is of eminent importance, because with the help of these 'opportunity costs' it can be investigated, what kind of selection-demands can be asked for what kind of army.

In paragraph 6.4. the third central subject of this chapter is discussed: the demand for volunteers. This subject is important for a distinction between a conscription army and an all-volunteer force, because the real demand for volunteers in an all-volunteer force shows which institutions in the armed forces should be changed, if the armed forces want to use all possible opportunities of the volunteers in order to keep the costs of an all-volunteer force as low as possible. Due to conscription, there are still a lot of institutions in the armed forces, that have a negative effect on an all-volunteer force.

§ 6.1. The supply of potential volunteers[1]

When analyzing the supply of volunteers and the opportunity costs of volunteers we shall use the traditional labour supply theory. From this theory, it follows that each element that is important for deciding to volunteer has to be discussed separately. These elements will be combined with the tasks and organization of the armed forces in paragraph 6.2. to complete a full labour supply theory for the armed forces.

The elements that influence the profession "soldier" can be divided as follows: 1) primary labour conditions in the armed forces, 2) secondary labour conditions in the armed forces, 3) labour circumstances in the armed forces, 4) the employment situation, labour conditions and labour circumstances in civil society, 5) the composition of the population that will supply the possible volunteers, 6) the information flow that reaches the potential volunteers.

Salary is the most important primary labour condition. Other parts of the primary labour conditions are the length of the contract, the tasks that should be performed in the armed forces and the bodily risk connected to the job.

Within the primary labour conditions different degrees can be found, because the armed forces offer different possibilities in tasks. This means that there is an opportunity for matching the wishes of the volunteer and the needs of the armed

---

1 This paragraph is among others articles based on: G.S. Becker, "Investment in Human Capital: a theoretical analysis, "Journal of political economy, vol. 70, 1962; G.J. Stigler, "Information in the labor market", The journal of political economy, vol. 70, 1962 and NorBerFN, Nordic Standby forces in United Nations service, Stockholm, 1974.

forces. Matching results in more people being engaged than first expected, because the greater variability of wishes and possibilities makes it easier to couple the preferences of potential volunteers with the wishes of the armed forces. In paragraph 6.2. this will be investigated in depth.

The second group of important elements are the secondary labour conditions. These elements include pension schemes, additional education, promotions and holidays. For the armed forces secondary labour conditions are very important. Probably more important then in civil society. This has to do with the closed personnel system and the pay-scales that exist in the armed forces. The armed forces have a closed personnel system, because it is impossible for volunteers to reach the higher ranks from an outsider's-position. The higher ranks are selected from their own resources. Moreover, the armed forces have an up-or-out personnel system. This means that a person can not fulfil the same job during his complete tenure. In a closed personnel system in principle everybody has to flow upwards through the hierarchy, to make place for newcomers. If someone does not want to flow up or there is no place higher up in the hierarchy for that person, no other choice remains than looking for a job in civil society. The secondary labour conditions are an important incentive for sitting personnel. Because these people are central in the investigation after the need for new volunteers, we point to paragraph 6.4. for further analyses. In this paragraph the pay-systems are also evaluated.

For a new potential volunteer the secondary labour conditions are of minor interest, except where attention is paid to additional civil education programmes. These programmes consider the building up of human capital in the armed forces, and can play an important role in the wishes of a potential volunteer. When matching the wishes of the volunteer with the wishes of the armed forces the additional training programmes play an important role in an all-volunteer force. See paragraph 6.2. for a further explanation.

The following group of elements that will interest a potential volunteer in deciding to join the armed forces are the labour conditions in the armed forces. These include the distance from residential areas to the barracks, the housing facilities in the barracks, the importance of the job, the amount of boredom, the personal relations between the members of the unit and the amount of unnecessary discipline. During the times of conscription the labour conditions are under severe pressure, because the 'indefinite' supply of labour brings too few incentives for the armed forces to meet the wishes of personnel on these issues. Bad labour circumstances do not only influence conscripts themselves, but all other personnel members who are dealing with conscripts too. Which constitutes practically everybody. Moreover, bad labour circumstances also have a negative influence on the incentives of a potential volunteer to join the armed forces.

So far, we have seen that if primary labour conditions, secondary labour conditions and labour circumstances improve, more people will join the armed forces. The question is, however, how far the armed forces should go in improving the different conditions. That is why it is important to compare the situation in the armed forces with the labour conditions and labour circumstances in civil society. In situations where the armed forces are far behind, it is necessary that they act as soon as possible to make up arrears, and in situations where the armed forces have a advantage or slight disadvantage, a smaller adjustment can be sufficient. If the armed forces want to come into the vision of a potential volunteer, they have to compete with other sectors in civil society, because a potential volunteer will make a decision between all available possibilities and will choose that job that will give him the best opportunities. Competition will be more severe if the needs of the armed forces are bigger, the population gets older or unemployment declines.

The last element that influences the supply of volunteers is the information that reaches the potential volunteer about the armed forces. One can think about recruiters in the fields, advertisements in newspapers and magazines, commercials on radio and television and publicity. The main goal of these recruiting activities is to make the potential volunteer acquainted with the possibilities of finding a job in the armed forces. An important additional condition is that the information is as real and reliable as possible and that the information concerns all possible elements that make a job in the armed forces attractive.

The above has shown a number of elements that can influence the decision to join the armed forces as a volunteer. If we restructure the elements, we can make the following volunteer-supply function:

$$E = f(W, P, S, A, BW, B, U, R) \tag{6.1}$$

whereby:

E = supply of volunteers
W = military wage
P = other primary labour conditions
S = secondary labour conditions
A = labour circumstances
BW = labour conditions and labour circumstances in civil society
B = composition of the population
U = unemployment situation
R = recruitment activities

Equation 6.1. can be simplified, if we assume that the supply of volunteers is proportional to the composition of the population and that the volunteers mostly regard the alternative labour conditions and circumstances in civil society as leading in their decisions.

$$E/B = f\,[W/BW], (P/BW), (S/BW), (A/BW), U, R] \tag{6.2}$$

When discussing all the separate elements of the supply of volunteers we already mentioned something about the sign of every variable in equation 6.2. We shall do this more extensively now.

The variable W/BW has a positive sign. This follows from the islands theory of Edmund S. Phelps.[2] This theory states that people use a reservation wage, when deciding about taking a job or not. If they want to accept a job, than the offered wage has to exceed the reservation wage. The reservation wage is based on expectations about what other people in the same job earn, advertisements, publicity and other factors. The potential jobs are separated on a few islands. In order to get enough information about the jobs, each job-seeker has to visit the islands to investigate the characteristics of the job. This search process costs time and the longer it takes to search, the longer will be the time of unemployment. As long as a job-seeker has access to correct information, he or she will find the most suitable job as soon as possible and will supply himself to the employer. However, in our world of islands imperfect information is more eminent than perfect information, because the information is spread out over all the islands. So, information is expensive. As long as the characteristics of the job do not reach the reservation wage, this potential volunteer stays a job-seeker. Only if the threshold of the reservation wage is exceeded he will supply himself and he will be part of labour supply. The island that offers the best characteristics will also have the greatest supply.

In other words, if the salary characteristics of the armed forces are better than the salary characteristics of an alternative sector, the armed forces will have an advantage in attracting volunteers. Whether a volunteer will also be engaged depends on the employer.

The salary as a component of the reservation wage not only possesses material aspects. The salary also plays a psychological role. This becomes clear if we compare the recruiting results of all the parts of the armed forces. From the results it follows that the Royal Navy and the Royal Air Force do not confront much difficulties in attracting volunteers. The Royal Army, on the other hand, has much more difficulties recruiting volunteers.

One reason for the recruiting difficulties at the Royal Army is the low status of the military profession in the army. As an indicator of status normally the average wage of that profession is used. The average wages in the Royal Navy and the Royal Air Force are much higher than the average wage in the Royal Army. The wages in the army are that low because of the presence of many conscripts with a salary that is far below the minimum wage. From the joining of the average wage to the status of the profession, it automatically follows that the Royal Army has a low status as an employer in many people's opinion. This is strengthened by the fact that as a result of cheap labour by conscription, a lot of

---

2 Edmund S. Phelps (et al.), Microeconomic Foundations of Employment and Inflation Theory, New York, 1970, pp. 1-27.

work that would have been done by machines if normal capital-labour ratios were applied as in other sectors in the economy, is done within the army by the production factor labour. Work that is often dirty and heavy.

Equation 6.2. shows us that the low status and the low salary average causes the supply of volunteers in the armed forces to stay behind the supply in other sectors. If military labour wants to find its place in the sight of scarce youngsters, than the armed forces have to compete with civil society. Or in terms of equation 6.2. the relation (W/BW) must equal at least 1.

After having taken a look at the salary as a component of the primary working conditions, we go to the other primary labour conditions. Parts of the other primary labour conditions are the length of the contract, the tasks that can be done within the armed forces and the bodily risk within the armed forces.

The length of a contract issue has two sides. On the one side a lengthy contract gives a degree of social security, but on the other side such a contract also causes trouble if possibilities for improvement are held up by contract obligations. The effect of a lengthy contract is not clear at first sight. The possibility for contract violation is important for those people who are already in the armed forces, and not so much for the new volunteers. Because this subject is investigated in paragraph 6.4. we will refer here to this paragraph. This will not say that this element is not important at all for new volunteers. But it is true that contract obligations do not have a high priority for new volunteers.

Lengthy contracts unquestionably provide lengthy social security and for this reason a higher supply of volunteers can probably be expected. Nevertheless the Social Council for the Armed Forces advises, in her report about contract length, to keep contracts short.[3] It comes to this conclusion by looking at the contents of the positions of soldiers. Professional soldiers primarily fulfiled a position in which only specific military skills were needed. A position that did not have a lot of content. However, because the international security situation has changed, the tasks of the soldier are also changed. In earlier times the Royal Army had to defend to Northern plains in Germany, now the NATO-tasks are not so clear anymore and the UN-tasks evolve quickly. These UN-tasks also bring more contents to a soldiers job.

The future soldier will be somebody who must be able to handle all kinds of combat actions, but he or she must also be prepared for a task of negotiation, mediation and reconciliation. He will have to fulfil more tasks, for which he needs training, but he will also remark that his profession has become much more complicated. All this demands lengthy contracts, both from the side of the volunteer as from the side of the armed forces as an employer.[4]

---

3 Maatschappelijke Raad voor de Krijgsmacht, Contractduur, advies 24, Den Haag, 1992, pp.2.

4 Variability in length of contract opens the possibility for matching. This is analyzed in paragraph 6.2.

Summarizing, we can state that lengthy contracts will lead to a larger supply of volunteers, if the jobs have enough content. Content can be created by expansion of tasks for which a soldier would be responsible.[5]

A job in the armed forces always has been associated with adventure. By lack of real action, there has been a lot of romance about this characteristic of the armed forces, because the adventure character had a positive effect on the supply of volunteers. But, because of changing tasks of the armed forces, this adventurous character has to be seen in another light.

A job in the armed forces is not that attractive, because the chance that a soldier is killed in action increases fundamentally when the tasks of the armed forces are changing, as they are nowadays. We therefore have to take a look at the downside of adventure too. What are the odds a soldier will get injured in action? In earlier times these were not very big , because the cold war threat was more important than the use of troops. Generally the soldier had the sense that the job was a dangerous job. But if the armed forces are considered closely, there is not much to worry about. Killed and wounded military are concentrated in a limited part of the armed forces: pilots and certain parts of the brigades. Moreover, Steven Canby[6] shows that deaths and injuries are mostly found under the newcomers in the armed forces. Professional soldiers most of the time escape bodily harm. Canby even states:

"Peacetime risk of life is now probably lower in the military than in civilian life. (....) An individual volunteering for a professional career in peacetime does not unduly increase his changes of dying, since (1) the peacetime incidence is no higher than the civilian average; (2) 87% are able to volunteer for the noncombat arms[7] and (3) his risk is mainly in being assigned a combat leadership position in wartime".

Because of the changing security situation in the world the tasks of the armed forces changed and so did the risks of life, because the possibility of sending troops is not just a theoretical one anymore. The risk of life within the armed forces will be evaluated subjectively by every individual soldier. Some people will have a high risk aversion and will not be prepared to fulfil dangerous missions. On the other hand less risk averse people will be attracted to the armed forces, being prepared to go further in excepting dangerous tasks.

Risk aversion is a subjective element and part of the preferences of potential volunteers. Because of degrees in risks, both in tasks of the armed forces and in preferences of the volunteers, the possibility of matching will be available here

---

5 In paragraph 6.4. further analysis will be made to assure that contracts are really served untill the end or that contracts are extended.

6 Steven L. Canby, Military Manpower Procurement, a Policy Analysis, Lexington 1977, pp. 65.

7 This shows again the possibilities for civilians in the armed forces.

too.[8] As the risk of action increases, the amount of adventure decreases and the supply of volunteers diminishes. The supply of volunteers also diminishes if the average rate of risk-aversion of individual military increases.

The secondary labour conditions have a positive effect on the supply of volunteers. For a potential volunteer the training and educational components of the secondary labour conditions are most important. When joining the armed forces a volunteer can fulfil some his social needs. In order to find a job after his service time it is necessary that he is prepared for a job in civil society. Education is necessary for this goal.

The armed forces can provide this need of human capital by educating the volunteer for a job in civil society. This is not only in the interest of the volunteer, but also in the interest of the armed forces. By introducing extended vocational training in the armed forces the volunteer receives future income in the form of human capital and the armed forces get trained soldiers, which they can use for specific tasks in the field of humanitarian aid.[9] During his service time a soldier is trained for a civilian function. The contract of the soldier has two stages. When serving six years, five years of military service are combined with a civilian training, and in the sixth year the study will be finished, including a period of internship of about six months. For the internship we can imagine a position in and out of the armed forces.

For this training schedule it is important that the civilian training is an integral part of the service time and is not done after the duty. If the training is not done within service time, the armed forces have to take the risk, that they will not have enough qualified volunteers, so they can not take part in humanitarian aid operations properly. Future income has a positive effect on the supply of volunteers, although the exact effect will be different for every volunteer.

Earlier in this chapter we have seen that bad labour circumstances have a negative effect on the willingness to apply for a job in the armed forces. The armed forces are burdened by the perception that labour circumstances in the armed forces are always dirty and heavy, to be done under most difficult and unusual circumstances, because that is a natural part of the job.

Partly they are right, and that is clearly understood by the employees in the armed forces. But it is entirely different thing if the measures of the armed forces in war times are also applied in peace time. In peace time other values and norms apply, although in peace time they have to be prepared for a war. In peace time the production of combat power prevails and not the war.

---

8 The risk of life does not only influence the willingness of potential volunteers to supply themselves to the armed forces. The relation is true the other way around too. The structure of the armed forces influences the risks that volunteers can meet. In paragraph 6.4.2. it will be explained that the risks in an all-volunteer force will be different than the risks in a conscription army.

9 With regard to this point also matching opportunities are possible, see paragraph 6.2.

In peace time the norms and values of civil society have to apply, whereby the employees are prepared for the labour circumstances of the war. Strictly using war circumstances in peace time scares a potential volunteer, and surely if these circumstances also appear in the barracks. In the barracks there is no reason at all to deviate from the circumstances that are normal in civil society. This means proper housing, normal working hours, normal labour relations, that are based on jobs and not on ranks, good food and normal social relations. Bad labour circumstances, that are a consequence of conscription should not be forgotten in this professional army.[10] In places where the armed forces lag far behind on these issues, immediate action is necessary, because bad labour circumstances hurt the armed forces enormously in acquiring the right personnel. In terms of the equation, the relation (A/BW) should equal at least one in the barracks, and should approach 1 as much a possible, no matter how difficult this last issue may be.

Just as in every labour market theory existing unemployment plays an important role in the supply of volunteers. Volunteers will lower their reservation wages to a certain level, if they can not get their desired jobs quickly. Moreover, the armed forces can be an alternative for lengthy unemployed, if the work will be combined with civil education programmes.

Larger unemployment, both in size and in length, will lead to a higher supply of volunteers. However, the exact size should not be overestimated. The armed forces should remain in competition with civil society, because if the promises of the armed forces do not meet the expectations of the volunteer, this volunteer will rethink their decision, even with expanded unemployment. An important aspect of this search process is of course the alternative benefit from searching.

Therefore not only the future income of a better job is important, but also the current income from social security benefits or labour. If a job in the armed forces does not offer enough in terms of material and immaterial benefits with regards to the current income, the search process will continue. The material benefits in the armed forces are sufficient most of the time, but the immaterial benefits are most of the time negative, so the reservation wage is not reached.

Unlike the commercial sector, the armed forces have the advantage, that they can hire people regardless of the economic situation. If in bad economic times the armed forces come with an appealing offer, the interest for a job will be quite high. Where else should the unemployed go?

Information is the last element that we will discuss here. In Phelps' island theory we have seen that the existence of imperfect information will lead to a search process. As more as the potential volunteer possesses perfect information, he will know on what island he can find the highest income. His search process will be shortened and his opportunity costs decline.

---

10 See chapter 5, paragraph 2.

From the island theory follows that the supply of volunteers in a certain sector increases if the supply of information increases. However, raising the flow of information is expensive. Therefore it is important that the given information is as complete as possible, with a minimum of cost as possible. Summarizing, we can state that the supply of volunteers will increase if the recruitment efforts increase, under the condition that these efforts are effective and efficient.

In this paragraph we have investigated the theory of labour supply. A lot of elements play a role in this process. Many elements, such as education, length of contract and risk-aversion can be combined, if we mirror these elements to the tasks of the armed forces. The wishes of the volunteer and the needs of the armed forces seem to be fitting each other in many occasions. They match. This matching opportunity can be the base for a contract between the volunteer and the armed forces.

If we consider the large picture, we see that next to the written contract also an unwritten contract appears between the volunteer and the armed forces. From this unwritten contract the real value of a job in the armed forces becomes clear. The armed forces have obliged itself to respect the volunteer as a person, to give the volunteer a useful job and the possibility for individual development. The volunteer has obliged himself in the unwritten contract to execute his job as well as possible in a disciplinary way. Bliven has the following to say about the two contracts:

"A reasonable bargain. My rough guess is that two-third of the new man at Ord are after remedial education or a skill that they can transfer at some later date to a civilian occupation. The idea that they are looking for 'permissiveness'- by that I mean toleration of their failures to meet established military standards- is completely wrong. It is the other way around: They want a vigorous, challenging program. The worst thing we could do is fail to give it to them".[11]

Matching can give the armed forces a suit to measure. This suit is the subject of the next paragraph.

§ 6.2. The Netherlands and the execution of UN-tasks: a real suit for the armed forces

The Dutch armed forces received a second main task after the end of the Cold War. The use of troops in UN-forces will be one of the most important tasks of the future Dutch armed forces. This use will probably take place in areas that are outside NATO-territory. This task requires troops that are highly prepared for this job. The feasibility of the Dutch soldier, the conscript, has declined, however. This is caused among other reasons by the shortening of service to one

---

11 Bruce Jr.Bliven, Volunteers, one and all, New York, 1962, pp.133.

year.[12] The period of one year is too short to train conscripts adequately for use in UN-tasks. The investments in the conscripts are too large to earn these investments back during the service time of the conscript. The shortening of service time is the result of a public choice process, that can not be turned back. Moreover, agreement has been made about the voluntarily will of the conscript to be sent to out of NATO-area operations. Without the voluntarily cooperation of conscripts UN-operations are not possible for the Dutch armed forces.

In this paragraph we will show how the Dutch armed forces should transform their organisation to become an effective and efficient organisation, that can both execute the tasks they are asked to do, and satisfy the wishes of the volunteers that have to fill the armed forces without conscription.

Arising from the international security situation and the public choice process, the armed forces have three kinds of main tasks:[13] 1. Defense of the 'borders of the state' in a NATO-environment and "UN-peace-enforcing" operations. These are operations that make use of violence. 2. "UN-peace-keeping-operations" and 3. international humanitarian aid. The two latter tasks are executed without the use of violence.[14] These tasks should have to be mirrored in the organisation of the armed forces. With the armed forces we generally intend the Royal Army, the Royal Navy and the Royal Air Force. In the remainder of this paragraph the armed forces will mostly be represented by the Royal Army. If parts of the paragraph are important for the Royal Navy and Royal Air Force, it shall be mentioned specifically.

Concerning the organisation of the armed forces, we take the view of an integrated organization. This means that the three main tasks will not be executed in separate units, but that every unit and every soldier has in principle three tasks. Tasks that follow from the main tasks of the armed forces.

The soldier in this organisation has to be a professional soldier, because only these volunteers can execute the three tasks adequately. Conscripts can not be sent to out-of-area operation against their will.

Strictly speaking the "UN-peace-keeping"-tasks and the humanitarian aid operations can be done by civilians, because these tasks do not have a character of violence. However, because we integrate the three operational tasks the use of civilians is not possible. Civilians can be used for non-integrated tasks.

The structure of the organisation follows in paragraph 6.2.1. The tasks of every unit are described in paragraph 6.2.2. Paragraph 6.2.3 concerns the training of the volunteers and paragraph 6.2.4. the recruitment. Conclusions are made in paragraph 6.2.5.

---

12 In 1996 it was even 9 months

13 MRK-advies nr. 25: Internationalisering van de krijgsmacht, Den Haag 1992, pp. 61.

14 For reasons of self-defence violence can also be tolerated here.

§ 6.2.1. The organisational structure

From figure 6.1. it follows that soldiers or units that are primarily situated in an army structure are matched to certain UN-tasks. These tasks can be humanitarian (technically or service orientated) or "peace-keeping". In the figure we see that medical troops should employ themselves with humanitarian aid, next to their NATO-tasks and the infantry is ear-marked to "peace-keeping" and technical humanitarian tasks. The mentioned examples are just indications, though should be treated as flexible.[15]

Tasks: Territorial defense (NATO-task, UN-peace-enforcing)	**Tasks:** UN-Peace-keeping and humanitarian aid
Army-structure	**UN-units**
- Food en logistics (B) - Medical (B) - Cavalry (A)	Humanitarian Aid A - technical B - services
- Artillery (A)	
- Engineers (A)	C Peace-keeping
- Armoured infantry[16] (A+C)	D Specialists-team
- Signal (A+C)	

Figure 6.1.: The organisational structure of the Royal Army

For specialist forces that are not available in the Army structure , recruitment can be done among the civilian population, according to the Nordic-system. This system will be explained in paragraph 6.2.4. Specialists enter the organisation as civilians and remain civilians, because they only have a task in the non-violence part of the organisation.

In figure 6.1. a clear distinction is made between on the one side "peace-enforcing", and on the other side "peace-keeping" and humanitarian aid. "Peace-keeping" and humanitarian aid are in continuation with each other and the two tasks can pass into each other easily without legal interference.

With "peace-keeping" and "peace-enforcing" the situation is different. Although it is theoretical possible that a peace-keeping operation turns into a peace-enforcing operation, in practice this is unlikely. "Peace-keeping"-units are separate units, most of the time occupied with specific tasks. If we want to enforce peace a combined action is necessary and the most effective structure to do this is that of an army structure. A "peace-keeping" unit in general does not

15 Therefore the left side of figure 6.1. can probably be extended.

16 Supplemented with the marine corps

possess the right combination of capital and labour to produce that combat power that is necessary for a peace-enforcing operation. In fact, peace-enforcing with a peace-keeping operation means self-destruction and is not effective. This also means, that every political pressure to take part in a peace-enforcing operation as a peace-keeping unit should be regarded as unacceptable.

§ 6.2.2. The tasks

The tasks on the left of figure 6.1. are well-known for many years. These NATO-tasks, which can easily be transformed into UN-peace-enforcing tasks, stay the same. We shall not discuss these tasks any further.

Tasks that belong to a "UN-peace-keeping" unit can in general be summarized under the following headings[17]:
(a) Monitor a cease-fire or an agreement to that effect
(b) To prevent an armed conflict between nations or within nations
(c) To contribute to the maintenance of the justice system and a return to normal conditions of a constitutional state.

Added to these tasks "peace-keeping-units" can also be used for tasks as the surveillance of refugees, protection of humanitarian aid operations, exchange of prisoners, etc.

The humanitarian units have to execute relief programmes. The programmes can involve tasks like the reactivating of functions within the government organization, the repair of devastated houses, medical treatment, food supplies, etc. Within the humanitarian units two lines can be discovered. One line which is mainly helping people and is called the service-line and the second line that is concerned with technical tasks. The technical team is an organization consisting of technical projectmanagers and assistants of different backgrounds, together with administrative personnel. The tasks of this team are repair and to a certain extent the rebuilding of devastated of damaged installations, public buildings, accommodations etc.

The work of the team includes:
(a) buildings
(b) electricity works
(c) road and water works
(d) telecommunication
(e) heating, ventilation and sanitation

Finally we have the specialist tasks. These tasks require people that have specific skills, that are not available in an army structure. The structure of an UN-unit often does not fit completely with the war structure of the Royal Army.

---

17 Source:Nordic Stand-by-Forces in United Nations service, NorBerFN, Stockholm, 1974, pp. 45.

The UN-basic organization will become more flexible, because of these extra specialists, and can be adapted to the circumstances that prevail. The specialists can make a unit "a measured UN-unit" without problems.

§ 6.2.3 Training

Every soldier has three tasks. To execute these tasks he or she needs training. For his or her NATO-task the training will not differ much from what it is now. For the UN-tasks additional training is necessary. In order to serve in UN-operational territory extra skills are necessary. In general, the following training goals can contribute:

(a) knowledge of the UN-operation and operating in a peace-force, and the conditions that involve taking part in an UN-operation

(b) knowledge of climatological circumstances and topographical conditions in areas, where UN-operations are executed and the questions that follow from these circumstances and conditions.

(c) an adequate capability of executing tasks -within the framework of the UN- that are assigned to an unit of an individual directly after arriving in UN-mission territory.

The training for UN-tasks have to provide the armed forces an ability to operate in an international context. This requires language education and attention for management skills in an international environment. The future soldier must acquire a mentality in his training period that is directed to negotiation, reconciliation and mediation.

A good preparation concerning the political, geographical, cultural, religious and language situation of the probable mission-country is highly desirable. The training should be adapted constantly to the results of the problem analysis per specific different situation.

For the humanitarian tasks a decent civil training is necessary. A training that should be given by the armed forces.[18] As we have seen in paragraph 6.1. when discussing the secondary labour conditions such a training provides a positive impulse to the attractiveness of the military profession.

The various needs and training shall be coordinated by a UN-institute, like the one existing in Sweden. It can also provide information for a proper training of UN-military. When thinking about such an institute we can look for connections with the United Nations university and its international network. We can also learn from the training programmes that are developed in the Nordic countries.

The specific UN-training for the specialists, in which the general goals and demands are explained, will take about four weeks. The specific knowledge they are hired for is brought from civil society.

---

18 In practice this means that the apprentice-system will be introduced in the army.

§ 6.2.4. Recruitment and matching

So far we have seen that military in the armed forces have to do different tasks. These tasks have different risk-profiles and these tasks also need different training sessions. The recruitment of personnel for these tasks should be adapted to this.

Every professional soldier in principle has three tasks and should get three kinds of training. For the humanitarian task it is necessary that the military get a decent civil education. This civil education should meet the needs of society as best possible, so the soldier will still enjoy this training when he has left the armed forces. By matching certain units to certain UN-units, there is a possibility to work selectively in the recruitment and there is the possibility to fulfil the wishes of the soldier regarding his civil training.

When recruiting, the different risk-aversions of people should also be taken into account. When thinking about being a volunteer it is very important to know the odds of getting in a life-threatening situation. The higher these odds, the less volunteers will apply.

The tasks of the organization also have a certain risk-character. By matching people with a low risk-aversion to tasks with a high risk, and by matching people with a high risk-aversion to tasks with a low risk a better allocation can be made between the needs of the armed forces and wishes of the military. Risk-differentation mostly involves the tasks on the right of figure 6.1., because there are relatively many peace-keeping and humanitarian aid operations with a different degree of danger. The total risk can differ from almost zero to a very reasonable amount of risk. The left of figure 6.1., "peace-enforcing", has a much higher risk in a single opportunity, but the chance of such an event is not that big, so that the general total risk is rather low.[19]

Practically this means that a volunteer chooses a job with a high or a low risk profile and he gets a civil training that is matched to the wishes of the soldier and the needs of the armed forces. The length of contract should be matched to the contents of the contract. In addition to this, pay should be differentiated to reflect higher salaries for jobs with higher risks and longer contracts.[20]

If the needs of the armed forces can not be matched easily with the wishes of the soldiers, than the armed forces should try to influence the volunteer with the help of scarcity-premiums. Differentation with regard to tasks, civil education and risk-aversion should be supported by differentiated payment.[21]

---

19 An example of such an event is the Gulf-war.

20 In paragraph 6.4. of this chapter we will take a further look at the joining of the salary to the length of the contract, the amount of risk, scarcity, etc.

21 In practice this means that the salary structure should be detached from the ranking system. As an example we can think about the salary of an infantry-soldier with a six-year contract. This salary can be higher than the salary of a lieutenant at the intendance, if it becomes clear that these lieutenants are much easier to get on the labour market, while soldiers for the infantry are much more difficult to get. See further paragraph 6.4.

In order to get the right people in the right spot without losing at lot of people, it is necessary that potential volunteers are adequately informed, so they can weigh the pros and cons of a job in the armed forces properly. They must be able to make a real judgment about the consequences of their own decision. Volunteers have a right to precise information about their legal position, payment and the circumstances they can confront. The size of the possible risk should always be clear to them. Only on the basis of complete information volunteers can agree to their contract. When after signing the contract a new fact appears, there should be room to dissolve the contract.

The recruitment of specialists is a problem with another dimension. This problem can be solved by using the system that is used in the Scandinavian countries and Finland. Within this Nordic-system, people are selected on the basis of voluntary participation and scrupulous screening. In the case of voluntary participation by a conscript in Sweden it is compulsory that the basic training of the conscript is finished. Agreements about the specialist team are made by contract and this contract is signed when the specialist is joining the team. The length of service is about a year and involves that volunteers follow a specific UN-training and are stand-by for the contract period. During the 'stand-by' period the specialist is not bound to his position, but he or she is obliged to be ready within a few days to serve in a UN-unit for about 6 months. The contract describes the terms of payment and the length of the contract in terms of availability and service-time. The financial compensation has to offer compensation for both the availability term as the UN-operation. Moreover, there should be no problem for the volunteer to go back to his old job when the service period is over. This should be supported by legal institutions. In order to fill the labour pool every time, recruitment efforts should be made among the civil population each year.

In this paragraph we used an all-volunteer force to set up our analysis. In an all-volunteer-force the Nordic-system is only necessary for the specialists, because the execution of the other tasks of the armed forces can be done by the voluntary soldiers without any problems. In a conscription army, it is necessary to recruit according to the Nordic-system for the tasks on the right of figure 6.1., because this system is the only system to arrange UN-operations without legal and organisational difficulties. The experiences of Sweden with its operations in Cyprus, Lebanon, Nigeria, etc., showed the success of this system. But this also means that two organisations will exist, because the right and left side of the organisation, like in figure 6.1. are not exchangeable. The costs of the armed forces will rise accordingly. The Nordic-system is effective, but can be improved in terms of efficiency. The efficiency of armed forces has to do with the choice between an all-volunteer force and a conscription army.

§ 6.2.5. Conclusions

In this paragraph we have shown how an adequate organisation of the armed forces in general and the Royal Army specifically should look like, if we want the armed forces to be effective and efficient, in regards to their tasks and the wishes of potential volunteers. From this paragraph we can see that:

(a) Only volunteers are suitable for the complete organisation. This does not mean that conscripts are not suitable in an army, but means that with conscripts an integrated organisational structure in the armed forces is not possible for both NATO and UN-tasks. In an all-volunteer force the double organisation is not necessary. Besides this, investments in conscripts to make them suitable for UN-tasks can not be recollected in the time that conscripts are obliged to serve in the armed forces.
(b) There is an integral organisation that executes on the one side traditional NATO-tasks and peace-enforcing and on the other side peace-keeping and humanitarian aid operations.
(c) Every soldier gets three kinds of training, whereby the civilian training, the humanitarian-UN-training and the personal wishes of the soldier are matched, whenever possible. The civil training should also prepare for the return to civil society.
(d) Recruitment of military should be adjusted to the wishes of the future soldier concerning education, risk-profile and length of contract. This can be achieved by matching units of the war organisation (left-side figure 6.1.) to UN-units (right side figure 6.1.). Differentiation in tasks and wishes should be connected with differentiation in wages.
(e) Effort should be put in founding a UN-institute, that coordinates the tasks, needs and training for UN-operations. Alignment with the existing international network in this field is emphasised.
(f) A labourpool of specialists for UN-tasks should be founded.

§ 6.3. The recruitment and selection process

The recruitment of personnel is one of the essential cornerstones in an all-volunteer force. During the times of a conscription army the recruiter has a passive job. Shortages of professional military can always be solved by taking extra conscripts. In an all-volunteer force the recruiter has an active task, because the supply of soldiers is not indefinite anymore.

In an all-volunteer force the supply of volunteers is originally zero and will rise only if recruitment activities are executed. The goal of the recruitment activities in the armed forces is to attract the appropriate amount of qualified volunteers, because the ultimate problem of an all-volunteer force is to attract the personnel to do the job. Attracting qualified volunteers is something else than attracting potential volunteers. The practical implication of this difference is that recruitment activities are not equal to attracting people, but that at the same time we have to take a look at the classification, selection and employment opportunities of volunteers.

In a broad sense it can be said that the recruitment system is responsible for (1) attracting volunteers who are looking for a job in the armed forces, (2) the classification of volunteers in their feasibility for military service, (3) the selection of volunteers, and (4) to decide when and where the selected volunteer can serve. We have said enough in paragraph 6.1 about attracting potential volunteers and the determination of the supply of volunteers. Point (4) is implicitly used in paragraph 6.2., because we used the 'matching-principle' as a starting point in our analysis. The job is assigned in mutual agreement, taken into account both the wishes of the volunteer and the armed forces. In this paragraph, elements (2) and (3) are central.

The quality of the volunteer is the most important element in the classification process. But the question: What is quality?, is difficult to answer, because there are no ready-made standards for quality. Quality is a relative standard.

When classifying volunteers in the Dutch armed forces a distinction is made according to school-records and mental en physical ability. The school-records are sorted on the basis of the type of school and the physical and mental ability are tested using principles from medical insurance activities and psychological tests. When tested not only the medical condition, according to the ABOHZIS-formula[22], is taken into account, but the test personnel also regards the risk volunteers oppose when they are exposed to severe activities.

With the help of all score results, a classification can be made. Such a classification system has advantages and disadvantages. The big advantage of a classification system is that it does what it is intended to do, which is that it allows for a selection to be made easily from all the volunteers that are potential candidates. Volunteers that pass a certain level in the classification record can be enlisted, the rest is turned down.

The reason to draw some kind of line for selection originates from three kinds of considerations. Volunteers that fall below the line are estimated to be less trainable for the military job, will have difficulties to execute their task in an appropriate way or will have problems with motivation and discipline. Whether this would be the case in practice remains unknown, because they are turned down beforehand. But we should not forget that in an all-volunteer force we have not filled all available positions beforehand, so we cannot put the demands too high. In a conscription army the situation is completely different and other selection criteria can be used.

---

22 The ABOHZIS-formula is a classification-system for the physical feasibility of the volunteer. Every letter represents a certain characteristic of the human body and gets value 1 till 5. A stands for Algemeen (general), B is upper limbs and longs, O is down limbs, H is hearing, Z is view, I is intelligence and S is stability.

In general we can see the process of stating quality standards like a statistic decision process, where the aim is to turn down those volunteers who are not suitable for the armed forces, but to keep in mind that the selection standards should not be expressed too high so suitable volunteers are eliminated by the classification system. Example: assume that an individual volunteer is suitable or unsuitable for military service. In addition, it is assumed that the selection standards are designed in such a way that every individual is accepted or turned down.

Figure 6.2. Statistical decision problem concerning the standard of selection

Acceptance	Accepted: x%	Refused: y%
Hypothesis		
Eligible	(1) Correct (1-Z_1%)	(2) Incorrect Z_2%
Non-eligible	(4) Incorrect Z_1%	(3) Correct (1-Z_2%)

From figure 6.2. we can see that there are four possible combinations in this simple decision problem: (1) the volunteer is suitable, and is accepted by the selection criteria, (2) the volunteer is suitable, but is rejected by the selection criteria, (3) the volunteer is not suitable and is rejected and (4) the volunteer is not suitable, but is accepted by the selection criteria. The second case, the rejection of a volunteer that is suitable, is named a fault of the first kind. The fourth case, the acceptance of a volunteer that is not suitable, is called a fault of the second kind. Because no single criterion can predict perfectly, we assume that a fault of the second kind happens Z_1% of the times a volunteer is suitable, and that a fault of the second kind happens Z_2% of the times, when a volunteer is not suitable. The relation between Z_1 and Z_2 is that if Z_2 declines, Z_1 rises in general, all else being equal.[23]

In order to make the correct selection strategy, we have to put the selection process into a cost perspective. Costs are attached to the making of wrong decisions and there are several administrative costs attached to the selection process. The costs that have to do with faults of the first kind, the rejection of a suitable volunteer, are the opportunity costs of rejecting a productive person in the armed forces. The costs of a fault of the second kind involve the costs made

23 This will say, the more strict the selection criteria are applied (less faults are allowed in the armed forces) the more suitable volunteers will be rejected. If the restriction of all else being equal is released, for example because there are better predictors, the figures for z1 and z2 are both going down. The development of better predictors is not with development and administration costs.

for recruitment, selection and training of an unsuitable person, because this man of woman will never fulfil its initial costs. The total costs attached to each selection process will be a function of (1) the costs of making an incorrect decision regarding the feasibility of a volunteer, (2) the possibility of making a wrong decision, and (3) the administrative costs of the selection process. If we assume that the costs of a fault of the first kind are C_1, the costs of a fault of the second kind C_2, the administrative costs A, and that b% of all volunteers are suitable, so (1-b%) is not suitable, the total cost of the selection process can be calculated as follows:

$$\text{Costs} = [b\%Z_1C_1]+[(1-b\%)Z_2C_2]+A. \qquad (6.3)$$

This costfunction helps us to explain, why the selection standards in a conscription army are so high, that only 73% is approved. The opportunity costs of a fault of the first kind are almost negligible, because for every individual that is declared unsuitable an alternative individual is available. In an all-volunteer force this alternative individual has to be recruited first, while at the same time the armed forces confront a loss of production, because not all positions are filled. The added value of the volunteer is missing, which does not occur in a conscription army, because the open positions are filled immediately.

In a conscription army the costs that are attached to a fault of the second kind are certainly not negligible. Training, equipment etc. cost a lot of money. Conscription supports the armed forces in developing selection standards that can be administrated easily (to minimize the costs) and that minimize the consequences of an expensive fault of the second kind. The transformation of a conscription army into an all-volunteer force now makes a fault of the first kind very expensive, because the rejection of a suitable volunteer implies a reduction of supply that is already scarce.

The abolition of conscription generally means lowering , and not lifting the selection standards in the armed forces. Conscription gave the armed forces an unlimited supply of excellent labour. In an all-volunteer force they are only allowed to make these demands if the supply of volunteers exceeds the needs of the armed forces.

When lowering the demands of the selection standards it is important to keep in mind, that this is not done in order to lower the quality of the volunteers, but to recognize that "standard quality" norms are not perfect predictors. The lowering of selection standards must go on until the level is reached where the marginal costs of a fault of the first kind are equal to the marginal costs of the second kind: $dC_1 = dC_2$, whereby C_1 is equal to the loss of production, the costs of extra recruitment and the extra selection costs. C_2 is equal to the equipment costs, training costs and the extra costs that are needed for the improvement of selection.

In the United States of America Chu and Norrblom[24] have investigated in 1974 the relation between costs of faults of the first kind, costs of faults of the second kind and the lowering of selection standards. They estimate that the costs related to faults of the second kind, like lost training costs, are about $ 5 to $ 7 million a year, when the selection standards are lowered in such a way that the amount of qualified volunteers rises with 5%. On the flip side is the calculation of the extra wages needed to raise the amount of qualified volunteers by 5% without changing the selection standards. These wages have to rise with $ 300 million each year. In other words, Chu and Norrblom conclude that the lowering of the selection standards, in order to get 5% extra volunteers, the term $[(1\text{-}b\%)Z_2C_2]$ in equation 6.3. raises with $5 to $ 7 million each year, but the term $[b\%Z_1C_1]$ declines with $ 300 million each year.

Both from an occupancy perspective as from a costs perspective it is expected that the transformation of a conscription force into an all-volunteer force will be accompanied with a lowering of selection standards. But this is not reality. Of all conscripts 73% is approved, but real volunteers are only approved one in eight times. Most of them being rejected on mental grounds.[25]

In the next subparagraphs we will see that is not necessary to maintain high selection standards to get highly qualified personnel. In paragraph 6.3.1. we will describe two projects from the United States. The first project, Project 100,000, has been part of the "war on poverty" of President Johnson and was meant to see if volunteers that were rejected on mental grounds, could perform adequately in the armed forces, if the armed forces would just give them a chance. The second project was a unconscious project, but became very interesting when it was clear that in the years 1976-1980 the classification systems did not function as intended and about 300.000 volunteers entered the armed forces with inflated test-scorcs.

In paragraph 6.3.2. a separate group of volunteers is investigated, where the armed forces uses different standards: the woman in the armed forces.

§ 6.3.1. The "Project 100,000" and the "ASVAB-misnorming"[26]

The US armed forces were the first institution in American society to start with test programmes on a large scale. The first tests were developed by psychologists during the First World War, although these test were only used much later. In 1941 the "Army General Classification Test" (AGCT) was

24 David S.C. Chu and Eva Norrblom, Psysical Standards in an All-Volunteer Force, The Rand Corporation, April 1974.

25 Rapport Commissie Dienstplicht, blz. 24. The one to eight figure only applies to the Royal Army. Other parts of the armed forces have higher figures.

26 This paragraph is based on the work of Thomas G. Sticht, Military Testing and Public Policy: selected Studies of Lower Aptitude Personnel, in: Bernard R.Gifford and Linda C. Wing, Test Policy in Defense, Boston 1992.

introduced. This test was meant "as a test of general ability and was intended to be used in basically the same manner as the Army Alpha".[27]

With the help of the AGCT and a few subtests every person achieved a total score and was classified. Smart students got category I, the above average group category II, average students category III, below average category IV and slow students category V.

After the Second World War military standards were lifted and people in category V were not considered anymore for military service. This exclusion was legally enforced. It concerned about 10 percent of all people.

In the middle of the 1960s, de AGCT was replaced by the "Army Forces Qualification Test" (AFQT) then, an additional difference was made between people who had a high school degree and persons that did not possess that certificate. Owners of a high school degree that scored higher than the 31st percentile in the AFQT were qualified without exception. If an individual was between the 21st and 30th percentile, category IV, then he was qualified if he had graduated from high school and scored above average on certain tests. Individuals without a high school degree were only accepted if they came above the 31th percentile, this is category I, II and III. This strict division into categories caused a lot of discussion in the United States, and not just because the levels were made legally binding. It often happened that commanders were basing their opinion about certain personnel only on the knowledge of the mental category they belonged to.

The Project 100,000 did not escape from this discussion. Project 100,000 was according to the initiators meant to improve the position of socially underprivileged youngsters. They believed that the armed forces were ideally equipped to improve the situation of these people, because the armed forces had a clear structure and the ability and experience to deal with a cultural and economically diverse population.

Project 100,000 was part of the "War on Poverty" of the mid-sixties. For the then minister of Defense of the United States, Robert McNamara, Project 100,000 was an efficient and effective way for the armed forces to deal with two national goals: social welfare and national security. The aim of Project 100,000 was to hire 100,000 volunteers each year, that would not be selected in a normal selection procedure. It would involve reconsideration of about 22,3% of the volunteers in category IV, the lowest suitable category. The costs of this Project were thought to be earned back in society by a higher degree of education, working skills and an enlarged self-confidence with hundred of thousands youngsters, who are considered now for military service because of Project 100,000.

McNamara saw Project 100,000 as a controlled experiment of the effect of the underprivileged youngsters on the armed forces and vice versa. Some members of the military establishment and members of parliament were of

---

27 Sticht, pp. 15. The "Army alpha" was the old test.

different opinion and argued that the hiring of less suitable volunteers would weaken the armed forces, as expressed in the words of Evans:

"The results were neither satisfactory nor equitable. The "New Standards" men flunked out of basic training at twice the usual rate, were court marshaled and dismissed with premature discharges twice as often. Among cynics in the Pentagon, the programme was soon dubbed McNamara's Moron Corps".[28]

Others had different complaints, like the story of Baskir and Strauss:

"In the opinion of many military leaders, social planners and liberal critics, Project 100,000 proved a failure. While it expanded the wartime manpower pool, it also required additional resources which there services could ill afford. But above all, it was a failure for the recruits themselves. They never got the training that military service seemed to promise. They were the last to be promoted and to first to be sent to Vietnam. They saw more than their share of combat and got more than their share of bad discharges. Many ended up with greater difficulties in civilian society than when they started. For them, it was an ironic and tragic conclusion to a program that promised special treatment and a brighter future, and denied both."[29]

Baskir and Strauss' conclusions are very much contrasted with the conclusion of the "Presidents Committee on an all-volunteer", that stated that:

"one cannot help but conclude that the Project 100,000 experiment has been a success and should be continued".[30]

To reveal the real truth Sticht collected a large amount of data that included two groups: a group with people from Project 100,000 and a similar 'control group' with non-Project 100,000 people. Sticht mapped out both groups and worked out the statistics in order to see if the goals of Project 100,000 were really reached, progress was made by the volunteers on different fields, and to see if the volunteers of Project 100,000 were really inferior like the critics said.

The basic training program was completed by 94% of the Project 100,000 volunteers. In the control group of more suitable volunteers this percentage was 98%. The figures about acquiring working skills showed also that the Project 100,000 volunteers were not far behind. More than 90% of the volunteers were not forced to do some program twice and more than 85% satisfied the condition of concentrated learning and testing and finished the training in one time. In the whole armed forces 86% of the volunteers of Project 100,000 finished their entire service time. For the control group this was 92%.

---

28 Evans, The Army and the Underclass: losing Battle, in Sticht, pp. 21.

29 Baskir and Strauss, Chance and Circumstance: the draft, the war and the Vietnam generation, New York 1978, pp 131, in Sticht pp.20.

30 Sticht, pp.21.

The volunteers that did not finish their term, less than half had to go because of bad behavior or unfitness. The majority dropped out because of already existing medical problems, died in Vietnam or other reasons.

In the Army 95% of the volunteers of Project 100,000 were seen as "highly efficient", so that one can say that no problems appeared here too. An important factor of critics in the Project 100,000 was that the underprivileged youngsters would cause disciplinary problems:

"Project 100,000 men were court-martialed and dismissed with premature discharged twice as often as non-Project 100,000 men."[31]

Literally, this was true, but what the critics forgot to say, was that the total percentage was 3,2, compared with 1,6% for the control group. More than 95% never saw the court-martial. Disciplinary charges were not really different for the two groups, so we can say that the supposed disciplinary problems were not confirmed by the figures.

In conclusion we can say that the Project 100,000 showed us that volunteers from category IV performed relatively well, both in training and at work. The results show that the differences between both groups are minor, in every case less than 5 to 10 percentage points. Lowering selection limits may cause additional training costs in terms of faults of the second kind, these costs are earned back doubly from a social point of view.

In Project 100,000 the selection limits were lowered because of a political decision. In the "ASVAB-misnorming" a technical error led to an non-intended and not recognized lowering of the selection limits. The technical error consisted because certain tables that were used to transform Armed Services Vocational Aptitude Battery (ASVAB) into percentile scores were not scaled adequately.

The ASVAB was introduced in 1976 and it took until 1980 before it was discovered that technical errors were made. In 1979 the Ministry of Defense in the United States thought that 5% of the volunteers in the armed forces consisted of volunteers in the category IV, but actually was 30%. When they discovered that hundred thousands less suitable volunteers had found their place in the armed forces, studies were set up to discover how the performances of these volunteers differed from volunteers that would be suitable under all test conditions. The technical error in the "ASVAB" lead to a neutral "experiment". In this experiment the military leaders were not aware of the fact that there were hundreds thousands category IV volunteers, who were actually "potentially ineligible (PI)".

Because the armed forces were not aware of the error, almost no commentary is heard about the quality of the troops in this period, contrary to the situation in the Second World War and in Project 100,000. Interviews with battalion commanders showed that almost nobody complained about the suitability of the

31 Ibid.

troops. In a recorded interview in 1979 in West-Germany Sticht asked a commander if the new soldiers could handle the complex armory.[32] The commander answered:

"You can talk to any of my commanders and any of my non-committeeed officers. I believe that 99 percent of them will tell you-I know they will- because they tell me the same thing; just what I'm going to tell you. That is baloney. We consider our soldiers to be outstanding. Our non-committeeed officers are outstanding. We've got outstanding officers. They're the best that I've ever seen. [When asked, What about the new guys?] I'm talking about the new guys, privates coming in. I have sergeants tell me every day, 'Boy these new privates that are coming in are great. We're really getting some good soldiers in.' Why do they say that; because that is the way we think about our soldiers. We choose to believe that our soldiers are damn good, from the day they walk in and to the extent that they aren't, that's our responsibility. We have the capability and space to see to it that they are helped".

The studies that appeared after the technical error in the ASVAB was discovered showed that the words of the commander were true for the greater part of the armed forces. The PIs were achieving only a little bit less than the eligible volunteers. The differences were not very big, like in Project 100,000, while in some cases the PIs even scored better. In the army the differences between PIs and personnel from the highest categories I and II were only small, in the navy and the air force the differences were more distinct. These differences are explained by the greater attention to pen-and-paper tests and study in the navy and the air force than in the army. Nevertheless, the drop out figures remained constant during many years. From the ASVAB-studies we can conclude that the feasibility of volunteers has much more to do with how people perform in their job, than with pen-and-paper tests. Volunteers from category IV perform less if the achievement is measured with paper test, although their actual performance is much higher, what is expressed in the appreciation of the work by their superiors. In 1987 this was again confirmed by the Ministry of Defense:[33]

"Upon looking at their performance, we learned that a surprisingly large number of them became successful members of the military. If the enlistment standards were working properly, those young people should have been marginal performers at best. As it turned out, not only did they not have marginal performance, many of them performed considerable above that level. They completed training; their attrition rates weren't unusually high; they were promoted at rates only slightly lower than their scoring peers; and they reenlisted. So, the question was not that training grades were somehow flawed, but that a quarter-of-a-million people who did not meet the enlistment standards and should not have been able to do the job did in fact do pretty well".

These results did not lead to a permanent hiring of many category IV volunteers. The discovery of the false scales in the ASVAB lead to the situation that the

---

32 Sticht, pp. 62.
33 Sticht, pp. 64.

amount of volunteers from category IV declined from 30 percent in 1980 to 4 percent 1986, although there actually was no real reason for this.

The Project 100,000 and ASVAB-misnorming studies show us that the actual qualification standards in the United States exclude volunteers that are at least 8 out of 10 times successful in every respect. Despite the fact that classification systems give objective measures the choice of a selection limit is a subjective, psychological and arbitrary case. The commanders want the best soldiers, because the performance of his sub-ordinates form the basis of their judgment. The lower the alleged suitability of his soldiers, the less prosperous the future is seen by the commander, although their may be no reason at all to think this way. Complaints of the commanders about the feasibility of his soldiers are most of the time a psychological matter, caused by thinking of his personnel in classification categories. When the commander is not aware about the suitability of his personnel or if they are misclassified, commentary disappear as snow in the sun. The same was true in the Second World war. A report of the Ministry of the Army of the United States in the Second World war shows that:[34]

"During World War II, commanders complained that they were getting too many men in the lowest mental category. The Department of the Army then arbitrarily decreed that the top half of that category would henceforth be classified in the next higher category. Commanders practically ceased their complaints, although they were getting the same number of low quality men as before-but now only half as many were designated as being in the lowest mental category."

The lesson that can be drawn from this paragraph is that the use of classification systems and maintaining selection limits has great social concern. Not only does high selection limits cost more money in terms of additional salaries and recruitment costs, much more important is to see the social effects of these demands. The refusal of "potential ineligible" volunteers does not only have consequences for the volunteer himself, but also for the family and the background from whence the volunteer comes. For the volunteer there is the loss of labour experience, education and self-confidence. For the families the additional income is also welcome, but even more important are the intergenerational profits by the experiences of the volunteer. His environment will have some benefits too, if the volunteer will serve as an example for the rest.

In the Netherlands of every eight volunteers, seven are turned down. This cannot be beneficiary to society. Social interests should be central in every public decision and not only the interests of the armed forces or the individual commander.

In an all-volunteer force the enlistment of conscripts is put out of order, the conscription law still exists. Only in emergency cases enlistment will be used and in such a case the armed forces will also use the potential ineligible volunteers. This creates a situation where these boys can do the dirty work in an emergence

---

34 Sticht, pp. 44.

case, but can not benefit in peace time, when casualty risks are low, from all the advantages of military service and maybe of his life dream.

All this pleads for as low as possible selection limits and a change of the standards that are used in the Dutch armed forces. Putting low selection limits has almost no effect on the quality of the armed forces, saves the tax payer a lot of money, and give youngsters a real chance and a social awareness in the armed forces.

§ 6.3.2. The woman in the armed forces

Conscription only exists for men. In the professional military only a few women are apparent. If conscription disappears, labour becomes scarce, and women become much more interesting for the armed forces. That only a few women are apparent in the armed forces has to do, among other reasons, with the physical demands that belong to the physical heavy functions in the armed forces. Because on average women are less strong then men, often the argument is heard that a large amount of women affects the effectiveness of the armed forces.

In this paragraph we will take a closer look at the position of women in the armed forces, in which two main lines will be discussed. The first line concerns the effectiveness of the woman in the armed forces, the second line concerns the efficiency of the women relative to the man as an employee in the armed forces. In this last analysis we consider a woman as being as effective and take a look at the additional costs and benefits that the presence of women in the armed forces will bring.

"Since 1982 in the Dutch armed forces there are no specific professional- or short-term functions for men or women. With this recognition of the right of women to fulfil every function in the armed forces the problems to really serve in the armed forces on an equal basis with men are off course not solved yet".

In this way the Social Council for the Armed Forces (Maatschappelijke Raad voor de Krijgsmacht; MRK) exposes the problem of women in the armed forces. The advise of the MRK[35] follows from a request of the ministers of the Ministry of Defense to advise about the way women can function in de armed forces. From this request for advise it becomes clear that the ministers were mainly pointing on the effectiveness of women, because, as we saw earlier, only a few women can satisfy the conditions that are necessary for the physical demanding positions. According to the request, under-minister Hoekzema accounts most of the combat positions to these physical demanding position.

From the description of advise it also follows that it should handle about an absolute qualitative problem here. But this is not true. The average woman is

35 Maatschappelijke Raad voor de Krijgsmacht, advise nr 7: "De vrouw in de krijgsmacht", Den Haag 1984.

weaker than the average man, but in practice no statistical averages count, but we have to deal with individual people, who differ in lots of respects from each other. There are, after all also weak men and strong women. If we really want to discuss the effectiveness of women in the armed forces, we should not specifically talk about women, but about the effectiveness of all weak people. An absolute qualitative problem becomes a relative qualitative then. It is not the difference between men and women that is eminent here, but between relative physical weak and relative physical strong people. Where we put the selection limits then is a political question. Not a political question between men and women, but the same political question that we have seen in last paragraph: "Where do we put the limits in our classification system?". From the MRK-report we can also learn, that:

"In civil society only for a few kind of jobs special body strength is demanded. By the existence of many technical resources the distinction between professions for men and women can only be declared on historical and cultural grounds. Besides, one of the most heavy professions is the job of housewife, a profession that needs a lot of heavy lifting every day. It is a dangerous and responsible job too, if we consider how many accidents happen in house."[36]

Once again this shows that the presence of women in certain professions does not depend on the physical conditions for the job, but is more culturally founded. Or stated otherwise: because in most professions only men work, the stronger physical condition of men has prevented a situation where the physically heavy jobs are made lighter, so that the entry barriers for women are extra high.

In the armed forces this applies even stronger. The armed forces have a lot of functions. Functions which we can divide in combat and non-combat functions, but also in physical heavy and physical less heavy functions. Next to that the armed forces also have conscription. Because of conscription a lot of work is done by manpower that would in normal conditions have been done by machines.

The allocation-effects by conscription not only influence the work that has to be done by conscripts, but also by professional military and civilians. The incentive to improve labour conditions and to lessen the damaging physical burden for the physical less strong is not apparent because of conscription. Therefore ergonomic measures to adapt the working conditions to the physical conditions where not executed and for a woman now, it is very difficult to keep her position in the armed forces from a physical aspect.

In chapter 5 we have seen that in a voluntary army the real costs of the production factor become clear. Volunteers are scarce and expensive, so there is necessity to substitute military for civilians, military for capital goods and inexperienced military for more experienced military. In the military-civilian substitution the distinction between combat functions and non-combat functions

36 See MRK-advise nr 7, pp 18 and 19.

becomes clear. In chapter 5 we have seen that the relation combat functions/non-combat functions in a voluntary army is about 1:1. This means that 50% of all functions are without question suitable for women.

If we take a closer look at the combat functions, it appears that after the appropriate military-capital-substitution only a few functions remain with a clear physical effort. Because of highly valued technology in the ships in the Navy, the planes in the Air Force[37], and the vehicles in the Army, often there is nothing more needed than a push on a bottom or the use of steering wheel. The needed physical effort to achieve is most of the time already reduced by the arms race of the Cold war.

Only the pure physical functions like the functions in the infantry are functions where the average woman will not be able to perform as well as an average man. In all other functions ergonomic investments can probably equal the performance of a woman to the performance of a man. However, this does not mean that women should be excluded from functions in the infantry. The situation that the average man can achieve more than the average women means that the relation men-women in physical heavy functions like the infantry will always bring a larger amount of man then women in these units.

Actual openness of physical heavy functions for women can bring an extra incentive to look for better labour circumstances for men too, that can lessen the burden of their physical heavy job. This search has never taken place really because of the availability of conscription, and thus the absence of real scarcity incentives.

The omission of the necessary ergonomic investments can be compared with a fault of the first kind, like we have seen in paragraph 6.3. The armed forces should decide between the costs of ergonomic investments and the costs of higher salaries. A further analysis should show where the marginal costs of both decisions equal each other. The raising of salaries is very expensive, because a pay raise of the lowest paid in the armed forces also effects the salaries in the rest of the wage building of the organisation, while ergonomic investment does not have these side effects. The cost relation between faults of the first and faults of the second kind, as shown by Chu and Norrblom in paragraph 6.3., can be used as an example here too, so there is almost no doubt that ergonomic investments are cheaper than raising salaries to attract new volunteers.

Despite all labour saving and ergonomic investments there will be a difference between heavy and less heavy functions in practice. When making function demands the Dutch armed forces distinct three function groups 1, 2 and 3. From this distinction a bigger nuanciation and differentiation in function demands automatically follows. However, this distinction does not work in practice, because differentiation is not made per function, but per unit. In these

---

37 An exception is the F-16 fighter. Practice shows that even the best trained women can not resist the pressures that become apparent during fighting missions. It is almost superfluous to mention that most men do not meet the standards either the resist these powers

unit all functions are declared more or less the same. For the relative easy job as a radarcontroller in the artillery functiongroup 2 (average heavy work) is asked, while the heavy job of wounded-carrier in the medical troops has functiongroup 3 (light work).[38] For a lot of women this practical function group distinction means that they can not function at all in some units, while there is no reason at all to restrict these units to men only on physical grounds.

This examples shows that exclusion mainly has an cultural basis and not physical one. For the Netherlands this is even more astonishing, because after the Second World War, when there were still women units, women were working in the armed forces satisfactorily in functions they are no longer allowed in now. Another disadvantage of restricting the physical demands per unit appears at the training of female military. Women succeeding the test and selection process, drop out more than men on average, because they do not fulfil the physical conditions of the training. In a voluntary army this can not be carried on anymore. The function demands should be put per function, not per unit.

The suitability for military service should be determined by testing and selection, and as less as possible during the training. The selection and training should be pointed at the function in the unit and in principle not on the whole unit. During the testing, selection and training period care should be taken by demanding things that are not present in the future task or will only be present in extraordinary circumstances. The lifting of the physical condition of women should not be forced and should take account of situations where injuries can prevail. Specific weaknesses should be taken into account and a good structure of the training programme is necessary, because it can not be desired that every one can do everything at once.

In conclusion we can say that it is not expected that the effectiveness of the armed forces is damaged by the on average weaker physical condition of a woman. Actually we should not speak about women here, but about the qualities of the physically weaker human beings.

Other than the resistance that is based on the effectiveness of the armed forces, the role of women is also discussed in matters that have to do with the relation between men and women, the always present field of tension between the sexes. The influence of differences in physical, psychological and biological respect between men and women are so large according to a few persons, that this will have a negative effect on the activities of the armed forces.[39] The question however is if this negative influence on the performance of the armed forces is really there and how these inefficiencies can be minimized. The efficiency of a female military relative to a male military can actually be seen in terms of costs of military in the same function. Female military have more hygiene demands then male. This has a biological origin, which should be supported by the armed forces. Buildings and clothes should be changed to meet

---

38 See MRK-advise nr. 7, pp. 52.

39 See MRK-advise nr. 7, pp. 33

the needs of female military. Women can get pregnant and have to deal with menstruation cycles. Because of this biological difference it can be expected that women are more absent than men. This absence could hurt the readiness of the armed forces. However, from the figures of the Navy in the United States it becomes clear (Table 6.1.) that the absence of men is twice as high as the absence of women.

Table 6.1 Absense

Reason of absence	**Average loss of days Women**	**Average loss of days Men**
Alcohol	0,09	0,12
Drugs	0,02	0,12
Nonallowed disapearance	0,05	0,24
Desertion	0,07	0,62
Abortion	0,03	-----
Pregnancy	0,37	-----
Total	0,63	1,10

Women have a better discipline and are often much brighter when it concerns tensions at work. Women are often more capable then men to fulfil the whole contract, which translates into a saving in recruitment and training costs. The mentioned examples show that most of the time it does not concern a raise of costs, but a change of costs when more women are present in the armed forces.

The relevant question is then, how much the armed forces will earn or spend when women are substituted for men. If more women come in the armed forces, the figures for women can deteriorate again, and the possible differences in cost can disappear. On the other hand women will take the position of the less able man, which means a cost reduction. As long as the marginal costs of an extra woman are less then the marginal costs of a man she replaces, substitution will save money, even if the average costs of women increase.

The most important financial consequence of an increase of the amount of women is the increase of the labour supply base. In this way the need for military personnel can be fulfiled without raising salaries. The success of voluntary army will among other reasons be measured by the way the armed forces are able to integrate female military in the organisation. This means that a clear integration process should be executed. This integration process can only succeed if the existing organisation is well prepared and managed in the process of functioning on a equal basis.

In an integration process of women in the armed forces the same facts appear as in the integration process of all discriminated groups in society. Other groups feel threatened in their position and take every argument to resist against this development. This is an important source of problems in the integration of women in the armed forces. Women run the chance becoming lonely in the men's world of the armed forces.

Up until now we have seen the woman as an individual, but we should not forget that a woman should function in a group. It is necessary to take a look at group behaviour. Binkin and Bach distinct two contrasting schools when discussing group behaviour in the armed forces.[40] One school implies that the integration of women in combat units or on ships can cause a lot of significant problems. The other school sees less problems.

The first school subscribes to the hypothesis that men concentrate in social groups, which exclude women. This would especially be true in institutions that deal with control of things that would conflict with the social order, like the armed forces, police and politics. The hypothesis says that cases that concern organized aggression "not only will males and females reject other females as potential leaders and defenders, but that males will reject females as colleagues". If this would have been true, then the presence of women would influence the effectiveness of a unit. This would often happen in units that have a macho-image. These units attract volunteers, because this unit has this image. By introducing women in such a unit the type of volunteer will change and therefore the group cohesion will lessen and with it combat power. The introduction of women on ships in the Navy has lead to discussion that is more or less similar to the hypothesis stated here. Research by both the MRK[41] and Binkin and Bach[42] shows that in practice there is no loss of combat power.

"The council (MRK) thinks that the negative influence of alcohol abuse on combat power is much easier to prove and much more severe than the influence of the relation between man and women and everything that goes along with that. Nevertheless there are much fewer voices to stop alcohol consumption in the Navy, than voices who say that women should be left ashore"

The second school puts less emphasis on the influence of social groups. Experiences from the Vietnam- and Korea-war have made the way free for a path that leaves group thinking and goes in the direction of a more individual approach.[43] According to this approach, that is based on quick relief in combat units during the wars in Vietnam and Korea, it is the personal self-interest of a soldier that is much more important than the obligations of this soldier to society:

"The ultimate standard of combat behavior rests on each individual's fight for survival".[44]

---

40 Binkin and Bach, pp. 89 and further

41 MRK-advise nr. 7, pp. 35

42 Binkin and Bach, pp 93-95.

43 See for example Charles C.Moskos, jr., The American Enlisted Man, pp. 143-146.

44 Ibid., pp. 145

The school states that the male ethic that is connected with a combat function is exaggerated. "Maleness" and "physical hardness" may get volunteers into combat functions, their interest decline drastically when volunteers are confronted with things of life and death. This interpretation is supported by experiences, as described by the MRK. It is also supported by experiences of the emancipation committee of the council police from The Hague. From the report "Vrouw in de ME" it follows that when it really gets tough, women act much more intelligently than men. In the armed forces situations as in the police do not happen often, but the experiences in the United States could support the statement that group behaviour is a less important factor when production is really taking place.

In general we can say that the theory of group behavior can not be supported. But what is the case when the amount of women in a group is very small, because only a few women are interested in a function in that group. Binkin and Bach say about this:[45]

"Research suggests that as long as women are in the minority, men will continue to view them according to preconceived stereotypes and to fulfil their own need to project the male image. This would tend to isolate women, keep the male group in conflict with them, and thus reduce overall group productivity.
Also meriting attention are the possible effects of social alliances and sexual pairings on unit performance. Integration studies found generally that, while the ideal mix was not surprisingly half and half, social problems were less likely to develop when the ratio of men to women was lower than three to one. Above that threshold, according to the researchers, some women tended to assume a 'superwoman' role and to make more friends than they would normally would, while the men tended to socially reject them as inferior".

The MRK considers the small amount of women in a group also as a problem. She proposes quota-measures to solve this problem: detachment of relative large groups of women in certain parts of the armed forces.[46] This prevents also problems like loneliness and insufficient attention of male cadre.

In the Netherlands all functions in the armed forces are open for women. The practical filling in of this problem stays out, however. During many years already the Dutch armed forces do not meet the demand of about 8% women in their personnel. This is largely caused by the fact that women should adapt one-sided to the armed forces, where through they are scared off and there are not enough women left to make an attractive environment for women either. Because the armed forces do not adapt enough to women, women are restricted from the possibility to profit from the good things of the armed forces, like working experience and training on several topics. The role of women in the armed forces will on a large scale depend on the way national institutions are prepared to support the integration of women in the armed forces.

45 Binkin and Bach, pp. 92.
46 MRK-advise nr 7, pp. 66

The politicians and the armed forces seemed to have shown their desire to integrate women by opening all functions to women as early as 1982. However, the policy of conscription remained. Because of conscription the integration of women in the armed forces became a failure; the armed forces had no incentive at all to adapt to the needs of women, who in general have a weaker physique.

Integration of women in the armed forces is among other reasons an ergonomic problem, which becomes evident, if the incentives for these ergonomic investment actually appear. The introduction of an all-volunteer force brings these incentives and will hopefully result in the true integration process. The percentage women in the United States and United Kingdom, countries with a professional army, allows for optimism. The United States armed forces employed 9% women in 1984 and United Kingdom about 6%, while the Netherlands had only a mere 2% in 1984.[47] On the first of march 1991 this percentage has risen to 5.2% of the total amount of professional military, or about 2.8% of the total amount of troops. This percentage has stabilized and certainly does not meet the stated norm of about 8%.

In an all-volunteer force people are scarce, and deserve every possible attention. This implies women especially. Fifty percent of our population are women and a proper integration of women in the armed forces enlarges the labour supply and will lead to a saving on salaries for the whole organisation. The woman in the armed forces is not only a men's problem, like the MRK states. It is particularly a problem that has to do with conscription.

§ 6.4. The demand for professional military

In the Meijer-report the demand for volunteers played a subordinate role. The labour market investigation the committee made used the assumption, that one conscript had to be replaced by one volunteer. The research team that made the labour market investigation, came to the conclusion that:

> "Enlargement of the interested supply and a better way of reaching the supply can mean that the need for volunteers can be narrowly accomplished, but for the conversion of a conscription army into an all-volunteer force it is necessary that the armed forces shed a light on its needs and procedures".[48]

In this chapter we have taken a look already at the supply of volunteers. The selection procedures have also been investigated and now it is time to discuss the need or demand of volunteers. The demand for volunteers or professional soldiers as we will call them further on in this paragraph, is extremely important in an all-volunteer force. Because labour is really scarce now, it is more urgent to

---

47 Ibid, pp. 101

48 Meijer-committee, Naar dienstplicht nieuwe stijl, Arbeidsmarktonderzoek, Den Haag, 1992, pp.49

see how many soldiers are really essential. We can also see, which hidden costs conscription brings next the costs we have already seen in preceding chapters.

As we have seen in chapter 5 the demand for new personnel in the long term is a decreasing function of the costs of labour. If new soldiers are relatively expensive with regard to other "input factors" in the armed forces, less new soldiers and more other input factors will be asked. In figure 6.3. the demand for new soldiers is reflected in the curve DD. In the short run the need for soldiers is relatively constant, because for a given armed forces structure it takes some time, before the mix of production factors is changed. In figure 6.3. the curve RR reflects this. The supply of volunteers is reflected in the curve SS'. Figure 6.3. shows that the feasibility of an all-volunteer force both depends on supply and demand.

The goal of this paragraph is to show, how the demand for military can be minimized. In terms of figure 6.3. this means that the DD- or RR-curve has to move as far possible to the left (R*R*), or an upside shift along the DD-curve should appear. This last shift has been analyzed thoroughly in chapter 5. By abolishing conscription the costs of soldier's increase. This cost increase sets off a substitution process, in which military are substituted for civilians and capital. During the transformation process of a conscription force into an all-volunteer force these substitutions are most important. However, after this substitution process the restriction of the need of new personnel remains a task of the highest order. Every year military leave the armed forces, because they die in combat action, retire, their contract expires or because they quit.

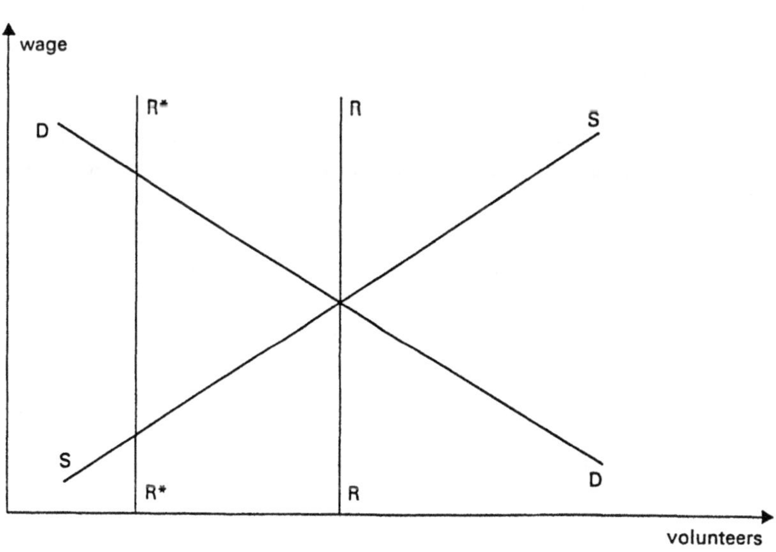

FIGURE 6.3 Demand and supply of professional soldiers

In chapter 5 we have seen that the abolition of conscription also brings a substitution of relative inexperienced soldiers with experienced soldiers. We mentioned a few aspects that had to do with the mix of experienced and inexperienced military personnel. This will be elaborated in the following subparagraph.

§ 6.4.1. The mix of experienced and inexperienced military

One of the central goals in the personnel policy of the armed forces has always been that young armed forces are the best armed forces. Why? In regards to the age profile a few factors play an important role.

First there is the observation that the armed forces have also put a premium on "young and powerful" armed forces. This is because the military profession demands a high degree of physical ability. This concept not only applies to the combat positions, but is also extended to the non-combat positions. The reason for this is that the non-combat positions in peace-time are seen as a labour pool for combat functions in war time. This demands a minimum of physical strength without many exceptions. The thought is reflected in this that fitter armed forces are also more effective armed forces. The younger the stock of personnel, the better.

Secondly, the military hierarchical personnel management system (the "up-or-out" system) has been constructed in such a way that a quick succession of people in a certain function is necessary. This creates a larger demand of young people, that is asked to serve only one contract period.

Thirdly, young armed forces have always been regarded as inexpensive armed forces, and a fourth argument is that a quick succession of young people in the armed forces is good for the enlargement of the reserves. Finally the argument for young armed forces is that a military system that contains a large amount of temporary youngsters is an advantage for the whole society.

The demand for young armed forces in not only heard in the Netherlands. But at first the idea of young forces also being the best forces is a little bit strange. In civil society experience plays an important role in the production process and the proportion elderly to youngsters plays a subordinate role most of the time. The armed forces also are an organization of capital and labour, whereby the factor human capital or experience can not be neglected.

The armed forces have to produce combat power, and for this combat power they need physical capital, human capital and labour. The fixation on young armed forces, and thus the factor labour, is therefore slightly naive, because physical labour and human capital play an equally important role in the armed forces.

The younger the armed forces, the less experienced they are. How inexperienced the armed forces actually are, is difficult to show. Conventional military power has always been measured in terms of quantity and never in terms of quality.[49] In chapter 5 we have seen that experienced armed forces need much less people to keep the same amount of combat power. Robert S. Gay concluded that 100 men with four years of experience can do the same amount of work as 180 inexperienced men without a loss of expected combat power. If we take a closer look at the mentioned arguments for young armed forces, it becomes clear that most of them can be called into question.

Military personnel considers the rank and the progress through the ranks in the hierarchical system, as the most important measure of individual progress. In the personnel policy a lot of emphasis is put on the promotion system. The rank serves as a kind of skill index without much consideration about the differences between the operational tasks. A personnel system that is mainly fixed on the progress through the ranks does not automatically mean that the armed forces should also be young. But this changes if we see the rank system in combination with the closed-shop character of the military system.

In civil society employees enter an organisation at every level and leave these organisations also on different levels. In the armed forces this is different. Most military enter the armed forces at the hierarchical bottom in the rank of soldier, are trained by the armed forces, and climb their way up through the organisation. Because the hierarchical military organisation gets smaller and smaller at the top, an upwards flow through the organisation means that experienced people have to leave the organisation and are replaced by inexperienced people. This happens because it is impossible to go up in rank. The quality aspect is of less importance. It is "up-or-out", with the consequence that the armed forces always have to hire a large amount of young people and therefor automatically gets younger. In part, young armed forces can therefore be explained by market principles. The armed forces are not able to compete with the market in the struggle for the experienced man, because the payment and promotion possibilities are attached to the service time in the armed forces and not to the skills of that person. The result is that the armed forces are forced to hire young inexperienced people.[50]

Young armed forces have also been seen as cheap armed forces. This opinion was prominently held during conscription times. For this statement all arguments have been used, that we have seen so many times already in preceding chapters. Up until now we had to conclude that conscription does not lower the costs of the armed forces. Conscription conceals the costs of the armed forces. The costs are really there, but are not carried by those who favour young armed forces.

Finally we have the social arguments for young armed forces. A large "turn-over' of youngsters would be a protection against a separate development of social ethics. Without considering much details (it will be discussed in chapter 7), the relation is empirically not significant and is somewhat controversial.

---

49 See also chapter 2, paragraph 1.

50 The last years a change can be seen in the armed forces concerning the use of skills in stead of service time for promotion possibilities.

The statement that young armed forces are the best armed forces, is false. This has also been concluded by the Defense Manpower Committee in the United States in America in 1976:[51]

"In noncombat jobs, the maturity, experience and judgment gained through longer service are more valuable than physical stamina and agility. (...) A longer maximum career is suitable for service members in noncombat jobs, particularly for those in technical and professional jobs. A person in these jobs could normally serve effectively until age 60 (...) In the field of radar detection, fleet evaluation shows that a destroyer equipped with standard electronic equipment and manned with personnel of excellent ability and experience has the capability of providing the same coverage as about three of the same ships operating in company if these latter are manned with personnel of average ability and experience. According to the committee: the effect of experience added to training can be seen in the field of guided missiles in all services. In general, missiles prepared and used by a group with a few years experience perform twice as effectively as missiles prepared by a group with similar training but no backlog of experience".

Because of the technological and organizational developments in the armed forces expertise and experience should be the most important element in the personnel policy. However, the practice of every day in the armed forces is difficult to transform to a situation that is equal to the situation in civil society. A civil society that shows that improvement of the use of personnel can be large, so that both inflow and outflow figures of personnel change drastically.

If we consider the arguments for young armed forces up close, we can see that young armed forces are a means rather than a goal. Young armed forces are a justification of conscription and a personnel unfriendly management system. Conscription takes care of a free supply of youngsters, that is justified by saying that armed forces have to be young if they want to be effective. The personnel management system that is used in the armed forces, puts experienced and older military personnel at a disadvantage, by replacing them place for younger people. This is also justified by saying that the armed forces have to be young. Both justifications are dubious and are at high cost to the armed forces and society.

§ 6.4.2. Conscription and the death[52]

In an all-volunteer force it is necessary that the need for new personnel is held as low as possible. This means that the armed forces need to create a situation that keeps presently enlisted soldiers as long as possible. This demands a clever

---

51 Defense Manpower Committee, Defense Manpower: the Keystone of National Security, April 1976, in: M. Binkin and I. Kyriakopoulos, Youth or Experience? Manning the Modern Military, Brookings Institution, Washington D.C., pp.31

52 This paragraph is based on Richard E. Wagner, Conscription, Voluntary Service and Democratic Fiscal Choice, in: Buchanan and Tollison, Theory of Public Choice, 1972, pp. 136-152.

personnel policy. However, the loss of personnel in the armed forces can never be avoided. The armed forces are an organisation that uses violence, and if they enter into an action situation, it is inevitable that people get hurt or die.

During the Cold War and the conscription force the Netherlands had at that time, the armed forces were organized in such a way that a quick succession of personnel had to be possible in order to keep war positions. Contrary to the British forces the Dutch armed forces had a large mobilization component. The British have a relative small mobilization component, because they have the opinion that an army must only be used as a defense instrument in the most extreme cases. Because the British have an all-volunteer force the scarcity aspects of such a force play an important role in this opinion. In an all-volunteer force soldiers are scarce and the waging of an unnecessary war can lead to a situation where the total army is wiped out if too many casualties occur.

The British view can not be found in the Netherlands. Per position in the Dutch first army, it is estimated that 5 to 6 people are necessary to cover the losses of personnel in a war. The difference between the British and Dutch opinions relating to this subject can be explained theoretically, and has its basis in the difference between an all-volunteer force and a conscription force and the chances of war with both forces.

Military are supposed to defend their own country in the case of war. Wars are rare happenings and mostly connected with the existence of a critical situation. The question, what is a critical situation, is often unclear. Therefore we state that a critical situation exists, when the people in power declare that such a critical situation exists. The institutional system of a country, which is responsible for the public choice process, declares if such a situation is critical or not. This means that if we think that a situation is critical under one kind of institutional system, it does not mean automatically that the situation stays critical, if the institutional system changes. In a changing environment the collective decisions may change also.

In chapter 2, paragraph 5 and chapter 3, paragraph 4 we used a median voter model, where public choices had to be made. In the following of this subparagraph we will continue with this model. In chapter 2 our public choice process consisted of the choice between butter and canons, whereby we assumed continuous variability regarding the amount of butter and canons. Decisions about waging war or not are not a continuous process, but have a more binary character. We go to war, or we do not go to war. Or, should we continue with the war, or shall we stop the hostilities we started.

When investigating the public choice concerning warfare, we should look at the threshold between positive and negative decisions. A positive decision to wage a war will not change by a marginal change in preferences, but will only be revised if the decrease in the preferences for war will pass a certain threshold. The relevance of the median-voter model, a model with continuous variability, seems to be small in this case. But this is not completely true. The relevance of these kind of models lies in the comparison of the results, that different institutions have, on the possible crossing of the threshold between whether to wage war or not, or to end a war.

By analyzing the differences between institutions in a continuously changing environment, the analysis can perhaps say something about the relative possibility that the threshold is crossed. The alternative institutions are in our case of course a conscription force or an all-volunteer force.

When analyzing the effects of conscription on the waging of a war, four possible situations can be distinguished. On the one hand we can make a distinction between the situation where a war is already happening and the situation where it is not. In addition we have the situation where the preferences for war increase or the situation where the preference for war declines. So according to this model, a war can happen now, whereby the preference to continue this war increases or declines. Or we have a situation of peace and the threats (preference for war) decline or increase.

From the four possible situations two are analytically interesting, because these bring the possibility that the threshold between peace and war can be crossed. These two are the decrease in preference for war, while the war is taking place, or a situation of increasing threats in peace times. Only the first situation will be discussed here, because the analysis of the second situation is symmetrical to the analysis of the first situation.

Let's assume that we are in a war situation now; a situation that appeared as a result of a normal public choice process. Since the decision to wage the war, the preferences for the war for a part of the population declined without increasing the preferences in another part of the population. In our median voter model this results in a change, if the preferences of the median voter are changed. If the preferences do not change, things remain the same. However, this is not always the case.

Things become more complicated, when we make a distinction between the conscription force and the all-volunteer force. In an all-volunteer force the decision to continue the war will be criticized, if the part of the population with less preferences for the war comes from the group that supplies military labour. This is even true, when no changes can be seen in preference by the median voters. If the situation is regarded as less critical by the people that supply military labour, these people will only continue the war, if they are compensated for this continuation. In other words: higher salaries should be offered to new volunteers to get the necessary amount of labour. People are prepared to join as a volunteer, if they are really sure that there safety is in jeopardy, not if they have doubts about the fact whether this is the case.

Higher wages for the military also means higher taxes for the rest of the population, because the necessary wage increase have to be paid one way or another. In a conscription army we do not have this mechanism, because conscripts are forced and they are not in the position to ask for pay rises.

If the preferences for war do not change in the population group that supplies the military labour, it makes no difference for the war decision if we have a conscription force or an all-volunteer force. However, if the population group that supplies the military labour shows a change in the preference for war, the distinction between the conscription force and the all-volunteer force is important. Because of the extra taxes the war will be more expensive in the case of an all-volunteer force. The higher the tax hike, the more there will be a chance that the median voters want to turn back the decision for war. A rise in tax payments does not have to be sufficient to cross the threshold of the war decision, but it is more probable that it happens in an all-volunteer force, because the conscription force does not have the interaction with the population by way of taxes.

In the case of an all-volunteer force there are two mechanisms that can change the decision for war: the preference for war and the price for war in the form of taxes. In the case of a conscription force we only have the former mechanism, the implicit cost-benefit analysis by price will be missing.

In summary, we can say that conscription increases the possibility of a war. If the members of the democratic community differ in their preferences for a war, a decision in favour of a war will be more probable in the case of a conscription force than in the case of an all-volunteer force. This is because the budgetary costs of a war will be lower under conscription.

A situation of war or "national emergency" can not be declared independent from the institutional structure in a society. Democratic procedures can lead to the declaration of an emergency situation under a certain institutional structure that never would have appeared under an alternative institutional structure.

In all-day practice we find these thoughts in the British all-volunteer force. The British have the opinion that an army should only be used to defend the vital elements of society and that a society should at least think twice before it would sacrifice scarce troops for an offensive action. In a conscription force we do not find these kinds of scarcity and therefore the thoughts about warfare are often much more aggressive in a conscription force.

For the individual soldier this means that the chance of dying in a conscription force is much higher than in an all-volunteer force, because a conscription force is much more likely to be called into action than an all-volunteer force. If we combine this with the fact the conscription forces are much more labour intensive than all-volunteer forces, we can come to the conclusion that much more casualties have to be expected in a conscription force than in an all-volunteer force.

The need for new soldiers because of death will be less high in an all-volunteer force, than we could have expected on the basis of the former conscription army. Although this fact is more of theoretical importance for armed forces in peacetime, it does have impact on the size of the reserves. The size of the reserves in an all-volunteer force can be much smaller in an all-volunteer force than in a conscription force. Protection of scarce people is an important goal in an all-volunteer force, which also means that less substitutes are necessary.

§ 6.4.3. Ranks and salaries

At the beginning of this paragraph we have seen that the emphasis on young armed forces can not be sustained in an all-volunteer force. Unfortunately a young army has become an inherent to the armed forces because of its second-best personnel management system. The present policy structures make it very difficult to fulfil all the demands of an all-volunteer force. In the last part of this paragraph we will therefore take a look at those instruments that can provide a situation where the personnel management system is in harmony with the demands of a modern all-volunteer force, so that potential volunteers are able to make a genuine judgement about applying for a job in the armed forces or in civil society without being disturbed by institutional obstructions.

The central question here is: "How can we take care of a situation where military stay in the armed force as long as possible". In literature[53] this is summarized into one concept: "the retention-rate". The higher this retention rate is the more experienced the armed forces is, and the less new personnel is needed. The most important obstacle in the armed forces to improve the retention rate is that the salary schemes in the armed forces are attached to the ranking system, the length of stay in the armed forces and the caring principle. Because these systems attach less value on differences in professional skills -differences that are very much valued in civil society- the military payment system is attractive for personnel with only few professional skills, while the system cannot retain the people that do possess these professional skills.

The final result is that the armed forces keep people that they could do without and looses the people that they need badly. The military payment system differs in many aspects from the payment systems in civil society. Two differences specifically attract much attention. The first is that the armed forces pay their personnel mostly on the basis of rank and years of duty, while in civil society, by emphasizing skills and profession, more is paid on the basis of achieved performances and opportunities. Moreover, the armed forces provide a lot of basic services to their personnel, like food, clothing, shelter and medical aid. This caring principle is rarely found in civil society. In the Dutch armed forces the caring principle is losing ground. Professional military mostly live outside the barracks and pay for their own food. Clothing and medical aid are still provided by the armed forces, although the medical aid is even now in discussion.

The reason for this payment system has a historic origin and touches the roots of almost every military establishment. Namely, that the military establishment is an institution rather than a profession. A civilian has a profession and *works for a* company. However, a military *is in* the armed forces and is supposed to follow some kind of mission to realize a highly esteemed good, instead of looking at

---

53 See e.g.: Martin Binkin and Irene Kyriakopoulos, Paying the Modern Military, Brookings Institution, Washington D.C., 1981.

himself in a materialized way. A soldier puts the institution of the armed forces first over his own demands. Although the payment of the military can not be compared directly with what we could have expected in a normal market situation, differences are mostly compensated by a series of social provisions and an amount of psychological income. In the case of problems at the workplace the members of an institution will not organize themselves quickly, but will try to solve these problems in a personal arrangement with their superiors, thereby trusting the ability of the institution to solve its own problems.[54]

The armed forces clearly have their own norms and values and therefore distinguishes itself from civil society. These norms and values take care of a situation in which an individual is completely at the disposal of the armed forces "which can decide what job he does, how and when he does them, what hours he works and the conditions in which he works and lives, entirely without consultation with the employee".[55] How to motivate these individuals however, is a completely other question, for which there is no simple answer:

"Traditionally, money has not been the only answer; service to the country has been more encouraged largely as a sacrifice to be made out of patriotism or a sense of moral indebtedness. Thus military leaders have gone to great lengths to create a professional identity-literally a different way of life in which cohesion, unity of purpose, and reciprocal loyalty are emphasized."[56]

In order to improve the unity and solidarity of the armed forces, the characteristics of the members of the armed forces are emphasized, that distinguish them from the rest of civil society. It is not surprising then, that the military payment system has adopted to this model of unity and solidarity. This payment system obliges itself to the payment of the same wage to everybody with the same rank, where it does not matter if this person is an infantry soldier, a hospital soldier or an administrative help. The underlying thought is that everybody delivers an equal contribution to the national defense of a country. A negative aspect of this concept of equality is that uniformity underestimates the relevance of the labour market, that can result into filling problems of vacant positions.

The personnel management system used by the armed forces has a large influence on the unique character of the military payment system. The armed forces have a closed-shopped personnel system, in which all personnel is acquired at the bottom of the hierarchy and flows further up. However, whether

54 See for a further explanation about the institution armed forces: Charles C. Moskos Jr., "From Institution to Occupation: Trends in Military Organization," Armed Forces and Society, vol. 4 (fall 1977), pp. 42.

55 United Kingdom, National board for prices and incomes, Standing reference on the pay of the armed forces: second report, Report 116, p. 6 in: Binkin and Kyriakopoulos, Paying the modern military, p. 21.

56 Binkin and Kyriakopoulos, pp. 21-22.

personnel systems are closed or not, they can not conceal the efficiency criteria it has to meet. This implies both the market sector and the government sector, because efficiency in payment structures is important to produce public services in the quality-price relation we would like to have.

In civil society there are large differences in payment between different professions. Differences that occur because of the kind of profession, the social importance of the function, the human investment that has been done for the profession, the alternative labour opportunities (scarcity) and the growing potential that is connected to every function. In the armed forces. however, we do not see these differences often.

On the contrary, the military payment system identifies itself, through the lack of professional differences, although there are a lot of different jobs to be done in the armed forces. As we have seen before, this lack of professional skills is not really unexpected, because it is the natural solution of a payment system that sees all tasks as equally important and therefore as equally productive. But such a system can only be restored in a world where scarcity aspects are not apparent, or in a world where enough people are present that can be satisfied with group satisfaction and psychological income. Unfortunately, there are only a few countries left in the world where people can be satisfied with psychological income, so the payment system of the armed forces can only survive, if the vacant positions in the armed forces are filled with people who are forced to join: conscripts.

Abolition of conscription brings scarcity of labour and therefore asks for a payment system that can handle the scarcity problem. Because of the present payment system and the pursuit for uniformity the armed forces are not able to see that some tasks are seen as less attractive, more difficult, better or worse than other tasks. The present payment system does not meet the elementary laws of supply and demand, which makes the filling of vacant positions in the armed forces even more difficult.

Abolition of conscription asks for a payment system in the armed forces that meets the laws of the labour market and is in agreement with the usual payment systems in civil society. This means that the payment system should be in accordance with the weight of the function, the human capital needed for the function, the sort of function, scarcity aspects and growth opportunities. This means that the armed forces should get rid of those characteristics in its payment system that make it different from their civil counterparts. The transition from a conscription force into an all-volunteer force means the transition from a normal suit to a tailor-made suit. A measured suit that is also necessary for payment schedules. In such a suit there is no place anymore for general pay increases, but much more attention should be paid to bonuses and scarcity premiums, extra increments and achievement payments:

"Expanded use of bonuses is certain to raise the basic issue of whether the military institution is willing to concede that on skill deserves higher compensation than another at the same rank and grade levels and more broadly, whether the reform of military pay policy should be reduced to provision of unequal pay for the same grade."[57]

With all possible labour market instruments it should be secured that the provision of the public good defense remains the same quality, while the financial consequences of changing a conscription army into an all-volunteer force remain modest.

Earlier in this paragraph we have seen that the closed-shopped personnel system in the armed forces and the upward flow through the organisation brings an automatic instrument into the armed forces, that brings a situation that experienced people have to leave the organisation, because there is no place left for them in the upper ranks. The number of positions with that rank are simply sold out.

There is also no space in the armed forces to fulfil the salary demands of experienced personnel, because a higher salary automatically demands a higher rank, while hierarchically seen there is no place for such people. The consequence is that these people will have to leave the organisation, and the armed forces are forced to look for new people who will have the experience of the former soldier a few years later.

The second-best solution, that the armed forces are forced to by its personnel policy, has its main cause in the strict joining of rank to salary. The rank is a personal title of the individual in the armed forces. The armed forces have ranks from soldier to general, with 16 intermediate ranks in the Dutch Army. The armed forces have so many ranks, because they point to the institutional character of the military organisation and not to the professional side. In an institutional system attention is not pointed at functions or tasks, but on persons and therefore the personal title of these persons, the rank. The difference in titles is made explicit by the hierarchical system, that has a clear sequence in titles.

A salary scale is a step or a grade in a value system, which is attached to a function. The salary scale simply reflects the amount of money someone gets for a labour achievement. Because rank and salary scale are directly related, the specific rank does rather than the salary scale indicates what someone earns. If the armed forces want to pay someone more, he or she has to go up in rank, because a closer subdivision of the salary system is not available.

Although the original form of military payment had no place for specific function value, the Dutch armed forces did not escape from some elements of a function specific value system. The origin of this fact has to do with the development of technology, that causes a demand for people with specific amounts of human capital. Personnel is awarded for this amount of human capital with a higher rank, which gives outsiders the idea that some kind of rankinflation exists within the armed forces.

---

57 Binkin and Kyriakopoulos, pp. 44.

In 1991 the Zuidema-bureau conducted a research after rank inflation in the armed forces. Its report "Is rang alleen rang als er rang op staat?"[58] concludes that it is not possible to irrefutably prove the existence of rank inflation. But a quantitative addition of functions with a higher rank ("upward pressure") is noted. This fact is also registered strongly in civil bureaucracies. This shows a development that refers to increasing complexity of society and technology in governmental functions.

The impossibility of showing rank inflation is not surprising, if we take a closer look at the definition of rank inflation developed by the Zuidema-bureau. This, very correct, definition is:

"Rank inflation is an asymmetric development of the level of the rank and the weight of the function, wherein the level of the rank exceeds the weight of the function during the time of development".

From this definition it follows, that there should be a connection between rank and function, if we want to show rank inflation, but as we have seen earlier, the armed forces do not emphasize the relation between rank and function, but do so for rank and persons. A relation that results from the institutional character of the armed forces. An investigation after the causes of rank inflation is therefore doomed to be a failure. The Zuidema-bureau does give a few recommendations to control the upward pressure on the ranks. Next to the recommendation of building a good registration system and a company wise standard model for the structure of the organisation, the Zuidema-bureau gives a third possibility, that is the real clue to solving the problems of the personnel management system of the armed forces, because it makes possible a much more stable organisation system. The Zuidema-bureau recommends:

"In this investigation we confronted the situation that better trained people were necessary for certain tasks because technology was getting more complicated. These people had to be paid more (market value) and therefore received a higher rank. It seems to be useful to break through this improper way of working by:
- choosing for a system with certain ranks (as long as one needs hierarchy, because of war situations, or because of performing tasks in international structures that require some ranks for reasons of culture or cooperation);
- cutting the direct links between payment and years of duty and thus the ranks, and to proceed with a joining of payment to objectively declared weight of function, with the accordingly connected form of performance assessment.
In this way one can react flexible to changes in organisation or to unforeseen external demands of labour, while one can better react to circumstances on the labour market,

58 N. van Dijkhuizen en P.H.J. Suiker, Is rang alleen rang als er rang op staat?, Leusden, 1991.

without changing the chosen structure of the armed forces or using improper adaptations to the payment system."[59]

The Zuidema-bureau hits the nail on the head with this remark. In order to adapt the payment system to the needs of an all-volunteer force, the salary has to be disconnected from the rank system. The salary has to be connected to the weight of the function, including all elements of the salary building that are present in a civilian function.

Ranks are predestined to function as a coordination mechanism, and the development of salary scales within the armed forces has to provide the possibility that soldiers can be rewarded according to the weight of their function and nothing else. If a company gets twice as big, the director gets a higher salary, but he or she stays director and does not become director-first-class!. There should be no difference in the armed forces.

The armed forces were already aware of the malfunctioning of their personnel system. But it took them until January 1, 1990 to attach more weight to the element "function weight". As a consequence the rank is indirectly attached to the function, and therefore there is an indirect link of payment to function. The recommendation of the Zuidema-bureau to change the payment system structurally is thought to be too much by the Minister of Defense Ter Beek in a letter to the parliament.[60] With this letter he admits implicitly that he persists on the direct link between rank and salary and does not feel much for the scarcity concept involved.

In paragraph 6.2. we have seen that the tasks of the Dutch armed forces are going to be expanded in the near future. Tasks that differ considerably regarding contents, risk and education needed. Because there will be a large differentiation in tasks the armed forces will need personnel with several different skills. Recruitment of these persons should be adjusted to the wishes of the future soldier, considering education, risk profile and length of contract. Matching of tasks and wishes is only possible, if this is accompanied by differentiation of payment. This differentiation is only practically executable if the direct links between ranks and salaries are cut trough and a flexible payment system is adopted.

In addition, the top-down approach in the armed forces should be replaced by a more bottom-up approach of the personnel policy. By introducing the subsidiary principle in the armed forces, we can get a situation that military only have a higher rank then others, if this is necessary for coordination issues between the different parts of the armed forces. Positions that are only used for supervising issues are eliminated in such a way, because the professional military can handle these positions themselves if they are really professional. Subsidiarity

---

59 Van Dijkhuizen and Suiker, on cit. p. 60. See for the same kind of words: Binkin and Kyriakopoulos, Paying the Modern Military, chapter 4.

60 Letter 90/377/23459 to the Chairman of the Tweede Kamer der Staten Generaal, 's-Gravenhage, 14 november 1991.

implies that for optimal decision making only those decisions that can not be made on a lower, more decentralized level, are made on a higher level. In the first place this saves a lot of scarce people, but it also improves the efficiency in a war situation, because there is a smaller chance that a unit disintegrates, because of combat actions. The bigger the group, the bigger the chance of disintegration. An accompanying fact of the subsidiarity principle in the armed forces is that the contents of the function of the lowest rank increases in value, making this function much more interesting for a lot of people.

The Dutch armed forces will need a tailor-made suit for their tasks to be executed. Without vision for the details this will never succeed. The organisation has to fulfil the demands on every aspect of this suit and this includes payment too. The present payment system does not only need redecoration, it actually invites for a drastic rebuilding. First there is the need for military managers to keep payment and rank strictly separate. The payment- and value system should be arranged in such a way, that there are still possibilities for promotion (today's soldier must be able to become tomorrow's sergeant), but the salary scales should be expanded mostly in function categories where training costs are highest (F-16 pilots), and where long contracts are most wanted. It should not be surprising that these functions nowadays have the most tightened retention rates of all functions. Especially, a larger amount of scales in such a function will provide the financial incentives to keep someone in the armed forces as long as possible.

The separate use of both personnel policy instruments - promotion and payment - will be an indicator for effective personnel policy. The disconnection of ranks and salaries will not only give an improvement of efficiency, it will also promote the quality of the armed forces, with a smaller demand on personnel as a result. Because of the smaller need of direct-productive personnel a multiplier effect appears, that will lessen the need for non-direct-productive personnel, so that the total personnel numbers will be reduced considerably. The possibilities of improving the retention rate and the quality of the armed forces through a change of the payment system are very promising, but can only be really a success if the retirement system is also reviewed.

The present retirement policy has as its main reason, that the armed forces need to be young armed forces. People in the Royal Navy retire at 50 and for the other parts of the armed forces the retirement age is stated officially at 55. The difference between the Royal Navy and the other parts of the armed forces are caused by compensation issues for navy people for the time they have been serving at sea during their service time. In a personnel policy that concentrates on experience, retirement at 50 or 55 is a strange fact. A revision of retirement policy should therefore be pointed at keeping a more experienced labour force and at the harmonisation of salary structures, to prevent experienced people to leave the armed forces when they are at the height of their possibilities.

The reason for "functional age dismissal" has always been the fulfiling of physical demands of the armed forces. In addition, the present retirement policy was intended to serve as an attractive part of the reward for the military and as a payment for the special institutional characteristics of a life as a military. At last the pension should help with the transition to civil life.

The emphasis on young and vigorous armed forces is already analysed at the beginning of this paragraph. Young armed forces are a misconception and that is even more true in an all-volunteer force than in a conscription force. Even if it is true that young armed forces are necessary to retain enough combat power, it is still doubtful if early retirement really contributes to this. Almost all personnel to be considered for retirement does not come from the combat forces. Quite a large amount of military has never seen any combat function at all. There is also no reason to doubt about the productivity and quality of the retiring employees. A large amount of the retired military takes on a new job in civil society when they are retired.

The present retirement system has the additional disadvantage, that it conceals the payment of a function in the armed forces. Although the armed forces want the military to see their job as a kind of vocation, for most persons this is quite different. For young military the pension scheme does not have that much importance, when applying for a job in the armed forces, because this future income is so far away that the value of this income is very low. Comparing the military job with the civilian job it means that the attention for a job in the armed forces becomes less.

The present retirement policy has to be changed therefore and the best way to do this is by linking the system to the pension system of civil servants.

The armed forces will have to adopt to the norms and values of civil society if they want to use the scarce resources of civil society in an efficient way. Holding on to its own norms and values, often off Napoleonic origin, can mean that the armed forces will always have to follow a second-best policy. This second-best policy can still be permitted in a conscription army, because the filling of their personnel is guaranteed. In an all-volunteer force, sticking to own norms and values means throwing in its own glasses. In an all-volunteer force therefore, the institution armed forces should not be prominent, but rather the military profession in itself. A profession just like every other profession in society.

§ 6.5. Final remarks

In this chapter we have taken a look at the labour market for military. From this chapter follows that the comparison of the armed forces with civil society in an all-volunteer force plays an important role. Unlike with a conscription force, the armed forces have to compete now with the other sectors in society in order to get scarce labour resources.

In this competition process the comparison of payments, both material and social, play an important role. Unlike a conscription force, this is not restricted to an internal comparison in the armed forces, but the comparison should be enlarged to the whole society. This means that differences in payment should be attached to differences in weight in function, differences in skills and the supply on the labour market. In stead of a macro approach of the personnel policy, personnel policy should concentrate on the filling of specific functions in the armed forces. The ready-to-wear suit should make place for the tailor-made suit. A tailor-made suit that does not fit a volunteer as if he is the possession of the general, but a tailor-made suit that takes into account the wishes of every individual volunteer. The armed forces are a company with hundreds of functions, so it will not be very difficult to fulfil the wishes of the individual volunteer. If this volunteer does not satisfy the demands of the armed forces or there are no alternatives available, then the armed forces should not feel restricted to try to make the volunteer conform in order to match its wishes with the wishes of the volunteer. An all-volunteer force asks for a human and real personnel policy. Not just because this will fit the volunteers, or because it is good for society in both human and financial perspective, but especially because it is a solution for the armed forces themselves, because they can easily solve the problem of vacant positions in an all-volunteer force by performing in such a way.

CHAPTER 7

The interaction between society and the armed forces

"[It is] a misunderstanding that privatization can not concern real public goods".
P.B. Boorsma in: Openbare uitgaven 16, October 1984, pp. 299

The armed forces are a part of our society. There have always been armed forces. We can not think about times without them. But, if armed forces want to survive than it is necessary that they are accepted by society. If society does not see the necessity of armed forces, than the armed forces will no longer have a right to exist. Beside the social acceptance of the armed forces in a general sense, the armed forces need a certain level of social acceptance in a specific sense too, in order to function:

"People do need the will to work there, not only related to the social accepted aims of the organization, but related to the legal status, the character of the work and the working conditions too".[1]

The notion of "social acceptance" has not been used that long by the armed forces as a notion of policy. Until the fifties Defense policy had two central subjects:[2]
- the effectiveness of the organisation
- the efficiency of the organisation

The personnel of the armed forces was completely available for the use of the organisation, 24 hours a day. Personnel policy meant nothing more than personnel control. The human being in the armed forces was only seen in his military role, and he was expected to be completely absorbed in this organisation. The military organization was a rather closed organisation in the fifties.

This closed character of the armed forces almost brought the fear that the armed forces would develop into a 'state within the state'. This concept is already very old and is mentioned by Niccolo Machiavelli (1469-1527) in his "Dell'arte della querra".[3] Machiavelli pleaded for the possibility of military conscription to

---

1 MRK-advies nr. 14, Maatschappelijke aanvaarding van de krijgsmacht, Den Haag 1988, pp. 5. and Maatschappelijke Raad voor de Krijgsmacht, Evaluatie maatschappelijke aanvaarding van de krijgsmacht 1988-1991, advies 14/1, Den Haag, 1991.

2 Ibid, pp.3

3 See e.g. M.L. Tiesinga, Dienstplicht: van militaire naar sociale?, Armex Defense Magazine (1992)

prevent a 'state-within-the-state'. He argued this because he saw military conscription as a obstacle for everybody who want to get into a position of power by force. According to Machiavelli an army that formed an average of the population was more reliable than an all-volunteer force.

Machiavelli's plead for improving interaction between society and the armed forces by conscription is also followed by others. The Ministry of Defense brings the following statement about conscription in the Defensienota 1968:

"The Royal Army has much more direct contacts with the Dutch society than the other parts of the armed forces, due to its nationwide locations and the many conscripts it has in its troops. Through that its habits, its ways of working and its existing relations are tested almost every day to what in the Dutch society is regarded as normal and just. Also because of this reason the army has to reconsider the correctness and fairness of its habits, ways of working and relations constantly. This is happening more often.[4]

It was the first time a Defensienota mentioned the social effects of military conscription, other than the procurement argument. More direct are the words in the Defensienota 1984:

"Conscription is not only an indispensable instrument for the procurement of the armed forces, it improves the interaction between society and armed forces too".

While in the Defensienota 1984 the procurement argument is mentioned first and the social interaction argument second, the Defensienota 1991 turns the arguments around. About the possibility of an all-volunteer force the Nota says:

"An army with conscripts ensures the involvement of society by its defense. A permanent flow of young Dutch people through the armed forces also leads to a greater acceptability of the armed forces for developments in society. Through that it is easier to ensure that the armed forces stay a reflection of society, to which it belongs. A more practical aspect is that we still have to see, if it is possible to attract sufficient volunteers".[5]

The question is if this statement is a practical development or a political choice. In 1991 a discussion was started about the possible abolition of conscription. Therefore it is possible that the Defensienota 1991 was an attempt to keep conscription on the basis of the argument of interaction between the armed forces and society, because it was already clear that the procurement argument was not completely valid anymore. Concrete indications for the validity of this statement are not available however.

In general the interaction between society and the armed forces can be described in such a way that the norms and values in the armed forces are a reflection of the norms and values in society. Moreover, society has to execute some kind of political control over the armed forces in such a way that the armed

---

4 VVDM-report "Einde oefening", Utrecht 1992, pp.6.

5 Ibid.

forces can not develop into a "state-in-the-state" and the government is the boss of the armed forces.

From this description we can derive the following questions. Which elements in the armed forces can lead to a situation where the norms and values of the armed forces deviate from what is normal in the rest of society and in such a way that they are a threat to the rest of society? Related is the question about which instruments can take over the role of military conscription concerning the reflection of social norms and values in the armed forces and the political control on the armed forces?

§ 7.1. The officers corps

The armed forces mainly have a closed personnel system and as we have seen earlier because of that a surprising personnel structure and culture. The culture in the armed forces is closely related to strong discipline, that is organized hierarchically. This culture can lead to a situation, where people are forced to do things that are unnatural to them, and can act against the values and norms of society. They have to do this because they are in a subordinate position. More than once soldiers have been used to commit a coup d'état.

International history shows us that is not important if these subordinates are volunteers or conscripts. Many coups d'état, like the one in Chile 1973, are committed with the help of conscripts. Canby writes about the empirical testing of this phenomenon:

"The assertion that a high-turnover, socially representative military is less dangerous to democratic institutions than a volunteer force is not empirically supportable. Although the refusal of conscripts to obey their immediate superiors was a key factor in the collapse of the French Army Coup against the Gaulle in 1960, other eclectic examples indicate that conscription is not a sufficient condition to insure against coups. Greece has universal conscription and Brasil and Peru have selective conscription. Not only is conscription no insurance against coups, the conscription/voluntarism issue is only loosely related to political threats from the military as an institution. This is because the military threats to any existing political order generally come from the officer corps, which control the military and is the most direct position to influence political institutions".[6]

If we want to control the democratic contents of the armed forces than it is important to control the hierarchical top. Hereby a distinction between an all-volunteer force and a conscription force is not necessary, because the execution of effective and efficient armed forces always needs a professional officers corps. This does not change if the recruitment system of the armed forces changes. This heart of the group, which can be a potential threat to society, will always possess the same people regardless the recruitment system. Statements about the

6 Steven L. Canby, Military Manpower Procurement, Lexington 1972, pp. 43.

necessity of a large personnel stream in the armed forces for social armed forces, can not be confirmed by empirical studies. This becomes even more clear if we see that young conscripts do not have much contact with older officers. If we want the officers corps to be really influenced, than it is necessary that the officers are personally influenced, where change occurs from their individual minds and behaviour.

A starting point for influencing the officers corps is that the influence is pointed at the political neutralization of this officers corps, without interfering in the primary tasks of these officers. Theoretically there are a few ways to neutralize the top of the armed forces. The first method uses indoctrination of the officers corps, by taking care that the military leaders share the views of the leading politicians in society. This method is often used in the former Warschau-Pact countries. In the Netherlands it sometimes happens too that an officer is asked to show loyalty to the leading politicians.[7]

A second method is the imposition of formal political control. This method is often supported by a large amount of informal political control. With informal and formal political control we can think about inspection organisations, environmental activists, anti-military groups, people living near military sites and training grounds, etc. The labour inspection, General Auditing Office and the ombudsman also belong to these instruments.

A third method is the splintering of the officers corps into different social-political groups. The aim of splintering is to break through the unanimity of officers regarding certain orders that can lead to undemocratic actions. A social-political mixed officers corps will face much more difficulties to melt together with a certain groups of civilians. If this group of civilians were to ask for the help of the officers, the result will be the split of the officers corps.

To get a diversified officers corps a few possibilities are available. First, far-reaching labour division within the armed forces will lead to a diversification of tasks and the possibility of attracting a larger potential of officers, or like Canby states:

"If the services would allocate their best talent by special assignments instead of dispersing them through standardized career patterns, the military would be more attractive to high opportunity-cost talent and fewer would be needed"[8].

Another diversification technique corresponds to the education of officers, and aims to strengthen the curriculum of military academies. In practice this means

---

7 This happened in 1992. A general of the Royal Army, general Couzy, showed his concerns about the restructuring of the armed forces on the opinion page of NRC-Handelsblad. Some politicians reacted that the general should keep his opinion to himself. According to these politicians they were there to do politics, generals should command his troops. As a consequence general Couzy was forced to sign a statement of loyalty, that did not resist him giving interviews about the specific tasks of the armed forces.

8 Canby, on cit. pp. 244.

that military academies will cooperate with regular universities and other schools, whereby the strict tie with the armed forces is loosened.

A fourth method aims to loosen the grip of the older and hierarchically higher personnel on the youngsters. Just like the third method these are ways to connect the values and norms of society with the norms and values of the armed forces from within. The first two methods are mainly external methods. According to Canby the loosening of the grip of youngster can best be done by influencing the intermediate chains and ranks:

"This means that the onus of blocking anti-state acts of senior officers is on career officers in the intermediate ranks. Given the vise-like control seniors have over their subordinates' careers, these intermediate officers are in a difficult position. Any questioning of the legality of an order, correct or not, may well ruin their subsequent military careers unless institutional protection is provided by a grateful government".[9]

The dependency of the young officer on the old officer can be weakened in several ways. Hopefully high selection demands for the officers corps will lead to a higher quality of officers, that are morally and economically independent because of their higher intelligence, more developed political conscience and better civil opportunities. In addition, it is to be recommended that the officers responsible for the communications and the decisions, also have the best possible education and the highest potentials.

However, the most important chain is the promotion system. The promotion system should be designed in such a way in the armed forces that the lower officers should be the least dependent on the goodwill of their direct superiors. A promotion system where a balance between achievement, that cannot be valued objectively, and intelligence, that can be valued objectively, is available, can diminish dependency. In such a system the emphasis is on the function demands to fulfil a certain rank and on not the length of service or the loyalty to the superior. This system also helps to diminish the weak management's elements that can be found in some parts of the armed forces. The management in the armed forces has the tendency to put too much emphasis on personnel leadership qualities and to neglect the cognitive elements that are necessary for this leadership. Since the beginning of the nineties the Ministry of Defense has changed its policy. It is putting much more emphasis now on function demands and cognitive elements.

Thus far we have taken a look at the middle management in the armed forces. The influence that soldiers have on their superiors must not be forgotten. Especially in the Netherlands soldiers have played an important role in loosening the grip of officers on soldiers.

Each soldier does not have much to say when he is on his own. He has to follow orders. The refusal of an order can lead to prosecution. Dutch history and

9 Ibid, pp. 47.

practice teaches us that soldiers can stand up for themselves, if they are able to unite, so they can defend their interests without hurting the general interests of the armed forces.

Especially for conscripts it is important that they can unite into an interest group or trade union, because these are the only ways in which a conscript can bring forward his dissatisfaction. They can not quit, if the situation does not satisfy them anymore. Volunteers can. The right of leaving the armed forces for a volunteer brings a new, more economic dimension to the interaction between society and the armed forces. Conscripts join the armed forces by force, are not allowed to quit, and because conscripts are cheap, the opportunity value of a conscript for the armed forces is low. If a conscript causes trouble or does not function, than this person is replaced quickly by a new conscript. If the armed forces are filled with volunteers, the situation is different. First, it is expensive to dump a volunteer- where does one find another one that quickly. Second, the armed forces have trouble with filling all their vacant positions, if the norms and values of the armed forces differ too much from the norms and values of society. The armed forces can place itself out of the market, if the wishes of the soldiers/volunteers are not taken into account. The mechanism that is working here, is the same mechanism as we have described in paragraph 6.4.1. In paragraph 6.4.1. we have seen that an volunteer-force will not go into action as quickly as a conscription army, because there is a chance that an volunteer-force has no personnel left if the war decision is not supported anymore by the group in the society that has to provide the soldiers. When soldiers are treated by their superiors in an inhuman way, the same can happen. Pressure on the labour market has to lead to the situation that the labour conditions and the labour circumstances of the armed forces has to equal more or less the situation in the civil society, otherwise the armed forces run the risk of having no personnel left.

But this not an absolute probability. A number of volunteers will accept a different working- and living climate, because they have no other opportunities on the labour market. According to the Social Council for the Armed Forces (MRK) this will mostly be true for lower-educated people.[10] Abolishment of conscription asks for attention to this phenomenon, the MRK states: the aim should be and stay at representative armed forces, both in norms and values as in composition. The MRK fears a situation where the majority of the volunteers originates from a group in society that can not be influenced by changes in opinion by the whole society. In terms of the median voter model this will say that this group of volunteers will never cross the threshold of, for example, going to war or not going to war.

The concern of the MRK on this point is understandable. However, in an all-volunteer force there are a few instruments that can be used, so that the pressure of the labour market really has an effect, like the right to quit. These instruments

---

10 Maatschappelijk Raad voor de Krijgsmacht, Standpunt van de Maatschappelijke Raad voor de Krijgsmacht about the Meijer-report, advies nr. 26, Den Haag 1992, pp.12

can take care of an automatic incentive for the interaction between society and the armed forces.

The tasks in the new volunteer force are more extensive than the tasks of the old conscription army. Volunteers should also be prepared to fulfil their UN-tasks. These UN-tasks ask for a high level of education of the volunteer, which can be achieved by initial education or through additional training by the armed forces. Tasks that concentrate on persuasion and convincing ask for more emancipated soldiers than were needed in earlier times. Moreover, the new tasks of the armed forces will help low-educated soldiers to climb up in the social hierarchy, whereby the representative character of the armed forces will increase.

In other words, there is a place in the armed forces for people with only little education. If the armed forces do not give these volunteers additional training, they mostly hurt themselves, because it will be much more difficult to recruit volunteers and to execute the humanitarian UN-tasks.

In the same way we think about influencing the top of the hierarchy, by making the middle parts or the hierarchy more independent, the lower parts can also be made more independent. A last remark here is that it is expected that the military interest groups keep on doing their work. They probably defend the interests and rights of the volunteers, and put pressure on the employer and the commanders in the armed forces in the name of these soldiers.

§ 7.2. The privatization of defense

In the armed forces both civilians and military are employed. In chapter 5 we have seen that abolishment of conscription or the payment and treatment of conscripts as voluntary soldiers, makes military labour forces expensive, so that they can be exchanged for civilians on places where this is possible. By exchanging military for civilians the armed forces become more civil society orientated, because the armed forces will depend more on civilians.

From a social point of view conscripts are often concerned as "civilians in uniforms". When these "civilians" disappear, the ratio civilians/military becomes worse, if we assume that this ratio represents the size of civil orientation of the armed forces. Conscripts must not be considered as military is this ration, but as civilians. Improvement of this ratio brings social benefits and the worsening of the ratio can be considered as a social loss. When conscription disappears the society is obliged to improve the interaction between the armed forces and civil society by using new instruments. These instruments have to take care of the fact that the amount of civilians influencing the armed forces directly are rising relatively to the amount of military. One of these instruments is privatization. Boorsma describes the notion of privatization as follows:

"Using more private initiative by the government".[11]

With the term privatization Boorsma both means the gaining of more independence of parts of the public sector, the transfer of tasks to the private sector, and intensifying the work of volunteers. In chapter 5 we have already spoken about contracting out, as the substitution of conscripts by civilians and capital. Contracting out is only a small part of the bigger notion privatization. Privatization of the armed forces is not only meant for improving the interaction between society and the armed forces, but can also bring an efficiency improvement.

At first sight privatization of the armed forces looks like a paradox. But if we take a closer look we can see that the armed forces offer all kinds of opportunities for privatization. Defense is a public good.[12] This public good is paid out of tax revenues from the government, but does not by definition have to be produced by the government. That the public good defense is produced by the armed forces, a part of the government, has been caused by the fact that the government possesses the monopoly on violence. A closer look at the armed forces shows us that the armed forces both possesses combat and non-combat functions. Because combat functions are connected with elements of violence, these functions have to stay in the government. Privatization by laying off tasks is not possible with these functions. The non-combat functions in the armed forces do not have the violence restrictions. So these functions can be privatized if feasible.

In paragraph 7.2.1 we will discuss the theoretical backgrounds of privatization. In paragraph 7.2.2. these theoretical results are assigned to the armed forces. The goal of these two paragraphs are not primarily efficiency results. In order to get the right size of the efficiency advantages of privatization two paragraphs will not be enough. Efficiency improvement may not be the prime goal, it certainly is one of the most important constraints. The main goal is to see if privatization improves the interaction between society and the armed forces. If this is really possible with the help of privatization, we will see at the end of this chapter.

---

11 P.B. Boorsma, Privatisering, Openbare Uitgaven 16, nr. 6 oktober 1984, pp. 284.

12 See also chapter 2.

§ 7.2.1 Privatization: theory[13]

Privatization can both be found on the supply side and the demand side of the economic process. When we look at privatization of the demand side we talk about assessing the benefit principle. This means that the costs of a public provision can be individualized and can be brought into account to the user. Defense as a final product for the consumer is a pure public good, so assessing the benefit principle is not possible in this case.

When talking about the supply side we can think about laying-off tasks, contracting out and giving more independence to parts of the public sector. When laying-off tasks the government leaves everything to the private sector, without bothering with things like policy and execution. By contracting out, the government still engages itself with the size of the tasks, but parts of the execution of this policy will be given -by contract- to private companies. When addressing more independence, tasks are transferred to independent organisations with a personal statutory body and indirect government control. This last form offers possibilities for variations.

Independence can be given internally and externally. In the case of external independence we most of the time talk about independent administrations. Independent or functional administrations are organisations according to private or public law that posses so much independence that there is no hierarchical subordination to a minister. In the case of internal independence we talk about things like contract management, self-control and agencies within the government administrations. The responsibility of the minister for the execution of the tasks stays, but the executive branches get more freedom to arrange a more efficient management. External independence has no hierarchical control, and

13 This paragraph is based on the following articles:E. Biesmeijer en W.C. Verbaan, Zelfbeheer I: de ambtenaar wordt manager, Openbare Uitgaven,16, nr. 5, september 1984, pp. 226-239; N.P. Mol, Zelfbeheer II: kostenplaatsenbudgettering, Openbare Uitgaven 16, nr. 5., september 1984, pp. 240-256; N.P. Mol, Bedrijfseconomie van de collectieve sector, Alpen aan de Rijn, 1989; N.P. Mol en H.A.A. Verbon, Institutionele economie en openbaar bestuur, perspectieven op de verzelfstandiging van overheidsdiensten, 's-Gravenhage 1993; P.B. Boorsma, Privatisering, Openbare Uitgaven 16, nr 6, oktober 1984, pp. 282-303; B.C.J. van Velthoven en F.A.A.M. van Winden, Privatisering, een politiek-economische benadering, Openbare Uitgaven 16, nr.6, oktober 1984, pp. 304-317; P. Felix, Verzelfstandiging als privatiseringsvariant, Economisch Statistische Berichten, 5 maart 1986, pp. 248-252; E. Boneschansker en H. de Groot, Verzelfstandiging van overheidsdiensten: wanneer en hoe?, Openbare Uitgaven 24, nr.3, mei 1992 ; D.J. Kraan, Bureaucratietheorie en organisatie van de rijksdienst, Openbare Uitgaven 24, nr.4, juli 1992; R.H. Coase, The nature of the firm, Economica 4, 1937, pp. 386-405; R.H. Coase, Accounting and the theory of the firm, Journal of accounting and economics 12 (1990), pp. 3-13; R.H. Coase, The institutional structure of production, The American Economic Review, september 1992, pp. 713-719; N.P. Mol en H.A.A. Verbon, Institutionele economie en openbaar bestuur, perspectieven op de verzelfstandiging van overheidsdiensten, 's-Gravenhage, 1993.

has the advantage that the cost of monitoring decline. On the other hand, the production costs may rise. So we have to take a better look at the conditions that will bring an advantage or a disadvantage.

Kraan[14] formulates the criteria for external independence as follows:

1. The desired quality and quantity of the produced provision must be sufficiently stable;
2. The minister must be able to posses the most actual and reliable information about the costs per unit of the produced provision;
3. An effective incentive should be available for the management of the independent government organisation in order to strive for efficiency gains.

If the desired quality or quantity of the product depends on quickly changing and unpredictable circumstances, independence is not efficient because of transaction costs. The existence of transaction costs means that alternative coordination methods are preferable to the market mechanism, even if these coordination methods bring costs and imperfections. Separate agreements per delivery with suppliers of production factors and intermediate products would lead to huge (transaction)costs. If the transaction costs and imperfections are much bigger than the prices the market mechanism generates, the market mechanism prevails and hierarchical supervision should disappear.

Hierarchical supervision is necessary if we want to guarantee that an organisation produces what the minister wants at any given moment. This is certainly true for a situation where the organisation has some kind of freedom in executing their tasks.

From the second criterion it follows that the product should be measurable and that a financial-management system should be used that is based on a cost-benefit-system. Only in this way it can be guaranteed that the needed cost information can be delivered permanently on the basis of actual facts. The management of production can only be efficient, if indicators can mirror relevant results. Every product should be defined properly, so that an internal financial-management-system can make clear the internal transaction costs that are made to produce the provision.

Cost accounting in the public sector is more and more necessary, because with the help of this instrument and the calculated cost prices it can be reasoned, which parts of the organisation should be managed hierarchically and in which part of the organisation the market mechanism prevails. On the basis of a good insight in the costs per unit it is possible to finance the independent service on norms costs per unit. Related to this is the necessity of juridical contracts that contain the needed results and the situation that independent services get some kind of statutory body.

The third criterion states that when hierarchical supervision is absent another incentive is necessary, so that 'additional' rents of the independent service are

---

14 Kraan, pp. 164-165

eliminated. This is essential because finance on norm costs does not mean an efficient production process yet. Information about the average costs is needed for this purpose that can not be deducted from the financial accounts, even if the books are organized in an economical way. It is possible that there is a difference between visible and pure costs. This difference can be attributed to the information gains management relatively has about certain things in the organisation and about the fact that management can use its position of power to get a price that is higher then the costs the politician is aware of. This situation equals the elements of Niskanens bilateral-monopoly-model as described in chapter 2.

The problem of additional rents can be solved by connecting the personal income of the management in some way to the difference between the granted budget and the visible costs: the efficiency gains. A system that brings full competition offers the best possibilities for this. Full competition introduces a few incentives that can eliminate additional rents in the long term. However, the question is if these incentives can be introduced in independent services of the government.

One way to design the efficiency incentives is to declare that the independent organisation can "keep" a part of the extra gains. This means that a part of the difference between the granted budget and the visible costs can be used by the service the way they like, without the possibility of adding the extra budget to the income of the managers. However, this does not lead to an effective solution. Firstly, this incentive will lead to complete waste, because the free consumption leads by definition to inefficient purchases or a political, too high, provision of the service. Secondly this incentive can not be effective, because the management of the independent service will never transform (invisible) additional rents into (visible) efficiency gains, if this means that only a part of these gains can be used free. If these rents can be acquired as invisible rents 100% can be used free.

A possibility to design the efficiency incentive in a successful way is by using the government company. However, for efficiency it is needed that the government acquires a normal dividend. The government company obliges the management to record all costs and benefits in a business manner, so that all efficiency gains can be read from the books. The fact that all deviations from a normal dividend are public also works as an important incentive in practice. Because the management of the government-company is released from the usual labour conditions in the public sector, it is also possible to make a relation between the realized efficiency-gains and the personnel income of the management. A separate question is how excessive margins of efficiency gains can be prevented. A few methods can be used for this.

The first method joins the system of full competition, whereby forced shopping is excluded. A second method is price regulation. By giving independence in a external way to parts in the public sector, we also have the automatic mechanism that efficiency gains, -that are by definition visible- can be put back to the general means by budget cuts or dividend payments.

Structural additional rents can also originate at the cost of the input factors labour and capital. As a consequence the quality of the service can be put at risk. Quality control, both related to input factors as to output and the production process is an essential part of privatization. Without these checks privatization can have negative consequences. A formal basis is needed to guarantee quality. This means that is quite possible that efficiency gains are only paid to the management if this has the approval of the quality officers. An example of such a quality check is a Board of Commissioners in the independent service.

The fear that large amounts of efficiency profits disappear in the pockets of private entrepreneurs is probably the most important reason why in practice external independence or internal independence is preferred to real privatization. But we should keep in mind that the absence of an adequate efficiency incentive in some kind of independent department within the government could influence the costs per unit within the public sector much more negative than the acceptance of a restricted - and therefor controllable - profit margin in an really independent service.

With external independence it is not really essential if there is a 100% government participation or not. The most important thing lies within the agreements or contracts between the government and the independent service. Moreover financial goals - for example less pressure on government means involving investments - can be a reason to consult the private sector into the production process.

The differences between internal and external independence remains limited if we form internal independence by dropping the hierarchical supervision regarding decisions of the management of a service over separate expenditures on appliances and personnel. The management of the service gets the command over an undifferentiated budget in this system. This implies that the efficiency elements of the production process should be guaranteed by the same demands that are stated with external independence, except for the fact that a statutory body is not necessary to sanction failures.

Some kind of statutory body is necessary if we want to have an adequate efficiency incentive within internal independence to skim overprofits. The "agency"-body is suggested for this, but it is not known yet if this form is also effective in practice.

If casting off, contracting off, and independence want to be a success, a few success conditions are necessary to get these forms of privatization introduced. The most important are:

- the management of the department must experience the system as useful
- the employees of the service must have an interest in the system
- the goals of the output must be clear for all parties, and
- there should be a good management-information system which can serve as basis for management decisions.

Next to that the culture of such a service should change too. The organisation culture of a conditioning, ruling and controlling government does not allow a culture that is necessary to deliver concrete products in an effective and efficient way. Practice shows that culture is often the main cause of failing reorganizations like privatization.

Privatization is a difficult process and does not take place because of general theoretical arguments pro and contra, but because politicians and civil servants are forced or feel forced to do this. If they do not feel forced the arguments against privatization can prevail. For example, privatization can mean a loss of jobs or quality of service in the government. A third reason is that privatization can be enormously expensive. For example, it can happen that a company gets a contract against a very low price. After some time the price rises. Since the party contracting out does not have the knowledge and technology anymore to do it itself, the government is forced to accept the price hike. A fourth argument that is used is that companies do not bother about non-economic values, like a clean environment and a fifth argument at last concerns social policy: a private company would burden its personnel sooner and more often and lay off easier than a government service. These arguments are very important in practice.

In what way we can use the theory of this paragraph in the armed forces is the subject of the next paragraph.

§ 7.2.2. The privatization of the armed forces

If we want to use the theory, described in paragraph 7.2.1., in practice, it is necessary to take a close look at the main elements of the theory. Hereby we follow the criteria that are set up by Kraan.

The first point is that the desired quality and quantity of the produced service, in our case defense, is sufficient stable over a long time. Although the international security situation has been moving the last few years and the public good defense gets a different appearance, there is no discussion concerning the instability of the provision. In the heart of the matter protection against influences from outside will always be necessary. The stability of the public good defense can be regarded as satisfactory nowadays.

This offers us the possibility to analyze the other elements. This analysis will not be precise, because a complete analysis will be out of the scope of the paragraph. The scope of this paragraph is to draw the general structure of privatization of the armed forces to see if privatization can improve the interaction between society and the armed forces.

The first step to do this is to define the final product of the armed forces in such a way that this output can be measured. From the definition of the final product we can deduct a few intermediate products which are necessary to really produce the final product. After that the different products should be attached to costprices. In order to calculate these costprices per unit the financial administration should be organized in such a way, that this administration can be used to generate costprices. At places were the armed forces still use a cash register bookkeeping the financial administration should be transformed into in a cost- and benefit bookkeeping.

The third step is then that the armed forces are divided in different service and production centers, that can get internal or external independence. Where possible services can be contracted out. The last essential thing that should be done is giving body to the quality protection institutions.

The armed forces produce combat power. Combat power is an abstract product, which is delivered to an unusual market: the security market. Combat power is formed by the presence of capital and labour. If we want to measure combat power we will discover some problems. Combat power is not directly measurable, so we have to find an alternative way to measure production, that can bring an indicator for the abstract concept of combat power.

Combat power is necessary to keep possible enemies out. If we really want to be successful in this, it means that the armed forces should be usable in such a way that they can resist the enemy. The combination of capital and labour must be effective, if we really want to speak about actual usability of the armed forces. To resist the enemy the armed forces have to exercise. By exercising, at a given moment they will have such a quality that they can be used within a certain time and they are so strong that they can resist the enemy. In other words the amount of exercising days can be seen as an indicator for the product combat power. How many days is necessary for every unit, until they get the quality certificate is different of course. When defining the product combat power the amount of exercising days that is normal now per unit can be taken as a starting point.

In a static situation the already present amount of personnel and material would have been enough to produce combat power. However, exercising costs time, and with time going on contracts of personnel pass trough, material breaks down and material has to be replaced because of aging. Moreover, during an exercise several raw and additional resources are used to allow production means to function, like food, clothes and petrol.

If a production unit, like a brigade or a paramedic battalion, wants to function it needs intermediate products, that serve as an input. These products need to be produced also. When we take a better look at these intermediate products we first take a look at the capital side of the combat power production process. In the armed forces people use buildings, grounds and machines. These material products are easy to distinguish. They are not abstract, but really there, like the building in the barracks.

The building of barracks, maintenance places, hangars etc., costs money, but the maintenance of all these kinds of buildings should also be brought into account. The costs of these buildings can be transformed into a costprice per unit used in the building. This costprice can then serve as a norm price for everyone who wants to use a building or a part of that building. The norm price can be put into account by a building service to the client. When calculating the value of a building in order to make up the cost price, the "opportunity costs" of the building can serve as a starting point for the calculations. This can be done to solve problems connected to the derivation of a cost price of these buildings.

When choosing what kind of privatization the building service fits, it is necessary to take a look first at the general security risks, which are attached to a service like the armed forces. The armed forces are an institute set up to keep external factors out. The enemy, competitor, must be held out of the door. It must not be in a position to get any information about the way the armed forces specifies its strategy and primary execution of the job. The further a unit is working outside the strategic decision process, the less it will be necessary to put that unit under direct hierarchical supervision. In the strategic decision process the use of the combination of capital and labour, combat power, is central. Without strategy of the armed forces a tank is nothing else than a bunch of steel on caterpillar tracks, which cannot be really used. Many products for the armed forces are not made by the armed forces itself, but by civil companies. Companies who benefit from there own protection of their products, otherwise the competitor will take it away and use it.

If we make a classification on the basis of the security risks of units that can be privatized in a certain way, then the strategy units will always be a part of the department. Combat units can get internal independence, because they can expect direct political orders and they possess the possibilities of using their violence monopoly. Direct hierarchical supervision is needed in this case. The suppliers of combat units can be privatized by external independence, whereby we can think about contracting off, if a large amount of competition can be expected in the supply of specific services or goods. A building service can be privatized by external independence, because the security risk is low. Buildings are built by private contractors, while these contractors have a comparative advantage on other contractors for specialized products like army buildings, which they can get by building theses buildings, and don't want to loose by being careless. For a building service it is desirable to be privatized externally, because in this way it can strengthen its way to finance certain things. In the statutory body of a unlimited company it is easier for the building service to get loans in the capital market.

Especially for a service where the good to be produced is a capital good, it is necessary that external finance is one of the possibilities, because in this way it can handle market changes in a flexible way. The market meant here is of course the market for security.

If the Defense-building-service-INC. wants to work efficient, it is necessary that enough incentives are found within the service that can help to let it be efficient. Theory states that for getting real incentives in services like the armed forces it is necessary that the personal income of the management is attached to the efficiency gains of the service, if we want to get the efficiency gains really visible. This theoretical statement should be put into practice, if we really want to see something. However, there must also be enough "checks-and-balances" build into the system, to secure that the efficiency gains are not acquired by “hurting” personnel and the quality of the buildings.

The quality control of the personnel can for example be ruled by taking up delegates of the personnel in a Council of Commissioners, that has to decide finally about the awarding of a part of the efficiency gains to the management of the Defense-building-service-INC.. In the Council of Commissioners also space can be made for member of the General Auditing Chamber, The Ministry of Defense and members of parliament to secure the quality of the service.

The quality of the Defense-building-service-INC. is also under control of its clients. These could be the combat units, but also other users. Problem in the relation between the clients and the Defense-building-service-INC. is that often a situation of forced shopping with each other will exist and a situation of a bilateral monopoly can not be avoided. This is because mostly there is only one supplier and one demander. For example, it is not allowed for combat units to establish themselves where they want, and buildings of the Defense-building-service INC. often have such a specific use that alternative use is impossible. The marketmechanism can not work here, so some kind of price regulation is necessary. The task of the council of commissioners of the Defense-building-service-INC., but also the council of commissioners of the clients, is to see if norm- or internal accounting prices are not the result of crooked positions of power.

Another necessary intermediate product is the use of grounds. Grounds should be equipped for exercises before they can be used. Grounds will also be used as a building site for barracks and other buildings. In this case the Defense-grounds-service-INC. is a supplier of the Defense-building-service-INC.. Price agreements should be based on the norm costs per unit ground, whereby some kind of regulation will also be necessary here. This price regulation is not necessary for the prices of the suppliers to the Defense-grounds-service-INC., which supply services and goods like guarding the ground or road construction. The Defense-grounds-service-INC. can be privatized by external independence. It will be managed and supervised in the same way as the Defense-building-service-INC..

A third group of products on the material side of the armed forces company is the stock of machines that is necessary to make all products in the armed forces. These machines do not only include tanks, F-16-fighters and frigates, but also the fork-lift trucks in the warehouses, the computers in the defense offices and the software for the computers. In principle the machine part of the armed forces deals with mobile capital goods that are supplied by the material service and used by various other parts of the armed forces.

Here, external independence of a Defense-machine-service-INC. is also the way to handle the machines in an efficient way. Besides, this Government-INC. can handle more flexible with investment requests from other parts of the armed forces, because external independence offers it the opportunity to use external finance.

The fourth group are the raw and additional materials that are necessary for the production of combat power. It concerns 'consumer goods' here, like clothes, kerosene, office equipment etc. The service that should deliver these products is actually nothing else than a purchase bureau, comparable to the Dutch Rijksinkoopbureau. It hires its buildings from the Defense-housing-service-INC., the machines from the Defense-machine-service-INC. and the grounds from the Defense-grounds-service-INC.. The logistic task of the Defense-goods-service-INC. costs money. These costs are reflected in the prices of the goods, that have to be paid by its customers. If the prices of the Defense-goods-service-INC. are the right prices, can be discovered by comparing prices of branch partners in civil society. When auditing the other Defense-service-INC.s, this is also a way to see if monopoly or other power relations are not abused in practice. But it should be kept in mind, that this is very difficult because of often lacking civil partners.

Up until now we have taken a look at four Defense companies. Three of the four companies deal with investment and capital goods. If we want to keep these goods in good condition, adequate maintenance is necessary. Neither buildings, grounds or machines will survive long without maintenance. Maintenance companies are available in large amounts in civil society. Although not every company would have the knowledge directly to maintain a F-16 fighter, a large amount of competition can be expected in this market. Because maintenance is again a step further away from the strategic decision process, maintenance is one of the parts of the 'armed forces company' that can be done by private initiative. The privatization form of contracting out is probably the most suitable form of privatization here. Competition will keep the prices for maintenance having a real basis. No extra supervision is necessary on quality, like is done in the Defense-service-INC.s. If a maintenance company does not fulfil the expectations, the replacement should already be there. The costs of maintenance will be charged at the account of the Defense companies. These companies will reflect the costs in their prices, that will be paid by their clients.

Graphically we can draw the relations between the combat units, Defense companies and maintenance companies, as done in scheme 7.1. The uninterrupted lines are flows of goods, while the interrupted lines represent the flows of money. The scheme is not complete, because mutual flows of goods between the several Defense companies are not drawn here. Besides this, it can be possible that the maintenance companies use buildings and machines that are possessed by respectively the Defense-building-service-INC. and the Defense-machine-service-INC.. Next to that we have the building contractors, the weapons producers, guarding service, which should also have a place in the scheme.

On the personnel side, we can also distinct a few intermediate products, just like we have done on the capital side of the combat power production process. We shall analyze these products by following the life cycle of a soldier in the armed forces.

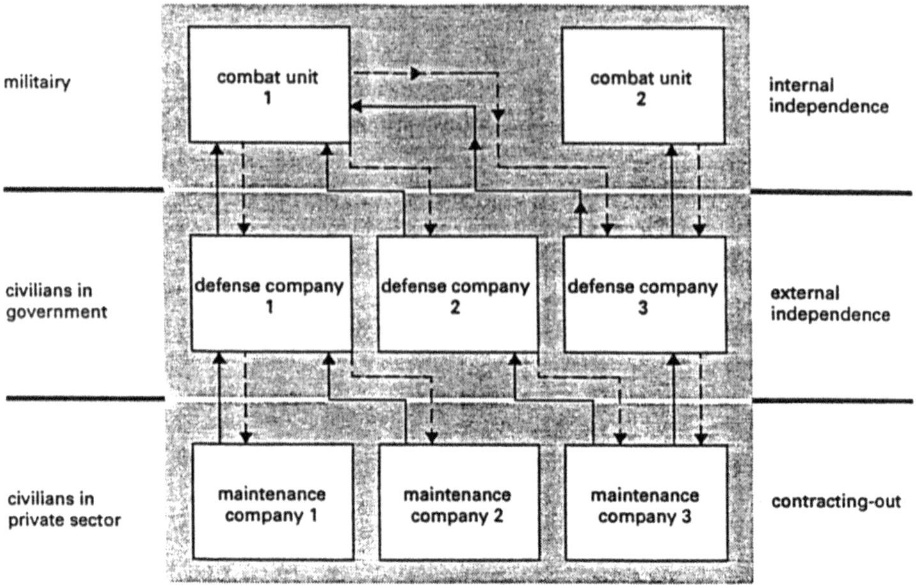

SCHEDULE 7.1 The link between combat units, defense companies and maintenance companies

This life cycle starts with the recruitment and selection of a military. Next, this soldier has to be trained, if he or she wants to meet the function demands that are necessary for producing sufficient combat power. After the training the military will be in active service. After his active service the military retires or leaves to a job in civil society.

In chapter 6 we had a lengthy discussion about the question of recruitment and selection of military. One of the problems we have seen there is that the wishes of a military are not picked up correctly by the armed forces. We also saw that a large amount of volunteers is refused, while actually there should be no real reason to do it that way. The cause of this indifference in policy has partly to do with the absence of incentives to handle really efficiently. Incentives that are among other reasons absent because of conscription.

Recruitment of new volunteers costs money. Expensive advertisement campaigns are constructed to attract volunteers. The selection of volunteers also costs a lot of money. The more volunteers are refused, it will be necessary to put more money in recruitment campaigns and selection efforts. If there are no incentives to maximize the differences between the real costs and the budget, this process will go on until the moment the budget is completely spent. Bureaucrats strive for budget maximization and in their pursuit of this they will argue that the quality of the recruited soldier is above all. This despite the practical observation[15] that the quality of soldiers only differs a little when they are at

15 See chapter 6, paragraph 3.1.

work and if even there really is a difference, this difference can be cleared by additional training.

If we regard recruitment and selection as a separate product, we can see what kind of possibilities there are to improve the production process of this good. Recruitment and selection is meant to bring a volunteer that is suitable to be trained to a soldier, or to be employed in another Defense company. The costs that are made for recruitment and selection can be transformed in a cost price per suitable volunteer. This norm price is then charged to the client in the armed forces company. If the recruitment and selection institute is put into the mold of a government INC. the management of this Recruitment-and-Selection-Institute-INC. is allowed to get some parts of the efficiency gains of the institute. If it is really sensitive for this profit it will probably be prepared to approve the suitability of a volunteer more quickly, because by doing this its costs are put down. The allocation of efficiency gains to the management of the Recruitment-and-Selection-Institute-INC. brings an incentive to hire volunteers, that would not have been selected otherwise.

In this process the Recruitment-and-Selection-Institute-INC. does not have a free hand, because it really depends on its clients. The Defense-Training-Institute-INC. and also the combat units will try to bring some counter pressure to avoid volunteers with low quality, because this will cause too many drop-outs. Drop-outs should be replaced again and these replacements cost a lot of money. On the other side the Defense-Training-Institute and the combat unit profit from a low cost price per suitable volunteer, because a low cost price is often connected with a lower salary. This is because, the refusal of volunteers has as a consequence that new volunteers must be found in a higher salary category. The sooner volunteers are hired, the faster recruitment costs are saved and the more economic rents connected with price skimming can be earned by the armed forces. The Defense-Training-Institute-INC. has a smaller incentive to do this, because a volunteer spends only a few months in training. However, in general the Defense-Training-Institute-INC. also profits when the suitable volunteer has a low cost price.

The Recruitment-and-Selection-Institute-INC. can be privatized by external independence. The supervision on the quality aspect is largely arranged by the market process. However, this institute only has a few clients, so it is advisable to allocate an important role to the Council of Commissioners here.

After the volunteer is declared suitable many of them will go to the training institute to be trained as a soldier, officer or other function that is necessary within the armed forces. The Defense-Training-Institute-INC. has the trained volunteer as a product. Training will differ per function. By taking the function demands per function as a starting point a few activities have to be done before a volunteer gets the mark 'trained'. The function demands will differ per function. This means that the costs per trained volunteer will differ also. If the management of the Defense-Training-Institute-INC. is stimulated by the allocation of possible efficiency gains, they will take care of the fact that volunteers have to do certain activities that do not fit with the function demands for a certain function. On the one hand these unnecessary activities cost money, but on the other side these activities can lead to a situation that the volunteer drops out, so that the costs will rise again.

The clients of the Defense-Training-Institute-INC. will also have an incentive to keep the cost price of the volunteer as low as possible, so from that side there will be pressure to restrict the training to the strictly necessary activities for the fulfiling of the functions.

The product of the Defense-Training-Institute-INC. is not restricted to the training of volunteers. It also has a task concerning long term suitability of the soldier, officer, material expert, UN-volunteer etc. or to take care of the situation that people in the armed forces fulfil the function demands to get up in the organisation. All the activities cost money, which are charged to the bill of the clients. These can be production-units or Defense companies, but also individual persons. The amount of products that the Defense-Training-Institute-INC. will take care of will be large. In chapter 6 we have seen that the training can not be limited to strictly military training, but space should also be created for additional civil education programmes and UN-training programmes. These trainings are necessary to fulfil the tasks of different parts of the armed forces, but also to keep salary costs down.

For the civil education programme and the UN-training applies that the clients will try to keep the activities for the training restricted to those activities that are necessary for the aims of the training. The Defense-Training-Institute-INC. does not have a free hand in these programmes either.

Finally the soldier will be in active duty in a combat unit. The combat unit is the place where the personnel side and the capital side come clearly together. Combat units have a monopoly on violence and should therefore be under strict supervision of the minister of Defense. External independence is not a possibility here. However, a combat unit is suitable for internal independence. Every combat unit gets a budget from the general budget. With this budget it has to fulfil the production norms for that unit in terms of exercising days. Combat units also will try to be efficient with their money, if the efficiency gains are in some way attached to the personal income of the management.

Combat units can be found in the production chain of the armed forces at the end of this chain. Special cases not considered, combat units can not get prices for their product. This has to do with the good characteristics of the defense of the common good, which are described in chapter 2. The combat units get their money from the general budget. With this money they buy their trained volunteers from the Defense-Training-Institute-INC., they hire their buildings from the Defense-Building-Service-INC. etc.

For a clear and efficient management it is necessary that the combat units are not too big. In the Army we can think about a brigade as a internal independent unit, in the Air Force we can think about a wing and in the Navy we can think about a task force. Other classifications are also possible.

In order to get an efficient management it is also necessary that the contacts with all suppliers are controlled adequately. Because this work can be a large burden for the top of a combat unit, it is advisable to assist the top of the combat unit by a administrative unit. This unit is responsible for the financial and logistic administration of a combat unit. It can also handle things that connect the logistics of two combat units, like the transportation of military from the barracks to a railway station. For these activities it naturally has to be paid.

The budgets which the suppliers to the combat unit use do not come from the regular budget. They have to earn their money independently and have to cover their costs with the revenues they get from their sales. For suppliers that have fierce competition from civil society this may be an unstable basis, but if they deliver good quality for a reasonable prices they must be able to survive.

The presented decentralized structure of the armed forces leaves a number of tasks that are presently done by the central organisation to the Defense-institutes and companies. For the central organisation of the armed forces a few tasks remain, of which the decision making role about the strategy of the combat units is the most important one. Part of this strategy is to keep unity of policy within the combat units. For example, it can never be the case that the same sort of combat units use different weapon systems.

The analyses of the international security situation is also a task that remains for the central organisation. From the financial tasks the allocation of budgets to the combat units according to norm prices is the most important one. The allocation of budgets to training, material etc., decays, because this task is taken over by the price mechanism. It is off course true that part of the financial work that was done in the past by the central organisation, is taken over now by the decentralized organisations. Concerning the quality controls and places in the several Councils of Commissioners, it is recommendable that financial experts of the central organisation get a place in these councils, because they ought be able to fathom the several norm prices and possible power situations.

From the personnel policy only the general personnel policy stays in the hands of the central organisation. The exact making of the personnel policy will be in the hands of the decentralized organisation parts, whereby every unit gets its own responsibilities concerning the tasks they have to do. This means that the Recruitment-and-Selection-Institute-INC. makes its own policy regarding recruitment and selection, just like the Defense-Training-Institute-INC. does for training.

If we turn back to the combat units we see that a large amount of activities are solved and reported there, because in order to deliver measured goods and services the situation can best be solved at the spot where it is happening. Do we have to lengthen the contract of a soldier? What is the ideal length of a contract considering capacities, possibilities and costs that are connected to a specific soldier? If we really want to get an efficient armed forces, than measured goods and services are a requirement, whereby we can get this by privatization. Privatization brings a situation where the armed forces are divided in a lot of "companies", that each have their incentive to work as efficient as possible. Not every armed forces company will use these incentives in the same way or are able to use them, but the start of working efficiently is there. This will improve the social acceptance of the armed forces considerable, both in a general as in a specific sense.

Incentives are available to give the underprivileged in society a chance in the armed forces, incentives are available to prevent a situation that volunteers have to do activities that are not functional, incentives are available to substitute military for civilians, because civilians are much less costly than military. Incentives care for an increased dynamic and increased dynamics is nothing else than a better interaction between two phenomena, in this case the armed forces and society.

Privatization of the armed forces shows the different parts of the armed forces which costs are involved with their acts. By privatization they are made clear that they deal with scarce resources, which have great value in society. Privatization of the armed forces diminishes the "free-rider" behaviour of the several units, because they are responsible for the costs and not another part of the armed forces, like in a situation without privatization.

It is the "free-rider" behaviour of certain units than can bring dangers for society. Although by privatization the dangers of for example a coup d'état can not be excluded, it can bring the feeling that such an action brings large social costs, that will finally be put on the account of the unit that pursued an action. Besides, combat units are largely dependent of government-INC.s. If they want to execute social unfriendly activities, they will need a lot of these companies behind them to succeed.

Before we finish this paragraph with a few schemes of the remaining central tasks of the armed forces, we still have to finish the life cycle of a military. After his active duty in a combat unit, he will leave this unit. If he retires, he won't be confronted anymore directly with the armed forces. He gets his pension from a pension fund, and that is it. If the military leaves the combat unit to work in civil society, he often likes the help that can be given to find a job. In this case the armed forces will have to take care in some form for the product "changing to civil society". When we talk about civil society, it is not necessary to look only outside the armed forces. It can be possible that there is a job in one of the Defense-companies. Because the costs of the product "change to civil society" can be attributed to a combat unit, the costs should also be attributed to that combat unit.

The central tasks of the armed forces will be executed by the combat units. The tasks it gets from the Ministry of Defense. The Ministry investigates the demand for security on the international security market, the armed forces delivers the supply (see scheme 7.2.). In this scheme the present structure of the Ministry of Defense, which has a place for both Army, Navy and Air Force is loosened.

The combat units use inputs on the personnel and on the material side. The combat units are central in the armed forces 'company'. This is expressed in scheme 7.3.. In scheme 7.3. only the mentioned directs suppliers to the combat units are taken. The catering, medical, psychological and social services are in practice available, but are not shown here for reasons of clearness of both the story and the scheme.

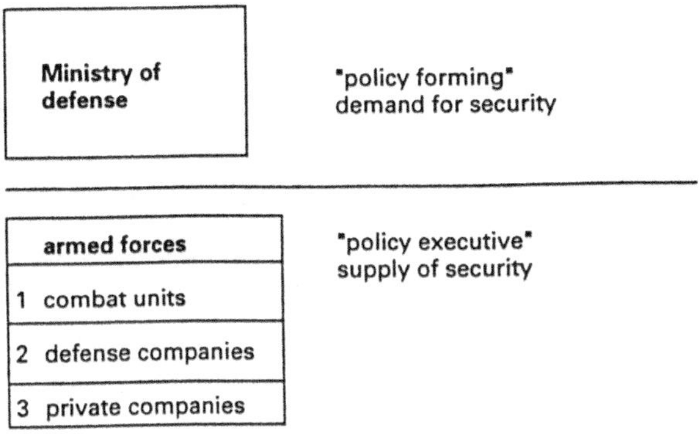

SCHEDULE 7.2 Demand and supply for security

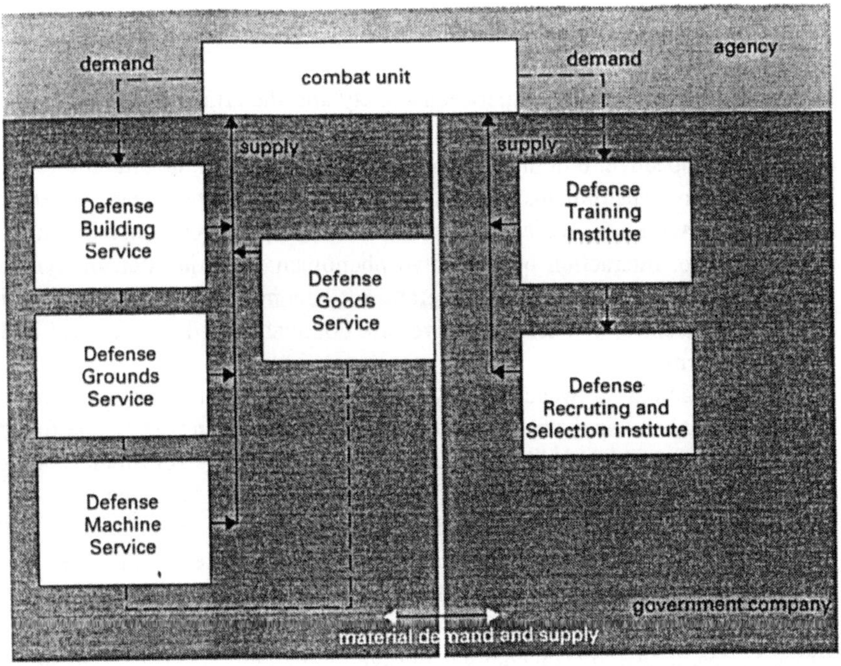

SCHEDULE 7.3 The link between combat-units and defense-companies

At last we have the several external independent companies that play an important role in the combat power production process, like the private firms. Scheme 7.4. is the last scheme in the privatization process, which started in scheme 7.2. from Ministry to agency, in scheme 7.3. from agency to government-INC. and in scheme 7.4. from government-INC. to private firm.

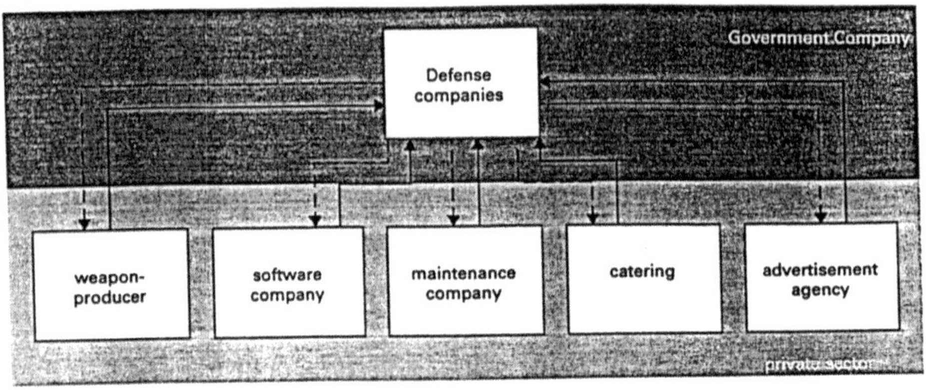

SCHEDULE 7.4 The link between the government company and the private sector

§ 7.3. Conclusions and final remarks

In this chapter the interaction between society and the armed forces was central. The interaction between society and the armed forces is approached from an economic perspective. It pointed at the internal dynamics of the armed forces and looked for those instruments that can take care of a situation that connects the armed forces with civil society in a suitable way, even when conscription is not there anymore. Interaction between two phenomena is a question of dynamics between the two. From economic literature it becomes clear that dynamics is a question of incentives. Where incentives are not available, dynamics will be lost in the long term.

The interaction between society and the armed forces is a search for incentives that can benefit from this interaction. These incentives can be found to give subordinates the possibility to operate independently from their superiors. Subordinates should be given the possibility to resist the superiors openly without repercussions for the subordinates. Examples are the promotion on the basis of objective measures and the possibility to quit whenever one likes.

Privatization is another possibility to improve the interaction in the armed forces. Privatization not only brings a better interaction between society and the armed forces, it also gives incentives to save tax money. Social benefits go hand in hand with budgetary gains.

In this chapter we have seen how privatization of the armed forces in peace-time can be organized. Besides this, the organisation structure is very much suitable in a war-time situation, whereby we should say that in war-time effectivity is prevalent and the efficiency aspect goes to the background temporarily. However, the dropping of the efficiency aspects is only valid for those situations that are directly threatening for the sovereignty of the own society.

If we have to deal with executing UN-tasks, than the allocation of extra budget is the way to finance these tasks, where efficiency rules are valid. If privatization of the armed forces is really feasible in practice, is a question of a complete other order. Privatization is technically possible, but the culture of the armed forces is a factor that should really be kept in mind. A lot of privatization processes failed because the culture of the unit to be privatized did not meet the requirements to privatize. In the next chapter that deals with the transformation of a conscription force to an all-volunteer force, we shall further discuss this important issue.

CHAPTER 8

The transformation of a conscription force into an all-volunteer force

"Under the volunteer army, there is no reason why we couldn't maintain a "stand-by" draft - a reserve mechanism to be called upon only in case of national emergency."
James C. Miller, A volunteer army for America, In: Miller J. (ed.), Why the Draft, the Case for the Volunteer Force, Baltimore, 1968, pp. 185.

The Dutch constitution, article 97, states:

"Alle Nederlanders daartoe in staat, zijn verplicht mede te werken tot handhaving van de onafhankelijkheid van het Rijk en tot de verdediging van zijn grondgebied".[1]

The constitution continues in article 98:

"Tot bescherming van de belangen van de staat is een krijgsmacht, bestaande uit vrijwillig dienenden en uit dienstplichtigen",[2]

From this formulation we can read that the armed forces always need conscripts, and that an all-volunteer force is constitutionally not possible. Article 98, section 1 of the constitution was formed in 1887 and intended to give conscription its constitutional basis. However, it was not intended in 1887 to oblige the legislator to fill the armed forces with conscripts actually if there was technically speaking no need to do this.[3] This means that there are no legal restrictions to transform a conscription army in the Netherlands into an all-volunteer force and vice versa.

Nevertheless the Council of State said that the abolition of conscription can not become reality without changing the constitution. She reaches this conclusion on the basis of the statement that the constitution uses the word "conscripts", and that the armed forces can not do constitutionally without conscripts. If we want to abolish conscription, according to the Council of State, the constitution has to

---

1 "All Dutch people, who are able, are obliged to cooperate in maintaining the independence of the Kingdom en the defense of its territory".

2 "To protect the interests of the state there are armed forces, consisting of volunteers and conscripts".

3 See N.H.M. Roos, NRC-Handelsblad, 3 november 1992, opinionpage

be changed. However, a few remarks can be made regarding this statement of the Council of State.

Conscription is an institution, consisting of a few elements. The first element is the registration of the conscript, then the conscript is tested, before the conscript is obliged to turn up for his first exercise. After the first exercise the conscripts has to go to the revision exercise. Abolishing conscription mainly concerns the termination of the enlistment procedure and the revision exercises. The obligation to register and test can always remain and are also in an all-volunteer force part of the personnel system in the armed forces. Conscripts are put at distance in this way in the armed forces, but are still part of the institution armed forces. If we interpret "conscripts" thus, a change of the constitution would not necessary at all. Conscripts would still be part of the armed forces, although not physically present. Apparently the Council of State was of a different opinion.

This chapter will consider the conversion question that is connected with the transformation of a conscription army into an all-volunteer force. Therefore we first take a look at the moment when a conscription army can be transformed into an all-volunteer force. Important is that this transformation has a political basis. The question here is in what way the welfare positions of individuals in our society are influenced by the transformation of a conscription force into an all-volunteer force. In paragraph 1.5. we have put the welfare positions of four groups central. If we consider the chapters so far, we have seen that the transformation of a conscription force into an all-volunteer forces, improves the welfare position of conscripts (chapter 4). The position of the general taxpayer also improves, because in an all-volunteer force the excess-burden of the conscription-tax disappears (chapter 5). Besides this the armed forces are confronted with the real costs of conscription and real scarcity of labour when conscription is abolished. This will lead to a situation wherein the interaction between society and the armed forces will improve in stead of deteriorating (chapter 7) and also to a qualitatively better armed forces, because scarce labour leads to a situation where the armed forces have to take their personnel seriously. If they do not perform in this way they mostly hurt themselves (chapter 6). The welfare position of all four groups improve in the long term. In other words, we clearly see a Pareto-improvement, that takes care of a situation where it is politically possible to change a conscription force into an all-volunteer force.

The chapter will also concern itself with the instruments that can be used in the conversion process, in order to make the transformation a success. Special attention will be paid to the transformation of a central lead organization into a decentralized organization, as described in chapter 7. We will also take a look at the reserve units. At last we will consider the change of culture that the armed forces have to deal with, if the transformation process will be brought to a good end. The legacy of conscription cannot stay too long, if we want the all-volunteer force to be effective and efficient.

§ 8.1. The choice between a conscription force and an all-volunteer force

Every society will try to defend itself against intruders. If a choice has to be made how to organize this defense, the question will be asked if we want to use a conscription force or an all-volunteer force. This question is more difficult to answer, than at first we might think.

As we have seen in chapter 4 and 5, an all-volunteer force nowadays is to be preferred over a conscription force in, because the costs of an all-volunteer force are lower than the costs of a conscription force. Besides, we have seen in chapter 6 and 7 that also on other grounds, the quality of the armed forces and the interaction between society and the armed forces do not bring problems, if the right instruments are used.

An all-volunteer force is efficient in using its production factors. It does not traverse the free choice between labour and capital, whereby the relative prices of these production factors are not disturbed and their is no excess-burden. The filling of the positions in an all-volunteer force is achieved by self-selection and therefore excludes the possibility that the opportunity costs of a volunteer are higher than the wage costs. In the used cost concept opportunity costs have been the central link. These opportunity costs also play an important role in determining, when the choice for an all-volunteer force or conscription force can be opportune.

Other than to the cost of the armed forces, a lot of emphasis is also put on the flexibility of the armed forces and the choice between a conscription force and an all-volunteer force. The choice between both possibilities can not be changed at any given moment. A choice that has been made, must last for quite a while. People say about an all-volunteer force that this kind of force is expensive and inflexible. Considering the costs of an all-volunteer force we have said already a lot. Budgetary an all-volunteer-force can be expensive. This will surely be true in times of military expansion. Socially an all-volunteer force is not expensive at all, and also in financial terms the costs can be controlled quite reasonable. When the armed forces are expanding the armed forces need to attract a higher part of the labour supply, what in terms of "economic rent" can be very expensive. But the use of temporary bonuses can take care of a situation where the extra economic rents can be controlled. Flexibility in an all-volunteer force can also be achieved with the help of bonuses without disturbing the normal salary structure.

The advantages of conscription lie mainly in a larger amount of flexibility and security. In addition, conscription brings the armed forces financial saving during war times. In peace times these financial gains play a subordinate role, because they pale into significance compared with the social costs of conscription. In war times this can be different, because in a situation of complete mobilization the complete national wealth is in jeopardy. During such times the social value of production factors exceeds their market value, during which the installation of conscription is opportune.

In terms of opportunity costs the choice between a conscription force and an all-volunteer force can be translated into the question when the opportunity costs for society in terms of war damage to people and capital stock are bigger than the opportunity cost for soldiers. Thereby we should keep in mind that the damage to people and capital stock will be zero during peace times, small during a restricted action and will be very large in the case of an invasion.

The opportunity costs for the soldiers will always be bigger in a conscription force, than in an all-volunteer force, but the damage to people and capital stock will always be bigger in an all-volunteer force than in a conscription force. Algebraically the opportunity costs of the soldiers in a conscription force (OCDs) can be given as follows:

$$OCDs = a_1 + b_1 X \qquad (8.1)$$

whereby X is a measure for safety, that can be translated in the amount of soldiers that is necessary. If $X = 0$ than the situation is very save and if $X = 1$ there is an invasion happening.

The damage to the people and the capital stock in a conscription force (OCDm) given by the following equation:

$$OCDm = (d_1 e^X)/(1-X) \qquad (8.2)$$

In a relative safe situation ($X = 0$) there is d1 damage and in a situation whereby $X = 1$ the damage is rather big.

The total costs in a conscription force OCD now are:

$$OCD = OCDs + OCDm \qquad (8.3)$$

For an all-volunteer force, the same kind of relation applies:

$$OCDv = a_2 + b_2 X \qquad (8.4)$$

and

$$OCDm = (d_2 e^X)/(1-X) \qquad (8.5)$$

whereby $a_2 < a_1$, $b_2 < b_1$, en $d_2 > d_1$

The total costs here are:

$$OCV = OCVs + OCVm \qquad (8.6)$$

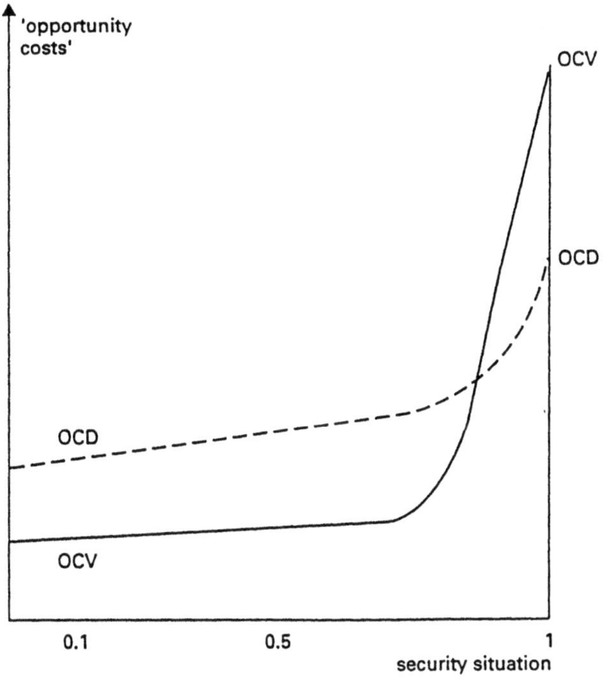

FIGURE 8.1 The costs of a volunteer force and a conscription force

Graphically the equations 8.3. and 8.6. can be shown in figure 8.1., in which the dotted line shows the costs in a conscription force and the uninterrupted line pictures the costs in an all-volunteer force. From figure 8.1. it becomes clear that the point of transformation must be there, where the damage to people and capital stock cannot be resisted anymore by attracting additional volunteers with any kind of incentive whatsoever. However, it is very difficult to show the real point of transformation. This point is connected with the possibilities of an invasion.

When an invasion occurs the costs are the highest possible, and conscription would have to be used as a way of defense. However, if we introduce conscription at the point of invasion it could be too late already. However, if we take the technological possibilities to foresee an invasion in consideration, we might say that an invasion will never be really unexpected, and besides this, all combat power to resist an invasion mainly depends on the available materials. If the combat material is not present anymore, a soldier cannot do much. There probably will only be place for carrying a gun and a uniform. Shooting can be learned in a short time and the practice of war makes everyone experienced with these kinds of material in a short time. So, conscription is not directly necessary in an invasion. On the basis of voluntary enlistment very much can be done, because in our world the amount of soldiers and the speed whereby these soldiers can be used in the armed forces, do not reflect upon the combat power of these armed forces. Combat power is a combination of capital and labour, whereby both components are equally important.

In this social cost-benefit analysis we can only speak in terms of insecurity about the costs of an all-volunteer force or a conscription force. Therefore we can not use a sensitivity analysis in this case, like Frank H. Knight made clear in his "Risk, uncertainty and profit". He states that sensitivity analysis can only be executed, if the specific chances of certain occasions are known. The international security situation does not know these chances, off course.

In conclusion we can state that the choice between a conscription force and an all-volunteer force, is only favorable to a conscription force, if the freedom and security of society is in very big danger and an invasion can not be stopped anymore by the regular armed forces with the help of their combat material and professional soldiers.

For conscription as a formal rule this does not mean, that conscription has to disappear from the constitution, if there is no conscription army. In an all-volunteer force conscription still exists, only there are no conscripts present. The obligation to show up in this case evaporates. In an all-volunteer force registration and testing of potential conscripts still remains. The registration and testing of conscription takes care of a situation, that the armed forces can always fall back on conscripts. They are available at a distance and are in such a way part of the armed forces. The choice between a conscription force and an all-volunteer force practically means the choice between enlistment or not. A choice which can be made without problems regarding the constitutionality.

§ 8.2. The transition of a conscription army into an all-volunteer force

From the preceding paragraphs in this chapter we have seen the attractiveness of an all-volunteer force. If we would have had such a volunteer force, it would worth a lot to keep such an army. However, it will be a gigantic task to transform a conscription force into an all-volunteer force, because the transition of one system to another system can be accompanied by gigantic costs. For the transition to an all-volunteer force a few adaptations are necessary. These adaptations have to do with to transition of a central lead system, the conscription force, into an all-volunteer force, that has the characteristics of a market system. Adaptations that deal with a change of combat power, will not be discussed here although they are present in the practical situation. This is because the change of combat power will only results in a change in dimension, not in a change of system. The adaptations that are needed, because the amount of combat power declines, will only be of size, not of another character.

The first step that is necessary to structure an all-volunteer force is to raise the salaries of conscripts to the level of professional military. This salary rise has three dimensions. First, the visible higher wage has a genuine effect on the attractiveness of the soldier's job. Because of a higher wage the supply of volunteers will rise, merely to the fact that the present conscripts get a better view on their current job. They get paid according to the value of their job, so their labour is much more liked also.

The second dimension of a wage increase is that the use of conscripts becomes more visible. Because the real costs of military labour is visible, a process will be started, which takes care of a situation that military labour is substituted by capital and civil labour. In chapter 5 we have seen that this process can lead to huge costs savings, if the conscript is not only seen as an expensive production factor, but also as an scarce production factor. A wage increase gives us the necessary incentives for the substitution process, but is not a sufficient of itself yet.

A third dimension of a wage increase is the compensation of income, that conscripts loose during their service time. This wage increase will not compensate their losses completely, because not everyone's opportunity costs are equal. Moreover, the wage rise to the level of professional military cannot offer compensation for things like the "sick-to-death"-premium and the loss of income that appears after the service time is over. However, the compensation will have its effect on the avoidance of the conscription tax. The compensation decreases the burden of conscription considerably, whereby avoidance behaviour will also decrease. This will certainly be so if the compensation in money also covers the "sick-to-death"-premium.

The rise of the wages to the professional level costs money, but it also delivers the necessary incentives to start an all-volunteer force. How much money is involved depends on the transition time of changing a conscription force into an all-volunteer force. On the one side we have a price effect, that will cause a budget increase for the salaries of conscripts. On the other side we have a volume effect, because the amount of conscripts will decline. The total effect of the wage rise for the budget is obscure. Much will depend on the speed the conscripts will be replaced. Just after the wage increase there will be higher costs, but if this situation will take weeks, months or years depends on the effectivity of the reorganization process.

A wage increase to the level of professional soldiers can be arranged in a few days, the disappearance of the conscripts depends on the amount of civilians and volunteers that can be hired to take over the tasks of the conscripts. The production in the armed forces has to proceed, otherwise it cannot be used.

The abolition route of conscription starts with an analysis of the amount of units that are really necessary to produce the amount of combat power needed. Conscripts that fill positions that are not necessary anymore, can be sent home immediately, because they only deliver useless services. Conscripts that are present in non-combat positions, have to be replaced by civilians. The hiring of temporary personnel can be useful to get a smoothly transformation, because conscripts on non-combat functions only fulfil functions that do not need a lot of human capital. Drivers, copierhelp or waiters are the most appealing examples in this case.

The conscripts that fulfil useful combat functions, will have to serve the longest. Before these conscripts can go home, voluntary soldiers should be recruited and trained. This costs some time, but can be resolved within one and a half year after the decision has been taken to transform a conscription army into an all-volunteer force.

Conscripts are not the only people that disappear in the transformation process, but also certain positions for professional military will disappear. In order to avoid people being fired, some solutions are needed.

The first solution is that a few professional military take the positions of soldiers. On first side this looks like a demotion, however this is not necessarily so. The reason for this is that the function of soldier in the future armed forces is completely different from the function of soldier in the former conscription force.

The armed forces will have a lot of new tasks, that will demand a lot more from the soldier. Another reason is that the subsidiarity principle in the armed forces demands that the soldier himself is responsible for most of the actions he does. Therefore, the function of soldier in the future armed forces is much more equal to the function of non-commissioned officer in the conscription force than the word soldier may seem. The big difference between a conscription force and an all-volunteer force is that in an all-volunteer most supervising functions are gone, because the supervisors in an all-volunteers force do the work themselves. Another advantage of the subsidiarity principle in the armed forces is that this can improve the reconstitution ability of the armed forces. If the international security situation may worsen in such a way that a conscription force has to be introduced again, the soldiers in an all-volunteer force can be pushed forward to a supervising position in a conscription force.

The implementation of the subsidiarity principle in the armed forces will probably cause a culture shock, however, if the rules of subsidiarity and the contents of the new soldier function are explained and executed well, only a few problems remain that can most of the time be solved practically. It can be possible that the change of function of the soldier will require some additional training for the former non-commissioned officers, otherwise these people are not fit for the future tasks of the armed forces.

The use of former non-commissioned officers in future soldier functions does not have to be connected with a change a rank and therefore salary. A fact that will be important to a lot of people in the armed forces. It can mean though that some units will not have military personnel with the rank soldier in the transformation stage, but only former non-commissioned officers. This does not have to be an objection, if we are aware of the fact that the contents of the function is the essential thing in the armed forces and the rank of a person is nothing else than his or her salary.

A second option is to put superfluous soldiers into a labourpool. During the period that these soldiers stay in this internal labour reserve, they will be trained by the armed forces in order to make a smooth transition to civil society. They can probably be placed out of the labourpool into positions that become vacant in the armed forces or in new units. Main task of the labourpool is to keep the human capital of the superfluous military up to date and to prepare them for the new tasks of the armed forces or a place in civil society. Loss of human capital should be avoided as much as possible, while other forms of human capital should be built up.

After the first stage of the transformation of a conscription force into an all-volunteer force with the disappearance of the conscripts and the reorganization of the superfluous amount of professional military is over, the second stage starts. This second stage involves the transformation of non-combat forces that are still filled with military into positions for civilians.

This process can be done slowly with all accompanying efficiency losses, by waiting for the moment that the military in such positions will retire. It can also be done quicker by excluding the non-combat functions from rotation schedules. With rotation the armed forces want bring some variation into the activities of the military and to give the individual soldier a more satisfying and complete military career. After a few years serving in a unit the professional soldier leaves his unit and goes from one function to the other. From an armed forces perspective the use of rotation serves two principles: the filling of vacant positions and the maintenance of personnel management goals.

When filling the vacant positions in the armed forces it is important to recognize that vacant position do not exists because of deaths, dismissals or promotion. It is also important to recognize that military personnel often do not want to stay in positions that are located in remote areas. The fact that most of the time it is not possible to give military extra salary for this specific reason strengthens the requests to rotate. The bonuses that are given to military for staying out of the country are not pointed at financial compensation for less utility, but are given only for the extra costs that staying in a foreign country brings.

The servicemen regard the rotation system positively most of the times, however, for the armed forces there are also negative aspects involved. Because of the relative short time in a specific function, the professional soldier will not be a specialist in this function. His added value at an often evolving function will not be optimal therefore. Besides this rotation costs of lot of money in terms of removal and traveling costs. A few military will not like the rotation system. This amount of people will rise if the rotation system becomes compulsory. Compulsory rotation will cause people to quit, a situation that benefits nobody.

If we do not use the non-combat position anymore as a rotation place, this means that less positions are available for the servicemen. This also means that less soldiers are necessary and that less people have to rotate. In the long term the decrease of the amount of rotation places, will not lead to any problems. The rotating group becomes smaller on a smaller amount of functions. In the short run the solution has to be found in a longer stay in certain positions, rotation not only within the own unit, but over all possible combat positions, less intake of new soldiers and more intake in the specialists team that is necessary to execute the specialist tasks for the UN.

The fact that non-combat functions are not available anymore for rotation does not mean that military are not allowed to fill these positions anymore. The individual military is free to apply for a job in the non-combat part of the armed forces, when he feels that his career in the combat unit is coming to an end. In some cases the former military are very useful to go on as a civilian, because they possess a certain amount of human capital that is very useful. Particularly in the starting stage of the transformation process several future Defense companies and Institutes will need the human capital of the military, that were working there already under the old system, because it will take some time to make civilians capable of doing such a job.

A third method to speed up the transformation process in the second stage is simply to revise the status of military into the status of a civilian. By revision of the status of military the armed forces can proceed quickly with the socializing of the armed forces, the privatisation of the armed forces and the collecting of efficiency advantages. Military proceed with the job they were working on, but as a civilian. This does not have to lead to salary consequences, because for every military rank there is a comparable civil wage. The transformation of a soldier into a civilian will have its consequences for the age of retirement. However, it is really the question if many military want to retire at 50 or 55, or they want to work on until they are 62 or 65. Very often retired servicemen take on another job after their retirement. Doing nothing is not amusing for them.

The big problem when transforming a military into a civilian is the change of the uniform for the clothes of a civilian. Many older military will regard this as a culture shock, when they were asked to do this. The culture of the armed forces is such a big problem in the transformation process, that we will discuss this issue in paragraph 8.5.

The transformation of a conscription force into an all-volunteer force also has consequences for the capitalside of the production process. The substitution of military by capital is one of the dimensions of this side of the transformation process. Mainly these items are dealt with in chapter 7, when discussing the privatisation of the armed forces and in chapter 5, when we spoke about the substitution of labour by capital. Some necessary measures in the privatisation process are not discussed in depth yet. This will be done in the next paragraph.

§ 8.3. The transformation of centralized armed forces into decentralized armed forces

In chapter 7 the privatisation of the armed forces was central in the analysis. This process introduces a lot of incentives that can improve the interaction between society and the armed forces and can lead to more efficient armed forces. If the incentives want to work properly, than it is necessary that these incentives are based on the right information. In other words the value of production factors that are used by the armed forces must be reflected in its price. If the price deviates from its true value, like in the case of conscription, a free-rider problem can exist. The consequence of this free-rider problem is that the real preferences concerning the use of production factors do not become visible and waste occurs.

When passing on services and products to other parts of the armed forces, the real price of the service or good shall be brought into account. Concerning non-durable goods, this will not cause any problems, however, the passing on of prices of durable investment goods can cause problems in the transition stage.

If the Defense-building-service-INC., the Defense-grounds-service-INC. and the Defense-machine-service-INC. want to control the investment goods that they have, it means that they have to possess the buildings, grounds and machines. Now these product are the possession of the armed forces.

The buildings have to be transferred to the Defense-building-service-INC. for the value in economic life. The users of the buildings hire the buildings from the Defense-Building-Service-INC. and pay a rent, which is deducted from the value of the building in economic life. This method is problematic. Because the users of the building are going to pay for the second time now for this building. First, an amount of money is paid at once, now rent has to be paid. Therefore, compensation of the Defense-Building-Service-INC. has to be paid to the original user of the building. This compensation does not have to be paid immediately, but can also consist of a debt. The Defense-Building-Service-INC. now has a debt to the user of the buildings, that can be paid back from the rents of these buildings. At first sight this construction seems to look like pumping around money, because the same can be achieved by giving the buildings at no charge to the Defense-Building-Service-INC., and abstaining from any rent to be paid by the user of the building. However, in the latter case the users of the building are not confronted with the real costs of using the buildings, whereby incentives for efficient use are not available.

When transforming centralized armed forces into decentralized armed forces one has to start with identifying the users of the buildings, grounds and machines. These users should be concerned as owners then. The second step is that the buildings, grounds and machines are sold to the several Defense-companies and leased backed again. The users of the buildings, ground and machines keep a claim on the Defense-companies, that is paid by the Defense-companies independently from the use of the buildings, grounds and machines. In this way the financial problems of the privatization process can be handled in an adequate way. If an unit of the armed forces does not use its buildings or a part of the building anymore, then the Defense-Building-Service is free to find other users for the buildings. These users can both be found in or outside the armed forces. The immigration service can be an example here, that needs space to shelter asylum seekers. The repayment of debt to the original user continues. This can be paid from the rents of the immigration service.

Buildings and machines are products that depreciate both technically and economically. Buildings and machines are built and after some time demolished again. We can say that the life expectancy of buildings is limited. With grounds this is different. That is to say, the soil that forms the ground. The pavement, sewerage, fences etc., that can be found on the grounds and form the actual grounds are also products that depreciate both technically and economically, and will therefore be treated in the same way as the buildings and machines.

With the pure soil this is different. The distinguishing mark of soil is its ever lasting life expectancy. This ever lasting durability is of such a kind, that in some cases we can speak about a perpetual means of production. Soil can have different functions as a means of production.[4] These functions are:

a) the function as place of residence
b) the function as bearer of replaceable matters in the vegetative production process
c) the function of bearer of irreplaceable matters in the extractable production process.

For the armed forces only the first function is of eminent importance. Soil in the function of a place of residence can not wear out, that is soil technically does not depreciate. If we want to confront parts of the armed forces with the costs of their uses, then on the basis of technical depreciation no costs will be charged. Soil can not worn out, but soil can be polluted. The costs of cleaning the polluted soil will be charged by the Defense-Grounds-Service-INC. to the polluter. Most of the time this polluter will be found quickly. If the user is not the polluter, than the user will take care of the fact that the real polluter will be found quickly, otherwise they have to pay for it themselves. Soil in the function of place of residence can not depreciate technically. In economic terms soil or grounds can depreciate. In general that place of residence will be chosen, that is relatively favourable to the place of the sales and the supply area of means of production, both of capital and labour. Movement of these territories can mean that the advantages of some place of residence disappear. As place of residence the value of the soil then depreciates.

For the armed forces economic depreciation of soil and grounds will be very difficult to specify, if it is not zero. Before 1989 the armed forces had to protect the plains in Northern Germany, now their tasks are much more elaborated to facts that can happen all over the world. The home-base will be the same for the

---

4 H.J. van de Schroeff, Kosten en Kostprijs, Amsterdam 1979, pp. 114.

armed forces with the new tasks, so economic depreciation of grounds will not be the case because of this. It can be possible that the new tasks ask for new practice grounds or barrack grounds. In this case the question is, who will finance these new grounds and who will pay the costs of finance. The Defense-grounds-service-INC. does not get a payment for the soil, because it does not depreciate in value. It can not finance it. The solution is that the finance of the grounds is done by the finance department of the Ministry of Defense, after the Defense-grounds-service-INC. has prepared the operation. The Ministry of Defense will be the official owner[5], all other burdens, like interests, on the grounds are the responsibility of the Defense-grounds-service-INC., which will charge the customers again.

Before we finish this paragraph, we will say something about the payment of rents for practice grounds that are not the property of the armed forces. Not all the grounds the armed forces use during peace-time training are their property. Now we have spoken about the fact that pure soil does not depreciate and no costs are involved, the payment of rent for practice ground seems a little bit strange. However, the rent is not paid, because of the depreciation of the soil, but is a compensation for the opportunity costs of the owner of the grounds. The reason for renting the grounds will possibly be that these particular grounds are not used often so that the costs of buying the place are too high, regarding the possible benefits of practising.

§ 8.4. The mobilizing forces[6]

If we want to change a conscription force for an all-volunteer force, we also have to find a solution for the filling of the mobilizing forces. Conscription brought an easy solution for this problem. After the initial training a conscript was stand-by, in order to show up in times of an emergency. The initial time a conscript spent in the armed forces was therefore called the first exercise. After this exercise revision exercises appeared to keep the conscript trained. In this way the armed forces were able to get a large amount of trained people for the use of their mobilizing units and the gaps that could appear in their regular units.

In an all-volunteer force this possibility will disappear in the long run. On a short term notice the transformation of a conscription army into an all-volunteer force won't cause any problems for the mobilizing forces, because in the case of an emergency we can still rely on trained conscripts. When the conscription army disappears, the conscription law is not abolished, only the obligation to show up for the first exercise disappears.

---

[5] This also means that the revenues of the sale of grounds will also go to the Ministry of Defense

[6] This paragraph is based on: M. Binkin, US-reserve forces: the problem of the weekend warrior, The Brookings Institution, Washington, D.C., 1975.

As time passes by the disappearance of the obligation to show up for the first exercise this will also bring a situation that the amount of trained conscripts becomes smaller and smaller and this shortage will have to be covered by the arrival of volunteers. These volunteers, called reserves, will have to fill the places in the mobilizing units. How many reserves are necessary depends on the goals of the armed forces, but in the preceding chapters we have seen that the amount of reserves needed in an all-volunteer force is much less than in a conscription force.

In the first place the amount of reserves is hence specified by the goals of the armed forces. From these goals it follows how many units in the armed forces have a mobilizing status. In the second place the amount of reserves is specified by the amount of physical capital that is available[7], because the combat power of a unit is a combination of capital and labour and not capital and labour separately. In the third place the amount of reserves will depend on the necessity to fill gaps that appear because of casualties. Especially this third element brings a big difference between a conscription army and an all-volunteer force, like we have seen in paragraph 6.4.2.

Paragraph 6.4.2. showed that scarcity in labour, brought by an all-volunteer force, has as a consequence that a military action is much less likely to appear than in a conscription force, because an action with an all-volunteer force can bring a situation where the all-volunteer force is totally without personnel. In other words, in an all-volunteer force, one will be much more efficient with its personnel, because in an all-volunteer force personnel is scarce. The personnel in an all-volunteer force will be much better protected, than in a conscription force. This all means that less reserves are needed in an all-volunteer force.

How many reserves are exactly necessary is an estimate. An estimate that has to be made by taking the amount of mobilizing units, the amount of physical capital, the risks that are attached to possible actions and an estimate of the amount of actions.

The disappearance of the conscripts involves the necessity to get voluntary reserves. The recruitment of the reserves can be done in two ways. The first possibility is to include the obligation for volunteers, that after their contract for the stand-by forces is over, they still have to serve a few years in the reserves. If this obligation is made compulsory without the necessary compensation, it may appear that the potential volunteer is discouraged by signing a contract, which he or she will be unable to foresee completely and that can go on for years and years. In order to prevent this there can be given a reward for availability. This reward can probably be matched with the second opportunity to recruit reserves. This second possibility has been discussed already in paragraph 6.2.4, when we were discussing the recruitment of specialists for the UN-tasks. In this possibility voluntary reserves sign a contract for a couple of years, whereby they declare to be stand-by for tasks to be done in the mobilizing units.

---

[7] See paragraph 8.1.

For this stand-by obligation the reserves get a reward. This reward could be attached to the reward that former stand-by volunteers got for the fact that they still had to offer themselves for being a reserve. If reserves are called for real duty, than they get full compensation. This also has to include the assurance that reserves can go back to their old jobs, if their task is finished. This also concerns the reserves that come forward from the real stand-by forces.

Reserves are also known as "weekend-warriors". This has to do with the fact the reserves have to practice if we want them to be operational. This practising will mainly be done in weekends. Next to that some initial training will be necessary, which will take a couple of weeks. After this basic-training programme these reserves can also go to the "weekend-training". For the reserves it will also be necessary that they will be respected as normal human beings, for which we should be glad that they volunteered for the job. This means that they should not practice with second-hand equipment, but they must also use that kind of material that is used in a war-time situation. Because this material is available in mobilizing barracks, this can also be achieved technically. Personnel to accompany the reserves comes from the real stand-by forces, because these people are placed above strength in the units.[8]

The recruitment of reserves can be done by the Recruitment- and Selection-Institute, while initial training can be given by the Defense-Training-Institute-INC.. The costs made by the reserves will have to be carried by the units the reserves are allocated to.

The way to fill the mobilizing units is identical to the system we use to fill the stand-by forces. Only the frequency for the reserves to appear in the armed forces differs from the stand-by soldier. For all the other aspects there should not be any difference.

§ 8.5. The culture in the armed forces

The armed forces are a hierarchical organisation, whereby the lines of hierarchy go from top to down. In the preceding chapters we have seen that a conscription force satisfies the characteristics of this hierarchical organisation. We have also seen that in an all-volunteer force the relation should be very different to get an effective all-volunteer force. This is not only expressed in the subsidiarity principle of paragraph 6.4., but for example also by replacing military for civilians. Civil society also has its hierarchies, but less visible than in the armed forces. In addition, it can be noticed that the armed forces are a bureaucratic organisation, where power, prestige and esteem are often more important than the income one gets. The transformation of a conscription force into an all-volunteer force will for a lot of people in the armed forces bring the unpleasant

[8] See chapter 5, paragraph 4, footnote 10.

feature, that those elements that bring them power, prestige and esteem will disappear in the reorganization process.

Niskanen's theory, described in chapter 2, gives an explanation for the budgetmaximizing behaviour of civil servants. Next to that it gives an excellent explanation for the existence of conscription. If we want to take a closer look at the culture of the armed forces, Niskanen's theory is not sufficient, like Haselbekke shows.[9]

Originally Niskanen's theory has been supported broadly. But slowly, the notion appeared that the hypothesis of budget maximization is too simple to explain complex bureaucratic behaviour and therefore the culture of the armed forces.

More or less traditional theories, like Niskanen's theory, are based on formal structures and variables that are connected with these structures, like budgets, formal rewards, sanctions, formal hierarchical relations and so on. Because next to the formal structure, there also is an "informal circuit" in bureaucracies with completely own characteristics, making the traditional theory insufficient. What is most important of all is that a bureaucracy should not be regarded as a holistic organisation, but as a pluralistic one: most bureaucrats have both bosses and subordinates. Decision making in the armed forces is most of the time specified "by exchange and trade and not by giving orders and directives that can be 'obeyed' or 'disobeyed'". In other words decision making is a process of exchange and negotiation, whereby the superior rewards the subordinate for its obedience. If the price or reward is not good enough the subordinates will not obey.

In Breton and Wintrobe's theory trust, selective behaviour and competition play an important role. These neo-classical instruments form important elements in their theory which is a reaction to Niskanen. One of the basic elements of neo-classical theory is that exchange and trade come forward from a property rights structure in an organisation. We trust that those rights are honoured; if not, than there is still the judiciary left to settle the conflict. Exchange characterizes the relation between the superior and the subordinate and also relies on property rights, although there are in general no legal institutions to guarantee these rights. So they have to rely on trust.

Individuals that trade with each other are part of a network, comparable to market situations. Organisation theorists call the structure of networks in organisations the informal structure. This informal structure is a variable, that is controlled by bureaucrats concerning size, complexity and influence. The formal structure is also important in this respect; this structure is a way to influence the behaviour of the subordinate. The supervision on the conduct of subordinates should be done for the most important part by the bureaucrats themselves. This supervision is completely different in a world that is based on trust that in a world that is based on relations than can be forced by contracts.

---

[9] The now following part is based on: A.G.J. Haselbekke, Profijtbeginsel en politieke besluitvorming, Leiden, 1989, pp. 176-183 and A. Breton and R. Wintrobe, The Logic of Bureaucratic Conduct, Cambridge, 1982.

According to the Niskanen's bureaucracy theory bureaucrats strive for their own interests. Thereby they can choose for a cooperative, efficient behaviour like in the Weber-model, or an inefficient, disloyal way like the Niskanen-model. So bureaucrats can behave selectively. Selectivity leads to minimization of output costs if bureaucrats behave efficiently and maximization of these costs when acting inefficiently.

What actually happens depends on the informal services, that bureaucrats deliver through their networks. These informal services come forward in a few ways, like the speeding up or slowing down of executing services, changes in the string of information or orders, when going through the hierarchy, variations in the size and quality of the information that leaks through to other bureaus and the media, etc.

When handing over information there will also be some kind of disturbance. The crucial fact is if this information is disturbed consciously or not. This is often very difficult to find out, because it is never sure if certain messages are really disturbed or there is normal white noise. Besides this it is almost impossible to prevent some information leaking away. Therefore there is space for bureaucrats to behave opportunistically. They are always able, unless the opposition of their superiors, to deform facts or leak out information if they think this is in their interests.

If bureaucrats want to use these instruments it is necessary that networks exists; trade and exchange is needed by using these instruments and that is only possible in networks that are based on trust. Selective behaviour is the result of a negotiation process between superiors and subordinates on the one side and between subordinates among each other on the other side and is decided by the 'reward' that is offered by efficient behaviour concerning the supply of informal services. These informal services are results of selective behaviour, sometimes what the superior wants, sometimes against the wishes of the superior.

Whether bureaucrats supply services in an efficient or inefficient way depends on the amount of trust there is between a principal and an agent, the amount of trust between the bureaucrats themselves and finally the risk there is when supplying an inefficient amount of services, which depends on the size and the costs of supervision. Trust is important, because property rights in the bureaucratic exchange process is not based on a legal basis, like exchange in a market. Informal services are traded against other informal services at another time and in another form. At the moment of delivery of the first service it is generally not known when the contra-service will be delivered. Within bureaucracies one has to trust the fact that one day the counter achievement will be delivered.

Within bureaucracies also conflicts appear. Conflicts, or competition problems are a dominant aspect of a bureaucracy. For example, there is competition regarding personnel, network relations or the participation in those networks ("the old boys network") and the competition among bureaus themselves. Competition will not also be the same as trust in these cases.

On the basis of the here mentioned theories Haselbekke concludes that the elements formal and informal structure, trust, selective behaviour and competition give a much better explanation for actual bureaucratic behaviour than can be expected on the basis of traditional theories. For us it is interesting now to see if the elements mentioned by Haselbekke are important for the culture in the armed forces. And if this is the case, whether these elements can give us instruments, which are important for the transition of a conscription force into an all-volunteer force.

For a successful transition of a conscription force to an all-volunteer force the culture of the armed forces is one of the dominant factors. Many reorganisations failed because the culture of the organisation did not meet the qualifications of the reorganization process. For the armed forces it is not unthinkable, that a transition, as described in this chapter, fails on the cultural aspects.

The armed forces are a strongly hierarchical orientated organisation with a deep passion for tradition and prestige. For many military the rank-system is a holy phenomenon and they perform their duty in the armed forces from some kind of vocation, and not because it is just an ordinary job. Their uniform plays an important role in this aspect. If there is one organisation left in the world, where the Niskanen model can be found, it will probably be the armed forces. Niskanen developed his theory, when he was working in the armed forces in the United States of America. If we should reorganize the armed forces on the basis of the theory of Niskanen, than such a reorganization will probably fail. The transition of a conscription force into an all-volunteer force will not differ much from building up an all-volunteer force on the foundation of the old conscription force. In other words: conscripts are substituted by professional military on a one-for-one basis. All other substitutions and changes will probably break in the budgetmaximizing bureaucratic process. An example of this sad scenario is given by the practice of the maintenance services in the armed forces.[10] The example shows that for good functioning of the maintenance services, narrow cooperation between the 30 maintenance services is necessary. However, according to a directly involved man:

"The difference in culture between the Army, Air Force and Navy are big. I can imagine that the military in the management are not so keen on our proposal. It means crumbling off their power. Nobody likes it to hand over power".[11]

The cooperation or merger of the services does not exist in practice. The substitution of military personnel in those organisations, which can only be found in the upper top of management, by civilians does not occur either.

If the transition from a conscription force to a all-volunteer force wants to be a success, it is necessary that other methods and techniques are used. It must be

---

10 See Abva-Kabo, "Aaneen", 29-8-1992, p. 8 "Niemand staat graag macht af".

11 Ibid.

clear for the people in the armed forces, who have to give up something, that they have to get a more or less equal compensation, otherwise they will rebel. In order to have a good view on what can be given, it is good to look for help at the elements given by Haselbekke. These elements can make the reorganization a success.

Decision making is a process of exchange and negotiation, which is based on trust. This is surely the case in a centralized armed forces, where there is no space for real property rights. When reorganising, the first thing to demand is a certain amount of trust. Trust is among others based on information flow. For a successful reorganization the amount of noise in the organisation has to be reduced to a minimum. In order to achieve this, every part of the armed forces has to cooperate.

A reorganization process starts at the top of the hierarchy. Here, the politicians have to see, that the original mission does not satisfy anymore and that change is necessary. Without the political will to change nothing will happen. Politics has to start the transformation process and will steer its direct subordinates to do this too. These subordinates will agree to this, if they think they have enough change, so they think they will not loose, one way or another. But these subordinates are the superiors of other subordinates. A negotiation process will also start here, which has to take care of a situation where subordinates think they will not be worse off after the process is over. These exchange processes will take place at every possible level, whereby the reorganization can not be refused and on every level achievement and counter-achievement should equal more or less.

For the transition of a conscription force into an all-volunteer force, this brings the following questions:

- How fast do the conscripts disappear and what kind of professional soldier will take its place?
- If the salary of the conscripts is lifted to a professional level, does this really improve the recruitment of professional military and the costs consciousness of the military or is the pay increase for conscripts nothing else than compensation for conscripts, which does not bring a return?
- Servicemen do not relinquish easily from their uniform, in order to go on as a civilian in the armed forces. What is necessary to get them that far. More salary, a longer contract?
- Dismissal is one of the possibilities, but what kind of social compensation plan is available?

All these questions and even more are relevant for the transition to an all-volunteer force. All the time achievement and counter-achievement are opposing each other. This permanent choice process costs money. Every successful reorganization costs money.

The reorganization process fails if achievement and counter-achievement are too far away from each other. This can happen because insufficient information is available on the basis of which decisions have to be made and a large amount of uncertainty remains. Information can also be intentionally inadequate.

Inefficiencies will also appear when no agreement will be reached, and conflicts develop.

It is almost impossible to show all the elements of all aspects of a successful transition from a conscription force to an all-volunteer force. But it is clear that a reorganization should follow the laws of the bureaucracy, where the elements trust, selective behaviour and competition play a decisive role. Omission of these elements will probably lead to the failure of the reorganization process. A clear view on the exact relations of these elements in the armed forces will benefit the reorganization process.

A reorganization is a process, which needs a long breath, whereby the culture of the organisation decides the amount of success most of the time. Even if the culture of the organisation is sensible to the correctness of the reorganization it will take some time before the reorganization process will show its results. Therefore, in a reorganization process not everything can be done at the same time. Otherwise the organisation gets overheated. The transition of a conscription force into an all-volunteer force will have to go in stages. These stages are explained in paragraph 8.2. and 8.3.

The armed forces have to be transformed first from an organisation that only has eye for its product, to an organisation that is also market-orientated; in other words the armed forces have to be transformed from an organisation without much scarcity-incentives to an organisation that is sensitive to scarcity. If this process is finished the decentralisation of the armed forces can continue. In the first period some provisions have to be set up, which can be helpful in the transition process, like the changes considering management accounting and information provision.

Although we are aware of the fact that many remarks can still be made in this paragraph, we finish this paragraph, because additional remarks are too far off the original research subject: military conscription. In this paragraph we have given an indication of the problems the culture of the armed forces can bring. A complete solution of these problems is not in accordance with the general problem of the book.

§ 8.6. Final remarks

In this chapter the transition of a conscription force to an all-volunteer force has been the central issue. Preceding such a transition we have to ask ourselves: do we really want such a transition? If we look back in this chapter and all the preceding chapters, we can say that such an all-volunteer force is preferable. If we would have had such a force already, it would have been worth a lot to keep such a force. Actually it is very strange, why such an all-volunteer force does not exist already, because from a societal point of view an all-volunteer force is both socially and budgetary far cheaper than a conscription force, and an all-volunteer force confronts the armed forces with the need of dealing with scarce means, so they will probably be more effective too.

Now, it is the case to transform that conscription force into the all-volunteer force of the future. This also means that we should look at the future and must forget the legacy of conscription. An all-volunteer force is a professional force that has eye for the capacities of the individual scarce human being, and is structured according to the law of the professional organisation. This implies that an all-volunteer force can not be the continuation of a cadre-militia army that formed the conscription force. The Netherlands did not have an all-volunteer force for 200 years. It will probably cost a lot of effort to hand over the conscription force, however the all-volunteer force will only be a success if the conscripts are forgotten as soon as possible.

In this chapter we have also seen the bottlenecks for a successful reorganization. The culture of the armed forces, which could cope without scarcity pressure for almost 200 years, will not change that easily. Foreign experiences, like the all-volunteer forces in the United States and Great-Britain, show this. In these countries the all-volunteer forces are built on the foundation of the conscription forces. The all-volunteer forces are a success, but they are also very expensive, because of insufficient consciousness of dealing with scarce resources. If we want to transform a conscription force into an all-volunteer force successfully, we also have to make this part of the transition a success. In this chapter we showed how this can be possible.

CHAPTER 9

Social conscription

"Nobody has ever said that it would be easy to make people aware of the luck they get. Neighbourly love does demand the severe, but also justified hand of social conscripts. In this moral combat there will be casualties, that is inevitable. Conscription happens to require warfare".
Paul Scheffer, NRC-Handelsblad, 16-10-1992, Opinionpage.

Military and social conscription are often regarded as brother and sister. A discussion about military conscription is often continued with a discussion about social conscription. In this book military conscription is central, however, a sidestep to social conscription is not completely off the mark, because the economic mechanisms that have been described earlier for military conscription are also valid for social conscription. Besides, an analysis of social conscription can shine a light on parts of military conscription, that are no longer important now, but could be important under other conditions.

§ 9.1. Introduction

Social conscription is described as:

"The obligation to participate in works during a certain period to fulfil demonstrable social needs"[1].

As a primary starting point to introduce social conscription the CDJA states that everyone should serve society according to the abilities one has. Thereby it is noted that there are a few tasks in society that are not done, because there is no money for it. A third argument is that there is an amount of dirty and unpleasant work in our society, that is not done. A fourth reason for social conscription is the equal burden for boys and girls that would appear then, because girls do not have to fulfil military service. As a fifth argument it is mentioned that unemployment can be tackled by social conscription, and social conscription can

---

1 Definition used by the CDJA, the youth organisation of the political party CDA (Christian Democrats). This definition can be found in Dutch in: E.J. Kleingeld en R. Rolleman, Sociale Dienstplicht, dwangarbeid of solidariteit? Utrecht, April 1990, p. 14.

give unemployed a chance on the labourmarket by giving them experience and education in society.

From these arguments it follows that the plea for social conscription is primarily fed by practical arguments. The obligation to do the work for a certain, often low payment, would be the remedy for this.

Social conscription has never been seriously investigated. Although requests have been made by the parliament to the Minister of Defense and Social Affairs, the requests were never followed up on. The Social and Cultural Planningbureau has put the 'in and outs' of social conscription together for the Meijer-commission. In the following paragraph we will do the same. Thereby we use the CDJA arguments as a starting point. Then these arguments will be linked with the methods used earlier in this book, when analyzing military conscription. In this analysis we will also pay attention to the possible benefits of military conscription, by investigating the learning effects of conscription on a meso-economic and macro-economic level.

§ 9.2. Social conscription: the theory

The characteristic element of social conscription is its compulsory character. This compulsory element will bring a tax-in-kind with the size of the difference between the opportunity costs of a social conscript and the salary the social conscript receives. The size of the total tax can be found by addition of all taxes of all conscripts. The opportunity costs both include material and immaterial costs.

The immaterial or social side of the opportunity costs is important, because especially the social costs and benefits explain why some people perform jobs as a volunteer, without asking money for it. Volunteers often do certain tasks, because they regard the benefits they experience personally of much more importance then the money they would probably have earned for an alternative task. If the benefits and costs for the volunteer are not in balance, the volunteer will not start the job, or he or she will stop. Volunteers are scarce, because it is their own decision to supply themselves on the labour market. In the case of social conscription, this is not the case. Conscripts are forced and therefore also the scarcity element disappears.

Social conscription introduces a tax-in-kind. This social burden is a burden for the whole society, like every tax . The only difference is that this tax-in-kind can not be found back in political indicators, like the public burden of taxation. It doesn't follow that the tax-in-kind is not present, but that political indicators give an insufficient picture of the whole burden for society.

The size of the tax-in-kind can give us a view of what amount of physical money is needed for a voluntary fulfilment of the jobs that are done by social conscripts. So, social conscription is not a means to provide public services without a social burden. Social conscription shifts the burden of taxation. Taxes in money are transformed in taxes-in-kind. The collective burden stays the same, because visible taxes are only replaced by hidden taxes with in principle the same size.

Social conscription is a tax that disturbs the relative prices of production factors. The social costs, that social conscription brings, are not reflected in the price of production means, so an excess burden arises. This excess burden comes forward in a few forms. First we have the costs of collecting the tax. The perception costs of the social conscription tax, are more or less equal to the perception costs we have seen in chapter 4 of this book. When introducing social conscription in the Netherlands about 200,000 youngsters should be put to work for a period of a year. Not everybody will get a function that corresponds with their skills. In order to take care that the social conscripts really can serve in its function, he or she should be trained first. In addition, someone should supervise this person, because of his or her inexperience. If this does not happen, the quality of the provision, like the service to the public, will come under pressure.

Supply and demand of work will have to be matched. Because with social conscription the scarcity element is gone, the coordination mechanism of the market should be replaced by another coordination mechanism. This transformation costs money. Supply and demand often do not match geographically either, resulting in money is also being needed for traveling and housing. A last directly visible burden of social conscription is the clothes social conscripts need when they have to work.

The disturbance of relative prices of the production means in the sectors in society where social conscripts will be used, also means that a substitution process starts. These substitutions are more or less equal to the substitution processes we have seen in chapter 5. Especially the substitution of capital for labour and experienced labour by inexperienced labour are of eminent importance for social conscription.

The possibility of replacing capital by social conscripts will depend on the technological possibilities. If we only regard the present technological possibilities the opportunities of substitution of capital by labour seem to be small. Efficiency losses will be small too. However, if we take a further look into the future this estimate becomes totally different. Because of the infinite availability of social conscripts there will only be a few incentives left to replace social conscripts by new technology, or to develop new technology. The lack of incentives brings a large amount of inefficiency.

Social conscription makes inexperienced labour forces cheap. Therefore after some time experienced forces will be substituted for inexperienced forces. In the armed forces we have seen that this will lead to a situation where almost no professional soldiers are present. In other words social conscription crowds out professional labour. These regular employees are set aside or get supervising non-productive functions. This process will very slowly be reality, when introducing social conscription.

Social conscription leads to a reallocation of production means. The production process becomes more labour intensive, but also much more inefficient. Social conscription has the implicit consequence that qualitative higher personnel is put out of productive functions by qualitatively less able people. If we still want to produce the same amount of public goods in society, this means that the production costs of production will rise. There will be no place for minimizing costs, both in social terms as in budgetary terms.

The consequences for unemployment can not be predicted at first hand. Social conscription obliges people to work somewhere. In these sectors the production process becomes more labour intensive, and unemployment will decline. This will probably be also true, if we take the disappearance of regular personnel in consideration. On the other side the public burden of taxation will rise, because of the inefficiency of the production process, if we want to keep the quality of the public provision up to date. The rise of the public burden will lead to all kinds of shifting processes, where through unemployment will rise again. This rise of unemployment is also caused by the fact that the disappearance of 200,000 people of the regular labour market will bring pressure on this labour market and an additional demand for higher wages. This will accelerate the shifting process and higher unemployment is the result.

The final effect on employment is rather diffuse, because of the many reallocation- and shifting processes. The hidden unemployment will only rise. Substitution of inexperienced for experienced personnel will rise the amount of supervisors and other non-productive personnel. Many people are needed to continue the process of social conscription, while in a world with scarcity this is mainly done by the market mechanism.

The hidden unemployment rises, because of social conscription, but at first sight is difficult to discover, off course because of her hidden character. However, the same applies here for what has been said when discussing the substitution of capital to labour; the long term effects will show the real effects. Although we can not look very far into the future to check this, experiences with social conscription in extreme forms, like in the former Eastern-European countries, can serve as a specter her.

Social conscription introduces also boredom, because the conscripts are not in a position to leave the job, when they do no longer like it. Boredom is an example of misallocation in a sector and has its origin in the compulsory character of social conscription. All these facts of boredom have its consequences for the image of the profession too.

The danger of social conscription is that the different mechanism that social conscription starts, will bring the sector in a downwards direction. Social conscription leads to social inefficiencies, which can lead again to the reallocation of priorities, from which new gaps occur, that have to be filled again by social conscripts. The history and the development of military conscription, as described in chapter 3 of this book shows the results of this process. And once a sector is going downwards, it will be very difficult to change its course.

After all these sad words about social conscription in theory, we will discuss the beneficial sides of social conscription. Social conscription has a learning effect. By social conscription young people see society from a different perspective. This can be both in a negative and in positive way, but both variances lead to an improved knowledge about society. One third of all military conscripts says that they learn something during their times in the armed forces, one third says that military conscription brings nothing special, and one third says that military conscription brought only negative and bad things.[2]

Up until now we have not paid much attention to the learning effects of conscription in a broader perspective then the learning effects of conscription on a micro-economic level. We have seen in chapter 4, paragraph 3 that conscription brings a setback in experience, because conscripts can not go further with the job they have been trained for during their compulsory service time. Their built-up human capital does not improve, or in most cases deteriorates.

We have just seen that one third of the conscripts thinks military conscription teaches them something, one third thinks nothing happens to them and one third thinks it affects them negatively. However, these are only the opinions of the conscripts themselves. Conscription can also have its effect for the direct environment where they are coming from, while it is even thinkable that the whole society can benefit from these learning effects by the conscript.

In the preceding chapters very little attention has been paid to the learning effects on meso- and macro-economic level. The reason for this is that nowadays these learning-effects do not play an important role anymore in the Netherlands. The learning-effects did not play an important role in the choice between an all-volunteer force and an conscription force and can not be found back in the figures of chapter 8. Why this is so, will be explained in the following part of this paragraph. Thereby we shall also show under which conditions the learning effects on a meso- and macro-economic level will be of eminent importance. On the basis of these conditions we will see if the learning-effects are important for social conscription too.

The best way to illustrate the learning-effects of conscription on a meso-economic level, is to go back to the contents of paragraph 3.1. of chapter 6, which deals with the recruitment- and selection process in an all-volunteer force. In this paragraph we stated:

> The lesson that can be drawn from this paragraph is that the use of classification systems and putting selection limits has great social concern. Not only does high selection limits cost a lot of money in terms of additional salaries and recruitment costs, much more important is to see the social effects of these demands. The refusal of "potential ineligible" volunteers does not only have consequences for the volunteer himself, but also for the family and the background where the volunteer comes from. For the volunteer there is the loss of labour experience, education and self-confidence. For the families the additional income is also welcome, but even more important are the intergenerational profits by the experiences of the volunteer. His environment will maybe have same benefits too, if the volunteer will serve as an example for the rest.

---

2 Research by SMK-VVDM, Dienstplicht: zin, tegenzin en toekomst, Den Haag, October 1992, p. 13.

Although at first it seems strange to explain the learning-effects on a meso-economic level by showing the possibilities of the all-volunteer force, the example shows, when these learning effects can appear. High selection borders exclude large amounts of young people to use the social advantages of working in an organisation like the armed forces. During a job in the armed forces youngsters can meet people in another environment. An experience they would not have had otherwise.

Exclusion from other groups in society especially plays an important role in cases, where conscription is not completely general, but only a part of the youngsters have to serve. By selection and the simple out-of-serve-order of many potential conscripts often those groups do not have to serve, that on the one side could need conscription to improve their skills and abilities and on the other side could give the positive learning-effects by their presence and skills. In chapter 3 this process is illustrated by the system of replacement in the nineteenth century. Although general conscription in the Netherlands does not leave large groups out of the system (see table 2, paragraph 4.3.), the amount of conscripts have become so small that a real general conscription does not exist. Besides this, the figures in table 2, paragraph 4.3., do not show the division of youngsters that did not join the armed forces, in regards to their education, so that possible learning-effects on a meso-economic level, if ever there, on the basis of the table do not explain everything.

In Great-Britain Mark Abrams has analysed the learning-effects of conscription on a meso-economic level. However, he only reaches the conclusion that:

"But if conscription in Britain seemed to have had very little direct effect on the quality of education, it apparently affected modestly career choices-understandably since deferment was based on occupation".[3]

In other words, because of deferments in the conscription policy youngsters moved to those occupations which where rewarded with a deferment for military conscription and education for these jobs where in the interests of many. The learning-effects of conscription did not arise, because people had to join the armed forces, but by avoiding the armed forces, while avoiding the armed forces where a consequence of a not completely general conscription system.
A similar development could be seen in the United States. Morris Janowitz states that:

"At the lower end of the educational continuum the incidence of military service declined sharply; only one-third of those with less than grammar school education served in the military. At the upper end of the continuum, those who entered graduate and professional school, similarly only one-quarter entered active service. The reasons are obviously different. Those with less than eight years of education were deferred on the basis of

---

[3] Mark Abrams, Some effects of British Military Service, in: Sol Tax, The Draft, p. 176, Chicago, 1967.

unfitness a direct expression of their low educational achievement and related medical and psychiatric conditions. Graduate and professional study produced exemption on the basis of educational deferment, often supplemented by martial deferment."[4]

Especially the groups that are socially disadvantaged, like the black community in the United States, are excluded by conscription. They are put aside, because the Ministry of Defense thinks they are not eligible for the task, considering the technological development of warfare. Here, the interests of society in terms of education and the interests of the armed forces collide. Because the armed forces are primarily intended for the protection of the people and not for educational purposes, in many countries like the Netherlands and the United States of America, there has never been a real general conscription. The learning-effects of conscription on a meso-economic level for the Netherlands should therefore be estimated rather low on the basis of this argument.

Summarizing we can say that a necessary condition for the existence of learning-effects by conscription on a meso-economic level is the availability of a real general conscription, a conscription system where everyone really serves.

However, this does not mean that the learning-effects are present if there is a general conscription. This depends on the existence of other institutions that can replace the role of conscription with regard to this point. The existence of alternative institutions also plays an important role when we want to analyze the learning-effects of conscription on a macro-economic level. Before we finish the analysis of learning-effects on a meso-economic level, we will therefore first take a look at the macro-economic level to see if something new appears before we come to a final conclusion.

When analyzing the learning-effects of conscription on a macro-economic level, it actually concerns the analysis about how much society profits from conscription in non-defense terms. We will illustrate these derivative learning-effects for society by showing the development of the modern German state in general in the Prussian state in particular.[5]

After the Thirty Year war (1618-1648) a real Germany did not exists. The country was divided in more than two hundred parts and was one big ruin. From these ruins the princes of a several states appeared slowly as absolute monarchs and the role of the central empire disappeared.

Barraclough writes about this Germany:[6]

"After 1648 it was no longer an empire at all, and scarcely even an federation: it had no common treasury, no efficient common tribunals and no means of coercing a refectory member. (...) It was neither a limited monarchy, as imperialists writers vainly sought to prove, nor a federal state, since effective means of federal action were lacking, particularly in the sphere of war and foreign relations."

---

4 Morrris Janowitz, The Logic of National Service, in: Sol Tax, The Draft, p. 77

5 The following is based on: Geoffrey Barraclough, The Origins of Modern Germany, Oxford, 1976.

6 Ibid, p. 383.

The absolute power of the monarchs mainly rested on two pillars, namely the administration and the army, whereby the monarchs were supported by the church. Almost every state in Germany in the seventeenth century satisfied this profile. Actually, in Prussia it was not much different. In the scattered territories, that were stretching from parts near the river Rhine until parts in present Russia:

"(......), there was no unity of common tradition; there was not, until the end of the eighteenth century, the unity of a common body of law; still less was there any common representative body; the one unity was that of common body of administration and a Prussian army."[7]

However, what the history of Prussia made different than the history of other parts of Germany was not its territorial history, that did not change until Frederick the Great launched his attack on Austria, it was more:

"(....) the subordination of all inhabitants, from the king downwards, to the service of the State. (.....) It was this sense of subordination to a higher duty, of responsibility to a higher power, which distinguished the Prussian state from the rest of eighteenth-century Germany. The famous doctrine that the prince is the servant of the state was a peculiarly doctrine. Its kings conscripted the lives of the peasants and the services of the nobles, but they also conscripted themselves."[8]

While other states languished under a old-fashioned and a wasting government, Prussia set the example of a government, that strove soberly to the development of all production factors in a country: a heavily disciplined army and a tradition concerning conscription that in a certain matter took the place of free political activities as a source of connection in society:

"(....) it remains true that the people of Prussia, under the constant pressure of royal precept and royal example, alone among the people of eighteenth-century Germany felt any sense of identity with the government set above them. It was a stern relationship, based on duty and obedience, on austerity and work; its substance was the obligation of every individual, low and exalted, rich and poor to serve the State with body and soul in life and death."[9]

Of eminent importance in this development is the role of the leader. The leader in society shows personally the importance of conscription. Frederick the Great and his predecessors had to do this personally, because other channels to achieve this in Prussia were not available then, or were not developed yet. Nowadays we would have used compulsory education, while we can also use a large amount of communication means to announce the common message. In the eighteenth century these institutions were not developed sufficiently and the king had to

---

[7] Ibid, p. 399
[8] Ibid, p. 398-399
[9] Ibid, p. 399

show the example of the conscription tradition all by himself. The great power of Prussia in this was that conscription involved everybody. No person was excluded and because the army and the administration were the only institution to be developed, conscription got the actual form of military conscription.

In 1763 Prussia was an European power, thanks also to the unity brought by conscription. This unity was initiated by outside threats and the pressure of a possible war, but the way to prevent these threats made Prussia a real entity and because of all the learning-effects included also a big power.

Barraclough translates this development a little bit further by stating that:

"The rise of Prussia to the rank of a great power modified the whole European constellation, and laid the foundation for the reconstruction of Germany after the French Revolution and the Napoleonic Wars had overthrown the old order and brought about a basic territorial simplification. Its emergence as a European power would have been impossible without the work of internal consolidation to which Frederick William I and Frederick the Great directed their energies."[10]

This citation does not only show the grandeur of Prussia, but also that Prussia was not unbeatable. Already in 1763 Prussia transformed its conscription force into an all-volunteer force. But with this transition the tradition of conscription also disappeared. A tradition that was hurt also by the death of Frederick the Great in 1786.

After the Napoleonic Wars Prussia returned to conscription quickly under the leadership of Scharnhorst, Hardenberg and Stein. They realized that is was almost impossible to get Prussia out of the depression it was in without reforming the political institutions and winning back the support of the people by giving them the right to speak about the transformations. The community feeling brought by conscription disappeared when conscription was abolished, and the role of conscription in this community building process was not taken over by other institutions, like education and communication.

From the Prussian example it follows that special conditions are necessary if conscription will bring genuine learning-effects for the whole society. If we want to say something about the learning-effects of conscription on a meso-economic and macro-economic level we should keep in mind that 'real' general conscription is an absolutely necessary condition, if any learning-effects may be available, while the gains of conscription should be estimated low in terms of positive learning-effects, if there are good alternative institutions which can bring the same, like compulsory education. Which alternative should be chosen in our times, conscription or compulsory education, will be analysed at the end of this chapter in a cost-and-benefit analysis. Here, we only want to say that when compulsory education is socially cheaper than conscription, the learning-effects of conscription at both levels are negligible.

From Prussia's history and the development of the conscription army in the Netherlands and in the United States, at least it becomes clear that:

---

10 Ibid, pp. 399

"An effective citizen army required (and requires) very special conditions to flourish. First, the technical level of warfare must be such that no elaborate equipment that is beyond the reach of ordinary citizens can have decisive effect in battle. (......) In the second place, a citizen army can only be effective as long as most citizens trust one another enough to fight side by side and back to back-not face to face against one another"[11]

The author of this citation adds to this, that in an all-volunteer force one should think very carefully about the way the leadership in society is attached to the military leadership, if you do not want an all-volunteer force to act against the will of society:

"If the United States decides nevertheless to accept the risks of relying upon long-term-service professional troops of the sort suited for conducting distant, low-grade wars and for garrison duty overseas, then devices must be found for linking military leadership more closely with the leadership of civil society. The existing policy of exempting the future leaders of civilian life from military service positively invites divergence of viewpoint and seems almost suicidal in a democracy."[12]

§ 9.3. Social conscription: practical implications

The choice for social conscription is a political choice. To make this choice it is necessary that the costs and benefits of social conscription are compared with each other. Although it is difficult to do this exactly, we will make an effort in this paragraph. First, we take a look at the positive sides of social conscription, like we have seen at the end of paragraph 9.1., to see if the value of these arguments are not changed by the results of the analysis in paragraph 9.2.

Departure point for social conscription is that everybody should put effort into society, according to the ability one has. What should be regarded as society? In chapter one of this book we used the assumption that society consists of a group of people. The people in this society call for the help of a government to care for those goods which they can not provide individually. Hence, the government is subordinate to the people in a society, and has to follow the wishes of this society. In exchange for the provisions provided by the government the people pay taxes. These taxes are levied in a couple of cases according to the ability-criterion, in which everybody gives to society according to its ability. If the tax is paid in kind or in money is not important here, because in both cases there is a payment to society. A tax-in-kind can be recalculated in money, if it is known what the value of the tax-in-kind is.

From this calculation, it follows that the use of social conscripts does not bring tax savings for society. The introduction of social conscription means the

---

11 William H. McNeill, The Draft in the Light of History, in: Sol Tax, The Draft, chapter 12, pp. 118.

12 Ibid.

introduction of a tax-in-kind, while the provision involved could also have been financed by the introduction of a tax in money.

If the government does not execute some tasks, because she does not have the money, it can not be done by social conscription. The costs to execute these tasks have not changed, they may have had a different appearance, but nothing else. A probable introduction of social conscription comes from a different choice of priorities, that was not made before social conscription was there. We could also say that the supporters of social conscription want to bring those provisions with conscription, that would not have been chosen if a normal priority setting on the basis of financial tax prices would have been there, because others think those provisions are not important.

It is often said that social conscripts should be used to do the tasks that are socially important. However, these tasks are not that important at every possible time, otherwise these tasks were already executed with the help of financial taxes. The same applies for dirty and unpleasant work. If society thinks, that the work should be done, than we have to reward this, by giving it the true priorities. If the priorities do not exist, the product will not be produced, or in other words the dirty and unpleasant works remain to be done.

The fourth point that will be discussed here is the question of equality. All youngsters have to do the work for society, in stead of only a selected amount of men, like in military conscription. Social conscription can lead to an equal burden for all youngsters, but for this condition it is necessary that all youngsters really serve and there are no exemptions at all. There has to be 'real' general conscription. This means that there shall be no testing of youngsters, because testing means that some youngsters will be declared unfit for a special kind of job, and the case of equal burden is broken.

On first sight it seems to be rather strange not to test youngsters for a job. Youngsters with several disabilities are not suitable for many kinds of jobs, and could be better declared unfit for the job, but in a long-term perspective this can be different.

By making cases of exemptions avoidance behaviour can occur. Besides this it is also a normative process the develop the test criteria. This has to do with infinite stream of labour supply, that social conscription brings. In a tree full with fruit, one does not miss one or two apples, which results in testing personnel getting the feeling to declare unfit those cases that are doubtful, because the next one is already available. In military conscription this has resulted in a situation, where 27% of the youngsters is sent away, while most men are not really disabled. The armed forces rather have the best people they can get, which is made possible by the infinite stream of conscription.

The same applies for the bureau that should execute conscription. On a short term schedule the costs of executing social conscription are not too high, like Charles Moskos describes in his book "A call to civil Service". But with the introduction of social conscription, the correcting, invisible incentives of the market mechanism also disappear and this brings the tendency for the bureau to grow to an enormous bureaucracy.

Concerning the last point in the discussion about social conscription, the falling unemployment figures, we will repeat what we have said in paragraph 9.2. The effect on unemployment is rather vague, because the different substitution- and shifting processes work against each other.

If we put everything together, it becomes clear that a lot of arguments for social conscription disappear and the question of social conscription is a balance of the knowledge people get by social conscription and the excess burden that conscription brings.

If the excess value of the knowledge by conscription is bigger than the excess burden of conscription, as described in paragraph 9.2. the choice for social conscription is justified. How big both elements are remains difficult, but with the results of chapter 5 about military conscription we can make an estimate. The excess burden of military conscription is about 2 billion guilders a year. Social conscription includes five times as much people as military conscription. When we extrapolate the amount of excess burden of military conscription to social conscription we get the sum of 10 billion guilders a year for the excess burden of social conscription.

The excess value of conscription according to the conscripts themselves is about zero, as we have seen in last paragraph. Although one has to listen to the conscripts in this respect, the opinion of the near relatives or community is probably better to judge the gain in knowledge.

However, it still is the question if the gain in knowledge by the youngsters brought by conscription, exceeds the value of the excess burden, here estimated on 10 billion guilders a year. It is probably much cheaper to give youngsters the missing knowledge about society and functioning in society by improving the normal education system. Then we would not be talking anymore about social conscription, but expanding compulsory education.

Compulsory education comes from the idea that young people have to be prepared for a place in society and to prevent a situation in which they are not prepared at all, because they take the wrong decisions. Decisions which they can not make properly yet, because of their age. Behind the reason of compulsory education is the thought of opportunity costs. With compulsory education it is intended to prevent someone of dropping out of school, where through its future possibilities are diminished. For every young person the opportunity costs are different. Many youngsters have the opinion that at the age of 15, the last year of compulsory education, they do not have sufficient human capital yet to take the jump into the real world. On the other side compulsory education also brings a waste of resources. Boredom in schools is an example of this. Although many youngsters go further with improving their skills by education and are not available for the labour market, compulsory education tightens the labour market, because young people are restricted by this obligation. Those who want to work are not allowed.

An important advantage of compulsory education compared with conscription is that compulsory education does not disturb the relative prices between production factors or puts the markets for these production factors out of order. This advantage will bring a much lower excess-burden for compulsory education, than is the case with conscription. The total cost-benefit analysis for conscription is negative, and therefore we have not paid much attention to the probable learning-effects of conscription in earlier chapters. Considering the present situation, the learning effects of conscription are too little to play an essential role in the complete analysis.

§ 9.4. Conclusions

In this chapter we have taken a glance at social conscription. In the first paragraph social conscription is defined as:

"The obligation to participate in works during a certain period to fulfil demonstrable social needs"

These social needs originate from general needs in society. Everyone's individual needs are restricted by the available opportunities. This implies both private and public goods. If the needs of society really can be fulfiled depends on the priorities of society. On the basis of the priorities decisions are taken and action is undertaken to meet the needs of society. In other words private and public goods are produced. For the production of these goods production factors are used. These production factors come from society, where they are scarce and can be used alternatively. On the basis of the list of priorities some goods will not be made, because apparently they are not that important.

According to the definition of social conscription, social conscription points at those goods that were not produced as an outcome of the priority list. If they would have been produced, there would have been no need anymore for the goods. With the help of social conscription people try to change the priorities of society. However, the costs of social conscription exceed the benefits enormously, because social conscription does not lead to a reduction of costs for society, but only a shift of burden from old to young, from visible to invisible costs and from a tax-in-money to a tax-in-kind. The total cost remain the same if we exclude the excess burden of social conscription. Including this, the burden will lead to a rise in social costs.

The excess burden of social conscription appears, because the market mechanism for production factors is eliminated. Because of the elimination of the market forces, where social conscription exists, there are no incentives left that lead to an efficient production of goods in those sectors. On a short term notice there will be no noticeable effect, but in the long run the disappearance of the automatic incentives will come to the surface, and the inefficiency losses will be enormous.

Social conscription can be compared with a computer program with the Pac-Man virus. First, the computer program will bring an excellent amount of figures, but with finishing the last bit of the program, the Pac-Man virus is started, which slowly eats all the bits and bites of the program, so after some time the complete program is gone and the user of the program has to start all over again. Social conscription looks nice on a short term notice, but destroys slowly the fundamentals of the market mechanism, because of which the production of sector with social conscripts collapses totally after some time.

Social conscription can never bring, what military conscription and compulsory education can bring, and that is that the opportunity costs of labour under the obligation of social conscription can never go above its market value. With military conscription this is possible during an invasion. While compulsory education brings 'gains of opportunities' considering the future value of labour. Hence, social conscription is nothing else than an expensive, bureaucratic and short sighted way of realizing the production of public goods, which would not be produced under a normal public choice process.

CHAPTER 10

Summary

In this book, entitled "Military Conscription: an economic analysis of the labour component in the armed forces", military conscription is regarded as an economic policy to minimize the cost of labour in the armed forces. The economic cost of conscription becomes clear when we analyse the opportunity costs of conscription. If conscripts were free to choose whether to join the armed forces, many would not under the present day conditions, since for them the costs of conscription far outweighs the benefits.

The principle of opportunity costs is always central in the economics of warfare. In this book the analysis begins with an investigation of these opportunity costs and then uses the results to analyse the formation of an all-volunteer force, which will in fact be achieved, if everything proceeds according to schedule, by 1998.

Chapter one concentrates on the structure of the thesis. One of the cornerstones is welfare economics. Welfare economics uses a mechanical view of the state. Translated to military conscription this means that the welfare of the conscript is a central point in the analysis of the economic aspects of military conscription. Also important is the fact that the concept of welfare concentrates on scarcity. Due to conscription the aspects of scarcity of labour in the armed forces are very weak, if not absent.

Conscripts are used in the armed forces to produce the defense of public good. The use of these means of production in the armed forces to produce defense leads to a withdrawal of the same means from the civil society, because these means are scarce with regard to the needs in that society. Therefore economic laws are also valid in the armed forces (chapter 2).

In the armed forces two specific functions can be considered: combat functions and non-combat functions. The latter supports the former without the use of violence. The use of violence is essential for combat functions. To fill the combat functions society has a choice between a conscription army and an all-volunteer force. In an all-volunteer force soldiers are recruited on a voluntary basis and salaries are paid from the yield of taxation. In a conscription army the obligation is prominent. Conscripts receive a salary that is lower than the income they could have earned in civil society, if they were not forced to join the armed forces. In other words conscripts pay a tax-in-kind (chapter 4). The burden of conscription, or conscription tax, is characterized by the difference between the salary and the opportunity costs of a conscript. The opportunity costs are equal to the sum of the alternative civil salary of the conscript and the "aggravation-premium" caused by the lost non-pecuniary advantages in civil society.

The conscription tax is about 10.000 guilders a year for every conscript not including the cost of conscription that will appear after military service because of the loss of working experience.

Without considering the collection costs of the conscription tax, the tax also causes a relative change of factor costs in the armed forces. Conscription makes labour cheap and this means that the armed forces are producing the defense of public good with a greater amount of labour than would be necessary. Conscription conceals the real costs of the armed forces and causes an "excess-burden" to the amount of 2.1 billion guilders a year, because due to conscription the substitution of labour for capital, military labour for civilians, and inexperienced labour for experienced labour does not occur. In addition, the misallocation caused by conscription leads to excessive forms of boredom and neglect of the primary living conditions of soldiers. However, conscripts are not allowed to resign if the situation in the armed forces is not satisfactory.

The excesses of conscription are not just a contemporary issue; in the 19th-century conscription had a massive influence on ordinary life (chapter 3). In an economic sense, the essential element of 19th-century conscription was the replacement system. Due to this system it became almost impossible to change the Napoleonic conscription system into an all-volunteer force.

In order to achieve an all-volunteer force, it is important that the armed forces are able to compete with civil society in terms of working conditions and working circumstances. In this comparison all the aspects of the conscription-tax will be illuminated once again (chapter 6).

In an all-volunteer force the soldier and the armed forces are confronted with two kinds of contracts. Other than the written contract, there is an unwritten one, in which the armed forces are obliged to respect the soldier as a human being, to assign the soldier useful work and to provide the opportunity for individual development. The soldier is obliged to fulfil the task to the best of ability in a disciplined manner.

The tasks of the troops in the armed-forces will be different in the future than they were prior to the fall of the Berlin Wall in 1989. Apart form NATO-tasks, the use of military personnel for UN-missions will be one of the most important tasks for the Dutch armed-forces. This means that the task of the troops will not be purely that of producing combat power. The future soldier must be able to negotiate, intercede and reconcile, while civilian education will be necessary for humanitarian aid operations. The civilian education programme should be provided by the armed forces, and will give military career a new and attractive perspective without raising salaries.

In an all-volunteer force the recruiting and selection process is an essential element of the system. Contrary to a conscription army, labour is scarce in an all-volunteer force. Potential volunteers must be treated with the greatest concern. If the supply of eligible volunteers is not enough to fill the needs of the armed forces, then research will be needed to see whether this is caused by overly strict selection criteria that are too strict. High selection standards do not only translate into a lot of wasted money in terms of extra salaries and recruitment costs, but high selection standards also cause high social costs, since eligible people can not obtain a proper job.

In an all-volunteer force supply of labour must be as great as possible. This means that the role of women in the armed forces should also be stressed. Without proper integration of women in the armed forces an all-volunteer force will never be fully efficient, because a sufficient supply of women will enlarge total supply, keeping salaries down.

Maybe more important than attracting new volunteers is to limit the demand for new volunteers. In chapter 5 it is stressed that the demand for military personnel is so large, because the cost of using these people is so low. The high demand is caused by conscription. If the real costs of personnel must be paid, demand will be expected to go down. Demand diminishes because the armed forces are confronted with real costs, but the demand for military personnel can also be lowered by different means. The armed forces have always stressed the concept of a 'young and vigorous force'. A young force also means an inexperienced force, while the physical element will be less important in the future armed forces. The 'up-or-out' personnel management system also causes a young-force, because experienced people will leave the armed forces when the armed forces can no longer provide any further challenge or promotion. This means that in an all-volunteer force the pay system should be separated from the ranking system. Rank is just a coordination mechanism, while pay is a scarcity mechanism.

If we want to change the conscription army into an all-volunteer force, we should also find a solution for the reserves. This is a long-term problem because on a short-term basis, it will still be possible to fill the reserves with conscripts (chapter 8). The amount of reserves needed depends on the objectives of the armed forces concerning the amount of extra units for mobilization, the amount of capital available and the losses of personnel in combat-action.

Especially in regards to the latter issue an important difference can be found between an all-volunteer force and a conscription army. Scarcity brought about by an all-volunteer force means that extreme care will be taken with regard to military actions, because an action with an all-volunteer force can mean that the volunteer force will run out of personnel. In other words the use of personnel will be more efficient in an all-volunteer force, because in contradiction to a conscription army personnel in the all-volunteer force is scarce (chapter 6).

The attractiveness of an all-volunteer force is great. But the choice for an all-volunteer force is not that simple. It is a balance between the opportunity costs of a conscription army and an all-volunteer force. Translated in opportunity costs, the choice between the two is a question of which is greater: the opportunity costs for society in terms of damages to people and capital by war or the opportunity costs sacrificed by soldiers (chapter 8). The choice for a conscription army can be sincere in case of an invasion, but it is important to notice that the point of transition between an all-volunteer force and a conscription army will be very close to the point of invasion, because combat power to stop an invasion of the country depends heavily on available material. Without that material a conscript can also not function.

Although currently an all-volunteer force is to be preferred over a conscription army, it will be difficult to realize the transition from a conscription army to an all volunteer force. Many groups in society benefit from the continuance of conscription. This is not just true for the leading military in the Ministry of Defense in their pursuit for budget maximization (chapter 2), but also public choice can lead to a situation whereby the transition to an all-volunteer force will be opposed. A lot of people benefit from the continuance of conscription, because it is a tax-benefit for them (chapter 3).

Nevertheless, the transition from a conscription army to an all-volunteer force can occur without any delay if some essential issues are addressed. Elements like formal and informal structure, confidence, selective behaviour and competition often provide a more accurate explanation for the practical behaviour of bureaucrats than budget maximization. If these elements are used in the transition period in a quid-pro-quo surrounding, the transition to an all-volunteer-force can be accomplished successfully. However, the culture of the armed forces will not be transformed that easily, which means that some amount of tension is expected to remain (chapter 8).

Concerning the aspect of public choice of the transformation; it is of eminent importance that all costs are considered. If it can be proven that the transition to an all-volunteer force saves money, the result will be totally different.

Military conscription also served a few secondary objectives. The most important one being the interaction between society and the armed forces by conscription. In an all-volunteer force this kind of interaction decreases, which will require the need for a compensating alternative to be found (chapter 7).

Interaction between society and the armed forces is a matter of incentives. The question is how incentives can be used in the armed forces to improve the dynamics between society and the armed forces. Other than the extra opportunities given to subordinates with regard to their superiors in the armed forces, privatization of the armed forces is an important opportunity to improve the dynamics of the armed forces. The primary objectives of privatization are to confront the armed forces with the costs of their own actions, through which they also see the costs of actions that are not beneficial to society.

After an in-depth analysis of welfare economics, public goods, bureaucratic behaviour, taxes-in-kind, cost prices, excess-burden, labour markets and labour market-instruments, privatization and opportunity costs, this book ends with studying civil service. Compulsory civil service has the same characteristics as military conscription, but can never compete with military conscription on one point. The opportunity costs of labour under civil service can never exceed its market value. In the case of military conscription this is possible during an invasion. Compulsory civil service is nothing but realizing the production of these public goods by way of bureaucracy and short-sightedness, a production which never would have come about in a democratic free choice situation.

REFERENCES

Abrams, M., "Some effects of British military service", in Sol Tax (ed), *The draft,* Chicago 1967

Abva-Kabo, "Niemand staat graag macht af", *Aaneen*, Zoetermeer, August 29, 1992.

Algemene Vereniging Nederlandse Militairen, *Verveling in dienst*, Utrecht, 1989.

Allers, M.A., *Kosten van overdrachten voor particulieren en huishoudens*, Researchmemo-randum nr. 483, Instituut voor economisch onderzoek, Faculteit der Economische Wetenschappen, Rijksuniversiteit Groningen, Groningen, 1992.

Altman, S. H and Fechter A. E., "The supply of military personnel in the absence of the draft," *American Economic Review*, May 1967.

Angrist, J. D., "Lifetime earnings and the Vietnam era draft lottery. Evidence from social security administrative records," *American Economic Review*,, June 1990.

Baakman, N.A.A. (ed.), *Overheid en onderneming, een inleiding*, Heerlen, 1991.

Barraclough, G., *The modern origins of modern Germany*, Oxford, 1976.

Becker, G. S. "Investment in human capital: a theoretical analysis," *Journal of Political Economy*, Vol. 70, 1962.

Bergeijk, P.G.A. van, *Economie van de oorlog*, Rotterdam, 1986.

Berger, M.C. and T. Hirsch, "The civilian earnings experience of Vietnam era veterans", *Journal of human resources*, herfst 1983.

Biesmeijer, E. en W.C. Verbaan, "Zelfbeheer I: de ambtenaar wordt manager", *Openbare Uitgaven*,16, nr. 5, September 1984

Binkin, M., *The military pay muddle*, The Brookings Institution, Washington, D.C., 1972.

Binkin, M., *U.S. Reserve forces: the problem of the weekend warrior*, The Brookings Institution, Washington, D.C., 1975.

Binkin, M. and S. J. Bach, *Women and the military*, The Brookings Institution, Washington, D.C., 1977.

Binkin, M., H. Kanter and H. Clark, *Shaping the defense civilian work force*, The Brookings Institution, Washington, D.C., 1978.

Binkin, M. and I. Kyriakopoulos, *Youth or experience? Manning the modern military*, The Brookings Institution, Washington D.C., 1980.

Binkin, M. and I. Kyriakopoulos, *Paying the modern military*, The Brookings Institution, Washington, D.C., 1981.

Bliven, B., Jr. , *Volunteers one and all*, New York, 1976.

Bogaert, K.A.M., "Aspecten van het economisch handelen in de militaire organisatie," *Maandschrift Economie*, nr 29, 1965.
Boneschansker, E. and H. de Groot, "Verzelfstandiging van overheidsdiensten: wanneer en hoe?", *Openbare Uitgaven* 24, nr.3, May 1992 ;
Boorsma, P.B., "Privatisering", *Openbare Uitgaven*, 14 nr.6, October 1984
Boorsma, P.B. and W.T.M. Bokkes, "De economische baten van hulpagenten", *Openbare Uitgaven* 23, nr.5, september 1991.
Breton, A., and R. Wintrobe, *The logic of bureaucratic conduct*, Cambridge, 1982
Buchanan J.M., *Cost and choice*, Chicago, 1969.

Campagne, G.T., "Over het ontstaan en de ontwikkeling van het instituut van de dienstplicht," *Kernvraag*, nr. 4, 1968.
Canby, S. L., *Military manpower procurement, a policy analysis*, Lexington, 1972.
Centraal Bureau voor de Statistiek, *Sociaal economisch panelonderzoek 1989 Vragenlijst A1*, Heerlen, 1989.
Centraal Bureau voor de Statistiek, *Statistisch Zakboek*, Voorburg/Heerlen, several years
Chu, D.S.C. and E. Norrblom, *Physical standards in all-volunteer force*, The Rand Corporation, Santa Monica, 1974.
Coase, R.H., "The nature of the firm", *Economica* 4, 1937.
Coase, R.H., "Accounting and the theory of the firm", *Journal of accounting and economics* 12, 1990
Coase, R.H., "The institutional structure of production", *The American Economic Review*, September 1992
Cooper, R.V.L., *Military manpower and the all-volunteer force*, Rand Corporation, Santa Monica, 1977.
Crane J.R. and D.A. Wise, "Military service and the civilian earnings of youth" in D.A. Wise (ed.), *Public sector payrolls*, Chicago, 1987.

DeTray, D. N., "Veteran status as a screening device," *American Economic Review,* march 1982.
Dijkhuizen, N. van and P.H.J. Suijker, *Is rang alleen rang als er rang op staat?* Den Haag, 1991.
Downs, A., *Inside Bureaucracy*, Boston, 1967.
Duindam S., "Beroepsleger of dienstplicht?", *Economisch Statistische Berichten*, 10-7-1992.

Duindam S., "De kosten van dienstplicht", *Economisch Statistische Berichten*, 29-4-1992.
Duindam, S., J. Leestemaker and R. Zaal, *"Rapport van het bezoek aan SCVR, Zweden door een delegatie van VVDM, Nederland, 15 t/m 19 augustus 1991"*, Commissie Internationale Zaken VVDM, Utrecht, 1991.

Engelberts, I.M., *Moet de plaatsvervanging worden afgeschaft*, Nijmegen, 1848.

Felix, P., "Verzelfstandiging als privatiseringsvariant", *Economisch Statistische Berichten*,, March 5, 1986.
Fisher, A. C., "The cost of the draft and the cost of ending the draft," *American Economic Review*, June 1969.

Gay, R. M., *Estimating the cost of on the job training in military occupations: a methodology and pilot-study*, Rand Corporation, Santa Monica, 1974.
Gifford, B. R. and L. C. Wing (eds.), *Test policy in defense,* Boston, 1992
Goldscheid, R. *Staatssozialismus oder Staatskapitalismus: ein finanzsoziologischer Beitrag zur Lösung des Staatsschulden-Problems*, Vienna, 1917.

Hansen W. L.and B. A. Weisbrod, "Economics of the military draft," *The Quarterly Journal of Economics,* Vol.81, 1967.
Haselbekke, A.G.J., *Profijtbeginsel en politieke besluitvorming,* Leiden, 1989.
Henderson, J.M. and R. E. Quandt, *Microeconomic theory: a mathematical approach*, New York, 1980.
Hitch, C. J. and R. N. McKean, *The economics of defense in the nuclear age,* Cambridge, 1960.

Janowitz, M., "The logic of national service", in Sol Tax(ed), *The draft,* Chicago 1967

Kleingeld, E.J. and R. Rolleman, *Sociale dienstplicht, dwangarbeid of soldariteit?*, Utrecht, 1990.
Knight, F.H., *Risk, uncertainty and profit*, Cambridge, 1946.
Koutsoyiannis, A., *Modern Microeconomics*, London 1975.
Kraan, D.J., "Bureaucratietheorie en de organisatie van de rijksdienst", *Openbare uitgaven*, 24 Nr. 4, 1992.
Kruseman, A., *Over de nationale militie en remplacement*, Amsterdam,1853.

Lingle, C., "On the real costs of military conscription," *South African Journal of Economics*, Vol. 57, 1989.

Maatschappelijke Raad voor de Krijgsmacht, *De vrouw in de krijgsmacht*, advies nr. 7, Den Haag 1984.
Maatschappelijke Raad voor de Krijgsmacht, *Evaluatie maatschappelijke aanvaarding van de krijgsmacht 1988-1991,* advies 14/1, Den Haag, 1991.
Maatschappelijke Raad voor de Krijgsmacht, *Verhouding burger- en militair personeel,* advies nr. 16, Den Haag, 1989.

Maatschappelijke Raad voor de Krijgsmacht, *Contractduur,* advies nr. 24, Den Haag 1992.
Maatschappelijke Raad voor de Krijgsmacht, *Internationalisering van de krijgsmacht,* advies nr. 25, Den Haag 1992.
Maatschappelijke Raad voor de krijgsmacht, *Standpunt over het advies van de commissie-dienstplicht (commissie-Meijer),* advies nr.26, Den Haag, 1992.
McNeill, W.H., "The draft in the light of history", in Sol Tax(ed), *The draft,* Chicago, 1967.
Meijer-commissie, *Naar een dienstplicht nieuwe stijl*, Den Haag, 1992.
Mierlo J.G.A. van, "Ambtelijk gedrag in bureaucratische organisaties," in A.F.A Korsten and Th. A.J. Toonen, *Bestuurskunde,* Leiden, 1988.
Miller J. (ed.), *Why the draft, the case for the volunteer force*, Baltimore, 1968.
Ministerie van Defensie, *Brief 90/377/23459 aan de voorzitter van de Tweede Kamer der Staten Generaal,* 's-Gravenhage, November 14 1991.
Ministerie van Defensie, *Defensienota 1991*, Den Haag, 1991.
Ministerie van Defensie, *Jaaroverzicht dienstplichtgegevens*, Den Haag, (several years)
Ministerie van Defensie, *Prioriteitennota*, 's-Gravenhage, 1993.
Mol, N.P., *Bedrijfseconomie voor de collectieve sector*, Alphen aan de Rijn 1989.
Mol, N.P., "Zelfbeheer II: kostenplaatsenbudgettering", *Openbare Uitgaven 16*, nr. 5. September 1984.
Mol, N.P. and H.A.A. Verbon, *Institutionele economie en openbaar bestuur, perspectieven op de verzelfstandiging van overheidsdiensten*, 's-Gravenhage, 1993
Mommersteeg-commissie, *Verplicht of vrijwillig dienen*, Den Haag 1976.
Moskos, C.C., jr., *L'armee de metier Americaine (1973-1990): constat de carence,* Fondation pour les études de defense nationale, Parijs, 1991.
Moskos, C.C., jr., *The American enlisted man*, New York, 1970.

Moskos, C.C., jr., "Form institution to occupation: trends in the military organization", *Armed forces and society*, vol. 4, 1977.

Niskanen, W., *Bureaucracy and representative government,* Chicago, 1971.
NordBerFN, *Nordic standby forces in United Nations service*, Stockholm, 1976.

Oi, W., "The economic cost of the draft," *American Economic Review*, May 1967.

Phelps, E. S. (et al), *Microeconomic foundations of employment and inflation theory*, New York, 1970.
Pigou, A.C., *The economics of welfare*, London, 1962.
Putten, J. van, "Geen reden te sterven voor de staat", *NRC-Handelsblad Opinionpage*, 31-10-1992.

Robbins, L., *An essay on the nature and significance of economic science*, London, 1962.
Roos, N.H.M. "Opiniepagina" *NRC-Handelsblad* November 3 1992.
Rosen, Harvey S., *Public finance*, Homewood, 1988.
Rosen, S. and P. Taubman, "Changes in lifecycle earnings: what do social security data show?," *Journal of human sciences*, zomer 1982.
Roux, A., "The economics of alternative national service," *South African Journal of Economics*, Vol. 59, 1991.

Samuelson, P.A., "The pure theory of public expenditure", *Review of Economics and Statistics 36*, 1954.
Schroeff, H.J. van der, *Kosten en kostprijs*, Amsterdam, 1979.
Siccama, J.G., "Militaire dienstplicht ondoelmatig en onrechtvaardig", in C. Homan and J.G. Siccama (eds.), *Dienstplicht, afschaffen of uitbreiden?* Den Haag, 1990.
Smidt, E. (et al), "Een verloren jaar; de relevantie van militaire dienstplicht voor de arbeidsmarkt", *Maatschappij en krijgsmacht nr. 14*, Den Haag, augustus 1992.
Smith, A., *The wealth of nations*, New York, edition 1937.
Spil, C.B.A., "Een economische waardering van de dienstplicht," *Economisch Statistische Berichten*, 8-10-1966.
Spits, F.C., "Klassedienstplicht in de negentiende eeuw, plaatsvervanging en afkoop", *Driekwart eeuw historisch leven in Den Haag,* 1975.
Stevens, L.G.M., *Elementair belastingrecht,* Deventer 1985.
Stichting Maatschappij en Krijgsmacht, *De prijs van defensie*, Den Haag, 1983.

Stigler, George J., "Information in the labor market," *The journal of political economy,* Vol, 70, 1962.
Swartz, S., "The relative earnings experience of Vietnam and Korean era veterans," *Industrial and labor relations review*, July 1986.

Theeuwes, J., "Een stilliggend doperwtje", *Trouw* , 12-20-1991.
Tiesinga, Marie-Louise, "Dienstplicht, van militaire naar sociale?," concept text for *Armex Defensie magazine,* 1992.
Tollison, Robert D., "The political economy of the political draft," in James M. Buchanan and Robert D. Tollison (eds.), *Theory of public choice*, Ann Arbor, 1972.
Tweede Kamer der Staten Generaal, *Rijksbegroting Hoofdstuk X*, Den Haag, several years
Tweede Kamer der Staten Generaal, *Vergaderjaar 1990-1991, 21.800 X*, nr. 39, Antwoorden op vragen van de vaste commissie voor Defensie, Den Haag, 1991.

Velthoven, B.C.J. en F.A.A.M. van Winden, "Privatisering, een politiek-economische benadering", *Openbare Uitgaven* 16, nr.6, October 1984.
Vereniging van Dienstplichtige Militairen, *Einde oefening*, Utrecht, 1992.
Vereniging van Dienstplichtige Militairen en Stichting Maatschappij en Krijgsmacht, *Dienstplicht: zin, tegenzin en toekomst*, Den Haag, 1991.
Vereniging van Dienstplichtige Militairen, *Maandblad "twintig"*, Utrecht, April 1993
Veterans administration reports and statistic service, *Research monograph 15: education and income characteristics of veterans maart 1979*, Washington, 1981.
Volkskrant, de.,"*In lopen hebben de soldaten van luchtmobiele brigade geen zin*," 20-11-1992, pp. 3.
Volten, H., "Dienstplicht, legervorming en de Nederlandse Economie," *Economisch Statistische Berichten,* 01-25-1967.

Wagner, R. E., "Conscription voluntary service and democratic fiscal choice", in J.. M. Buchanan en R. D. Tollison (eds.), *Theory of public choice*, Ann Arbor, 1972.
Wolfson, D.J., *Publieke sector en economische orde*, Groningen, 1988.

Contributions to Economics

Hagen Bobzin
Indivisibilities
1998. ISBN 3-7908-1123-8

Helmut Wagner (Ed.)
Current Issues in Monetary Economics
1998. ISBN 3-7908-1127-0

Peter Michaelis/Frank Stähler (Eds.)
Recent Policy Issues in Environmental and Resource Economics
1998. ISBN 3-7908-1137-8

Jessica de Wolff
The Political Economy of Fiscal Decisions
1998. ISBN 3-7908-1130-0

Georg Bol/Gholamreza Nakhaeizadeh/Karl-Heinz Vollmer (Eds.)
Risk Measurements, Econometrics and Neural Networks
1998. ISBN 3-7908-1152-1

Joachim Winter
Investment and Exit Decisions at the Plant Level
1998. ISBN 3-7908-1154-8

Bernd Meyer
Intertemporal Asset Pricing
1999. ISBN 3-7908-1159-9

Uwe Walz
Dynamics of Regional Integration
1999. ISBN 3-7908-1185-8

Michael Carlberg
European Monetary Union
1999. ISBN 3-7908-1191-2

Giovanni Galizzi/Luciano Venturini (Eds.)
Vertical Relationships and Coordination in the Food System
1999. ISBN 3-7908-1192-0

Gustav A. Horn/Wolfgang Scheremet/Rudolf Zwiener
Wages and the Euro
1999. ISBN 3-7908-1199-8

Dirk Willer
The Development of Equity Capital Markets in Transition Economies
1999. ISBN 3-7908-1198-X

Karl Matthias Weber
Innovation Diffusion and Political Control of Energy Technologies
1999. ISBN 3-7908-1205-6

Heike Link et al.
The Costs of Road Infrastructure and Congestion in Europe
1999. ISBN 3-7908-1201-3

GPSR Compliance

The European Union's (EU) General Product Safety Regulation (GPSR) is a set of rules that requires consumer products to be safe and our obligations to ensure this.

If you have any concerns about our products, you can contact us on ProductSafety@springernature.com

In case Publisher is established outside the EU, the EU authorized representative is:

Springer Nature Customer Service Center GmbH
Europaplatz 3
69115 Heidelberg, Germany

Batch number: 10726322

Printed by Printforce, the Netherlands